Visual Q

PageMaker 5.0
for Windows

Carrie Webster

with Paul Webster

Webster & Associates

Peachpit Press

PageMaker 5 for Windows: Visual Quickstart Guide
Webster & Associates

Peachpit Press, Inc.
2414 Sixth Street
Berkeley, CA 94710
(510) 548-4393
(510) 548-5991 (fax)

© 1992, 1993 by Webster & Associates Pty Ltd

All rights reserved. No part of this book may be reproduced or transmitted in any form or by any means, electronic or mechanical, including photocopying, recording, or by any information storage and retrieval system, without prior written permission from the Publisher. For information, contact Peachpit Press.

Notice of Liability:
The information in this book is distributed on an "As is" basis, without warranty. While every precaution has been taken in the preparation of this book, neither the author nor Peachpit Press shall have any liability to any person or entity with respect to any liability, loss, or damage caused or alleged to be caused directly or indirectly by the instructions contained in this book or by the computer software and hardware products described therein.

Trademarks:
Throughout this book, trademarked names are used. Rather than put a trademark symbol in every occurrence of a trademarked name, we are using the names only in an editorial fashion and to the benefit of the trademark owner, with no intention of infringement of the trademark. Where those designations appear in this book, the designations have been printed in initial caps.

First published 1992
Second edition 1993

ISBN: 1-56609-034-2
Printed and bound in the United States of America

Printed on recycled paper

Why a Visual QuickStart?

Virtually no one actually reads computer books; rather, people typically refer to them. This series of **Visual QuickStart Guides** has made that reference easier thanks to a new approach to learning computer applications.

Although conventional computer books lean towards providing extensive textual explanations, a **Visual QuickStart Guide** takes a far more visual approach—pictures literally show you what to do, and text is limited to clear, concise commentary. Learning becomes easier, because a **Visual QuickStart Guide** familiarizes you with the look and feel of your software. Learning also becomes faster, since there are no long-winded passages through which to comb.

It's a new approach to computer learning, but it's also solidly based on experience: Webster & Associates have logged thousands of hours of classroom computer training, and have authored many books on computer applications.

Chapter 1 provides an overview of how to install PageMaker 5 and its basic features.

Chapter 2 through **16** graphically overview the major PageMaker features; these chapters are easy to reference and, with the extensive use of screen shots, let you quickly grasp the concepts.

Chapter 17 covers the two utilities that come with PageMaker 5—Table Editor and Dictionary Editor.

Acknowledgments

The authors wish to acknowledge the effort and dedication of the following people:

- Jenny Hamilton
- Sean Kelly
- Tony Webster

Special thanks to the following people from Aldus Australia:

- Graham Freeman
- Carrie Platt
- Fergus Hammond

Thanks also to Peachpit Press for editorial assistance.

Contents

Chapter 1: Introduction

Installation Summary 1
Starting PageMaker 6
The PageMaker Screen 8

Chapter 2: Setting up a Publication

New or Existing Publications 15
Placing Files 19
Column and Margin Guides 29
Saving Publications 31

Chapter 3: Linking Files

Link Options 33
Linking Files 34

Chapter 4: Text

General Editing 41
The Type Menu 44
Exporting Text 59
The Control Palette and Text 60
Story Editor 69
Manipulating Text Blocks 74
Transforming Text 80

Chapter 5: Master Pages

Master Page Concept 85
Automatic Page Numbering 86
Guides on Master Pages 87
Removing Master Page Items 88

Chapter 6: Creating Graphics

    The Drawing Tools 91
    Drawing Graphics 92
    Moving and Resizing Graphics 94
    Altering the Appearance of Graphics 95
    Editing Graphics 99
    Setting Graphic Defaults 100
    Constraining Graphics 101
    The Control Palette and Graphics 102

Chapter 7: Imported Graphics

    The Formats PageMaker Supports 113
    Loading Graphics 115
    Cropping Graphics 118
    Wrapping Text around Graphics 119
    Irregular Wrap-arounds 121
    Inline Graphics 123
    Image Control 125
    Imported Graphics and the Control Palette 126

Chapter 8: Working with Templates

    Creating Templates 129
    Opening Templates 130
    Using Templates 130

Chapter 9: Aldus Additions

    What Are Aldus Additions? 133
    Acquire Image 133
    Add Cont'd Line 134
    Balance Columns 134
    Build Booklet 135
    Bullets and Numbering 140
    Create Color Library 142

Create Keyline 144
Display Pub Info 145
Display Story Info 146
Display Textblock Info 146
Drop Cap 146
Edit Tracks 147
Expert Kerning 149
Find Overset Text 150
List Styles Used 150
Open Stories 151
Open Template 151
PS Group It 152
PS Ungroup It 153
Printer Styles 153
Running Headers/Footers 156
Run Script 158
Sort Pages 159
Traverse Textblocks 161
VP Converter 162

Chapter 10: Defaults

Application and Publication Defaults 165

Chapter 11: Using Styles

What is a Style? 169
Creating Styles 170
Editing Styles 172
Removing a Style 173
The Control Palette and Styles 176

Chapter 12: Color

Spot and Process Colors 179
Applying Color to Text and Graphics 180
Creating Colors 183
Editing Colors 187

Chapter 13: Printing
Print Dialog Box 189

Chapter 14: Multiple Publication Features
Book Command 197
Creating a Book List 198
Copying and Pasting between Publications 200

Chapter 15: Creating a Table of Contents
Table of Contents 203
Creating Contents 204

Chapter 16: Creating an Index
Indexes 207
Creating Index Entries 207
Topic and Cross-Referencing 211
Show Index Command 213
Creating the Index 214

Chapter 17: Utilities
Table Editor 217
Table Manipulation 219
Importing Files into Table Editor 228
Saving tables 229
Exporting Files from Table Editor 230
Placing Files in PageMaker 231
Dictionary Editor 233

Index 237

INTRODUCTION 1

INSTALLATION SUMMARY

Installing PageMaker 5 is a relatively simple operation. The following instructions summarize what you need to do.

Figure 1. The first step in installing PageMaker is to select *Run* from the **File** menu in the Windows Program Manager.

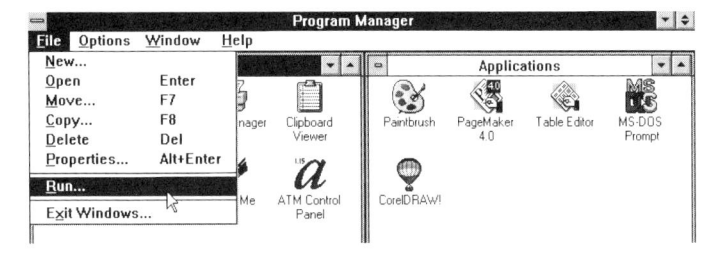

Figure 2. Put the PageMaker Disk 1 in the floppy disk drive. In the *Run* dialog box type in *a:\aldsetup* or *b:\aldsetup*, depending on which disk drive you are using. Then select *OK*.

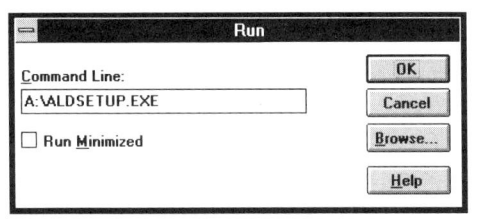

Figure 3. This activates the *Aldus Setup Main Window*. Select the PageMaker options you want installed, then click on *Setup*.

Figure 4. The *Select directory* dialog box appears with an automatically selected installation directory. You can override this by typing in a preferred directory. Then click on *OK*.

1

Chapter 1: Introduction

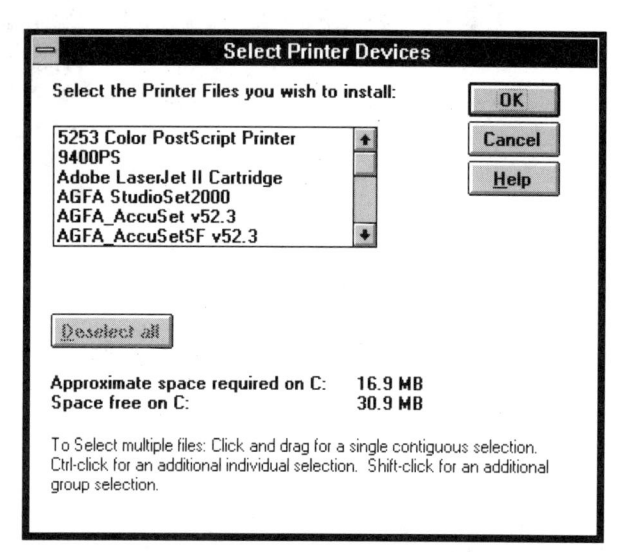

Figure 5. Next, choose the printer devices you want to install in the *Select Printer Devices* dialog box.

Figure 6. The next dialog box to appear is the *Personalize your program* dialog box. Type in your name, company and serial number and click on *OK*.

Figure 7. Click on the *Yes* button if you want to run the tutorial at the end of the installation procedure.

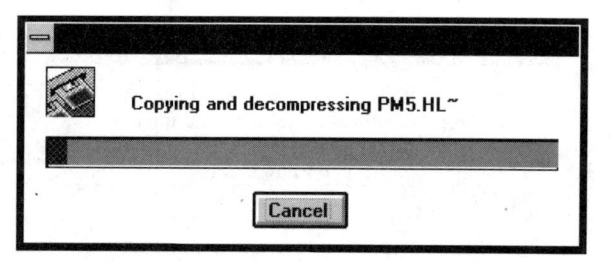

Figure 8. After clicking on *OK* in the *Personalize your program* dialog box, PageMaker begins the installation procedure. Further instructions follow as shown in Figure 9.

Chapter 1: Introduction

Figure 9. After a few moments, the *Please insert the disk labelled (2)* window appears. Insert Disk 2 in the drive you are using, change the path if necessary, and click on *OK*. Soon you will be asked to insert the remaining disks. Follow the same steps as for Disk 2 and click on *OK*.

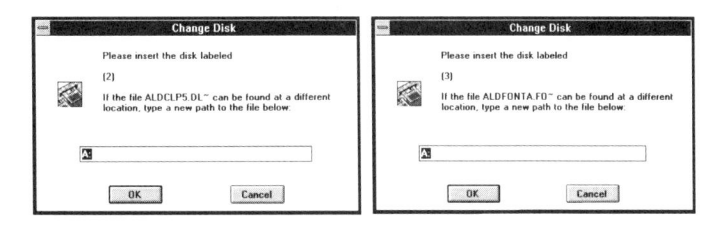

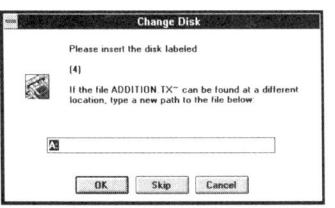

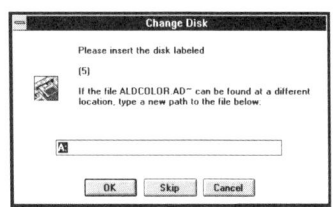

Figure 10. Once you have inserted the last disk and the installation has finished, this screen prompt will appear confirming that you have installed the program. Click on *Continue*.

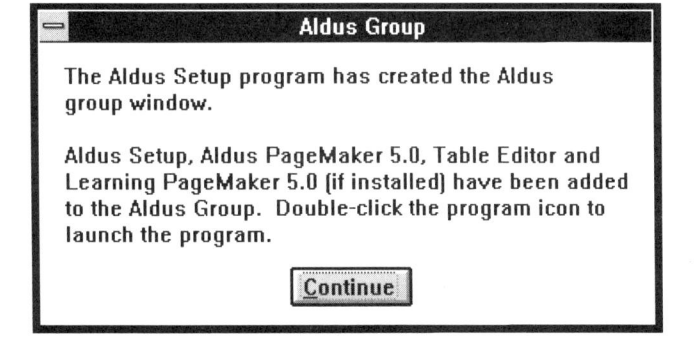

Figure 11. This dialog box lets you know that you must separately install your printer drivers through the Windows Control Panel—select *OK*.

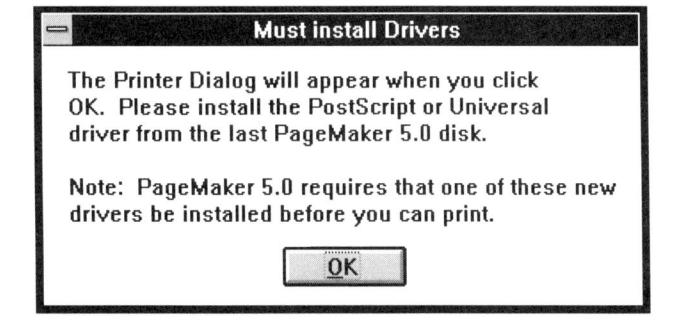

3

Chapter 1: Introduction

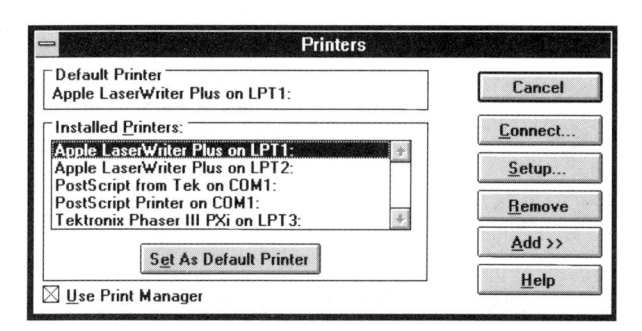

Figure 12. When the Windows Control panel appears, it will automatically open up in this *Printers* dialog box. Click on the *Add* button to extend the dialog box.

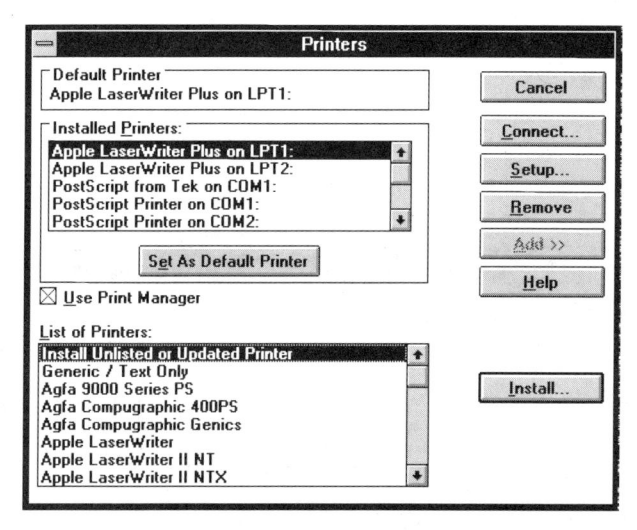

Figure 13. Select the printer driver you wish to install from the *List of Printers* box and click on *Install*.

Figure 14. The *Setup complete* dialog box lets you know you have successfully installed PageMaker. Select *OK*.

Figure 15. Here is a final message from the Aldus Install program.

4

Chapter 1: Introduction

Figure 16. When you are returned to the *Aldus Setup Main Window*, click on the *Exit* button to return to the Program Manager.

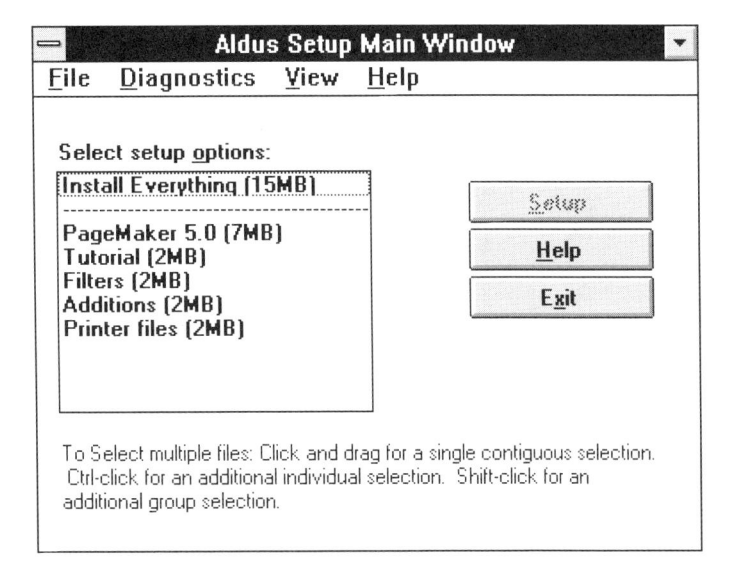

Figure 17. PageMaker is now sitting in its own group in the Windows Program Manager.

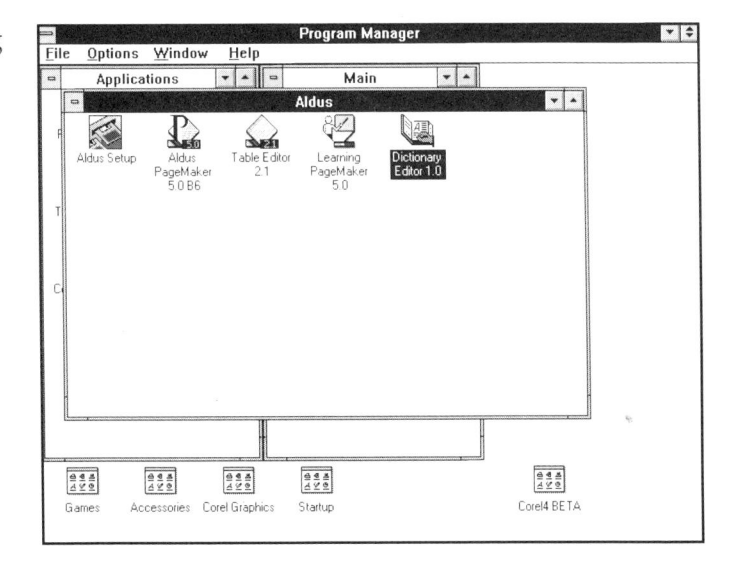

5

Chapter 1: Introduction

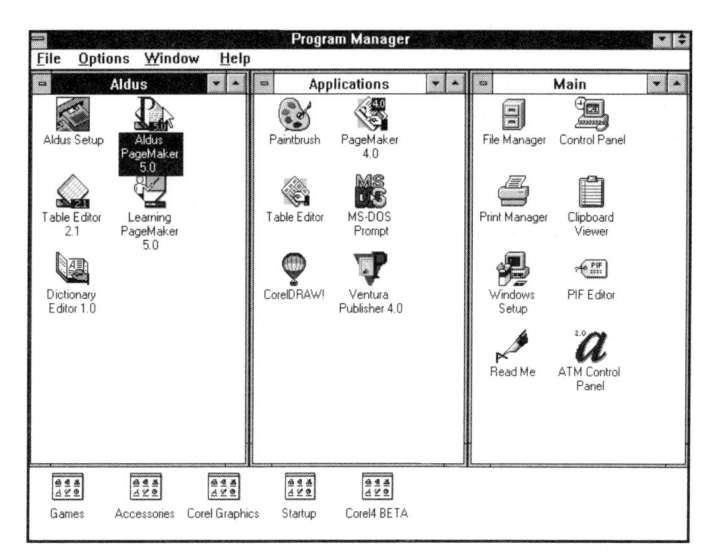

STARTING PAGEMAKER

Figure 18. Opening PageMaker 5 is a matter of locating its icon on the Windows desktop and double-clicking on it.

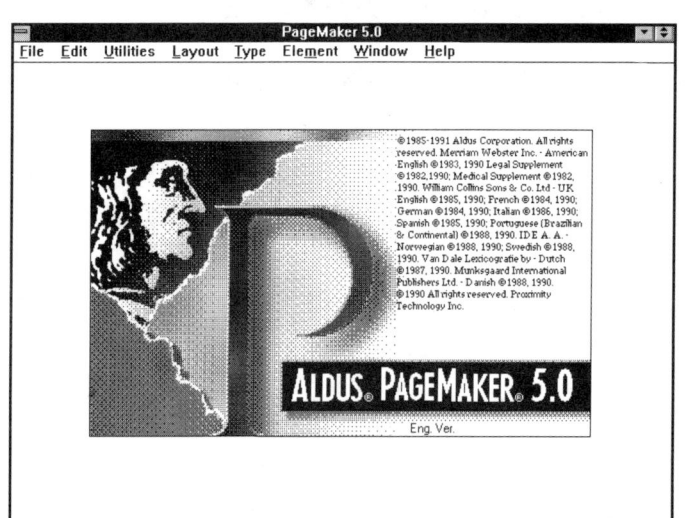

Figure 19. Once you have opened PageMaker, your screen will be similar to the one shown here. At this point you have the choice of creating a new publication, or opening a previously saved one. You can find these commands in the **File** menu.

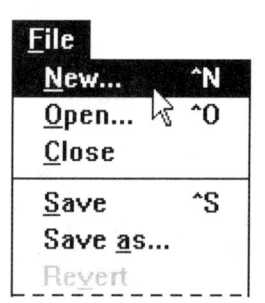

Figure 20. To create a new publication select *New*. Similarly, to open a previously saved publication, select the *Open* command.

PAGE SETUP

Figure 21. The *New* command activates the *Page setup* dialog box. This allows you to define attributes for your publication.

In Chapter 2, **Setting up a Publication**, we will be changing dialog box options. For now, click the mouse once on the *OK* button.

Figure 22. After selecting *OK* in the *Page setup* dialog box, this is how a new publication looks.

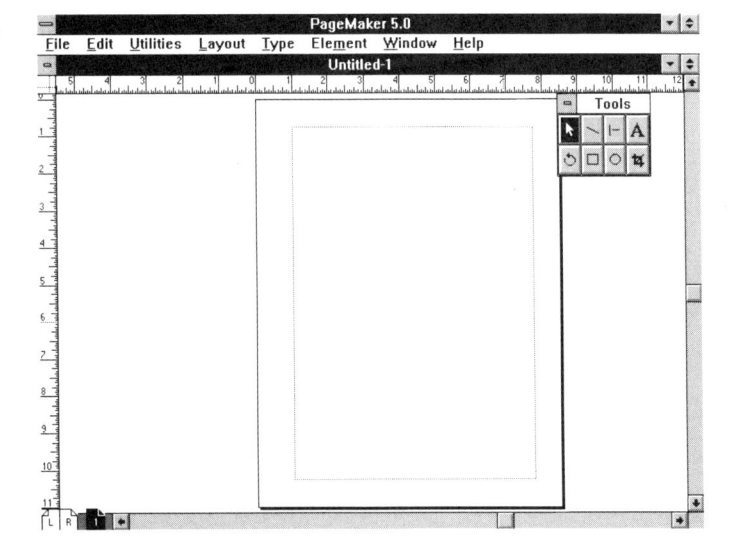

Chapter 1: Introduction

THE PAGEMAKER SCREEN

Figure 23. This is the PageMaker screen. Your screen may not contain all these components when you first open PageMaker.

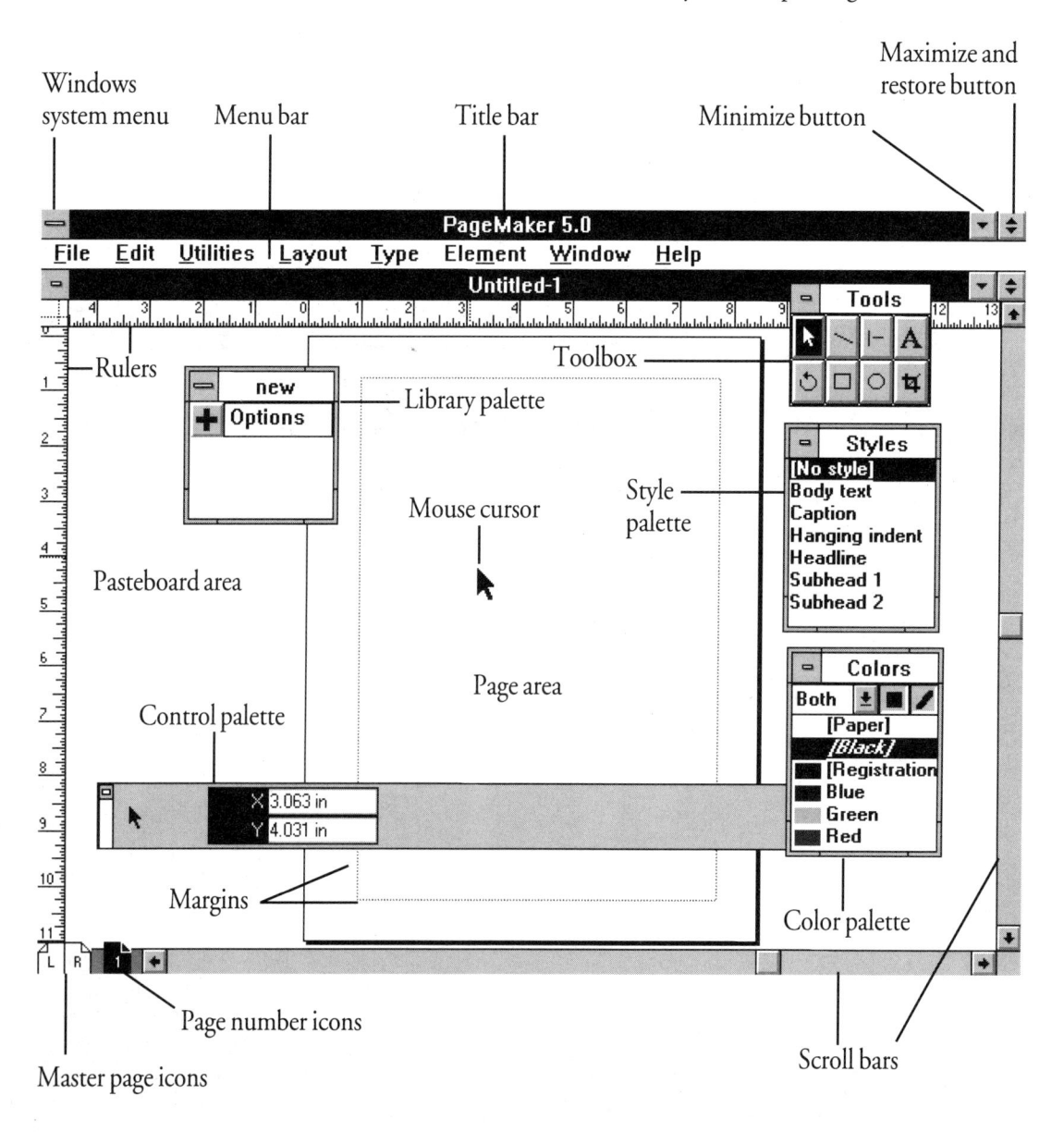

[Figure 23: Annotated screenshot of the PageMaker 5.0 interface with the following labels: Windows system menu, Menu bar, Title bar, Minimize button, Maximize and restore button, Rulers, Toolbox, Library palette, Style palette, Mouse cursor, Pasteboard area, Page area, Control palette, Margins, Color palette, Page number icons, Scroll bars, Master page icons. Menu items shown: File, Edit, Utilities, Layout, Type, Element, Window, Help. Styles palette lists: [No style], Body text, Caption, Hanging indent, Headline, Subhead 1, Subhead 2. Colors palette shows: Both, [Paper], [Black], [Registration], Blue, Green, Red. Control palette shows X 3.063 in, Y 4.031 in.]

8

Chapter 1: Introduction

SCREEN COMPONENTS

THE MENU BAR

Figure 24. Clicking on any name in the menu bar produces the drop-down menu commands you use to operate PageMaker.

| File | Edit | Utilities | Layout | Type | Element | Window | Help |

THE TITLE BARS

Figure 25. The program title bar displays the program name—PageMaker 5.0.

PageMaker 5.0

Untitled-1

The current publication title bar contains the file name of the PageMaker publication. If you haven't named it, it reads **Untitled-1**.

MINIMIZE, MAXIMIZE AND RESTORE BUTTONS

Figure 26. These three buttons are located in both title bars. You use them to increase or decrease the size of the current window.

Minimize button — Maximize button — Restore button

PAGE NUMBER ICONS

Figure 27. Page number icons indicate how many pages are in your publication, and which page or pages you are currently viewing.

MASTER PAGE ICONS

Figure 28. Clicking on the master page icons takes you to the master pages in your publication. You can have left and right master pages, or just a right master page for a single-sided document.

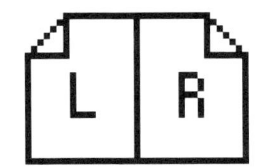

9

Chapter 1: Introduction

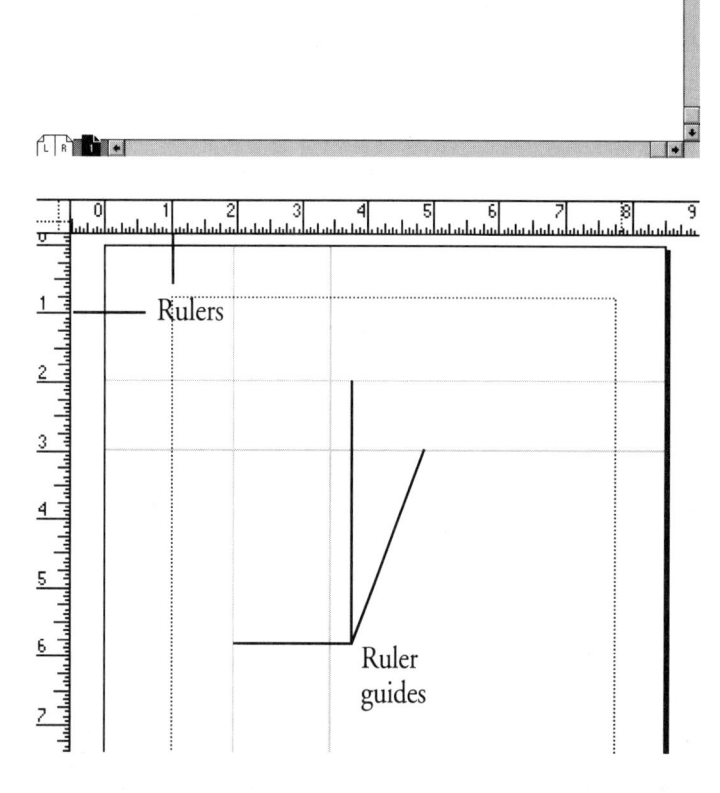

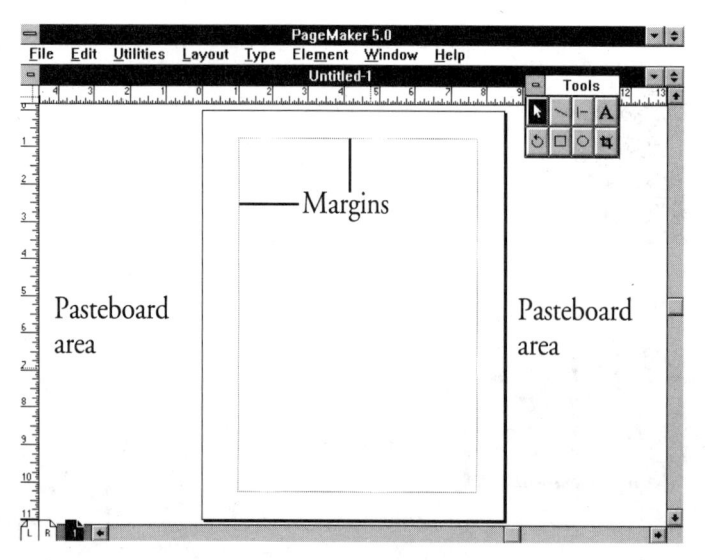

SCROLL BARS

Figure 29. Use the *scroll bars* for moving around the screen to view different parts of your page.

RULERS AND RULER GUIDES

Figure 30. Use the rulers to measure distance on the screen. You can change the measurement units and move the zero point to any area on the screen.

Ruler guides are non-printing guides that you drag with the mouse onto the page from either of the rulers. You can move them with the mouse once they are on the page.

MARGINS AND PASTEBOARD AREA

Figure 31. Margins are non-printing guides that indicate the defined print area.

The pasteboard area is like a desk around your page where you can put text or graphics. PageMaker will save any object on the pasteboard with the publication.

PAGE AREA

Figure 32. The *page area* represents your page and its boundaries.

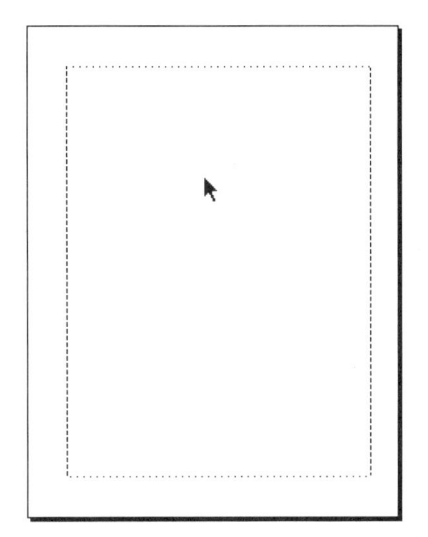

STYLE PALETTE

Figure 33. You use the style palette in conjunction with the text tool to apply styles to paragraphs of text.

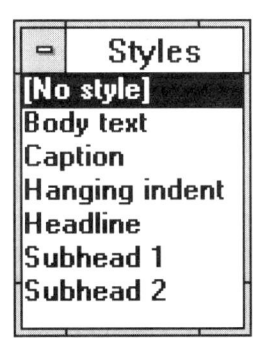

COLOR PALETTE

Figure 34. You use the color palette to apply color to selected text or graphic areas on the screen.

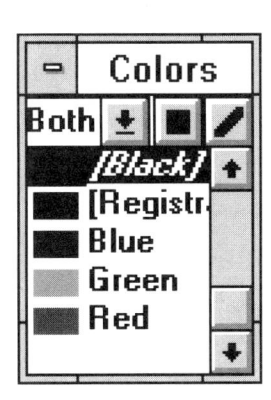

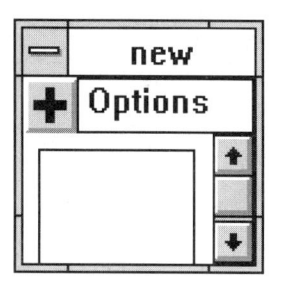

LIBRARY PALETTE

Figure 35. You use the Library palette to store and retrieve images and text files that you frequently use.

CONTROL PALETTE

Figure 36. Use the Control palette to place, rotate, skew and resize selected objects precisely on the page.

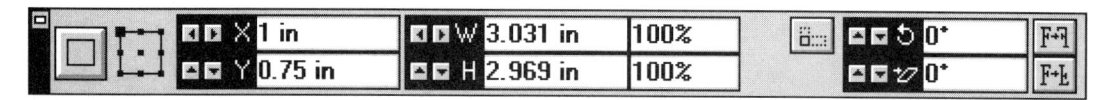

Figure 37. If you are using the text tool, you can also use the Control palette to apply fonts, point sizes, leading, kerning, styles, indents, and more, to text on the page.

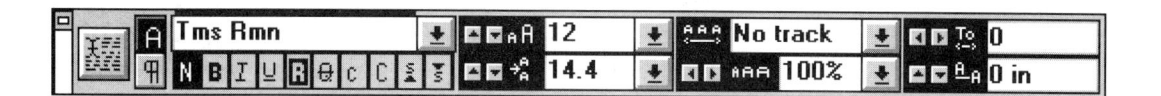

MOUSE CURSOR

Figure 38. The mouse cursor is the icon that you move around the screen by moving the mouse. The shape of the cursor changes depending upon what tool you have selected and what you are doing with PageMaker.

TOOLBOX

Figure 39. The toolbox contains a number of tools that you use to manipulate, create, resize and move text and graphics on the screen.

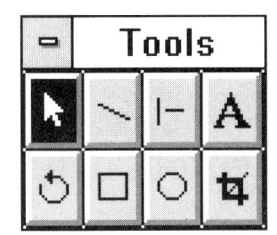

Use the pointer tool to select, move and resize text blocks and graphics on the page.

Use the line tool to draw straight lines at any angle.

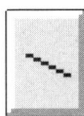

Use the constrained line tool to draw lines at 45 degree orientations.

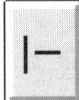

Use the text tool to edit and apply attributes to text, as well as to create text files.

Use the rotation tool to rotate objects on the page.

Use the rectangle tool to draw squares and rectangles.

Use the ellipse tool to draw circles and ellipses.

Use the cropping tool to crop imported graphics files.

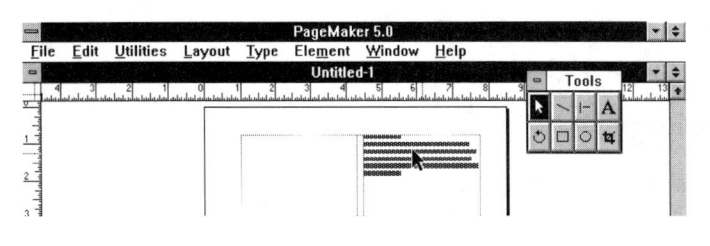

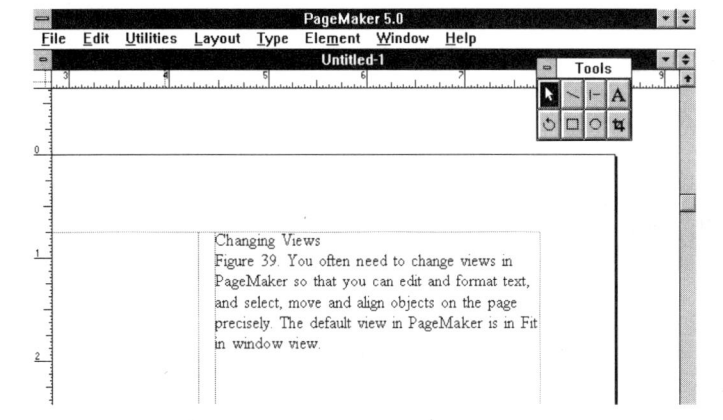

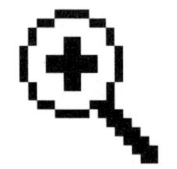

CHANGING VIEWS

Figure 40. You often need to change views in PageMaker so that you can edit and format text, and select, move and align objects on the page precisely. The default view in PageMaker is in *Fit in window* view.

Figure 41. The quickest way to change to *Actual size* is to position the mouse on the area you would like to enlarge and click the right mouse button. Click the right mouse button again to return to *Fit in window* view.

You can also use the right mouse button with the Shift key to change to 200 percent view.

Figure 42. An alternative to using the mouse is to select a view size from the *View* command submenu in the **Layout** menu. You have more of a range here, as well as a series of keyboard shortcuts, displayed to the right of the commands. When you use the menu, you cannot specify which part of the page PageMaker magnifies.

Figure 43. Hold Ctrl+Spacebar to activate a magnifying tool. Click the left mouse button to enlarge an area on the page, (Ctrl+Spacebar+Alt to reduce) or hold the mouse down and drag it over the area you wish to enlarge.

SETTING UP A PUBLICATION

NEW OR EXISTING PUBLICATIONS

After opening PageMaker, you have the choice of creating a new publication or opening an existing one.

NEW PUBLICATION

Figure 1. To create a new publication, select *New* from the **File** menu. This activates the *Page setup* dialog box. In this dialog box you can set up various options for your publication: the page size, orientation, and number of pages, whether it is double- or single-sided, the margins, and the starting page number. It is important to select your printer type here as well.

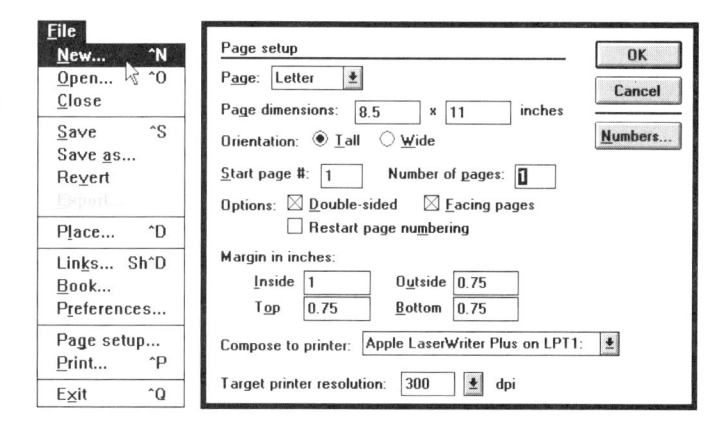

OPENING AN EXISTING PUBLICATION

Figure 2. To open an existing publication, select *Open* from the **File** menu to activate the *Open publication* dialog box. In this dialog box you have access to all directories and drives on the hard disk, including floppy drives. Make your selection and click on *OK*.

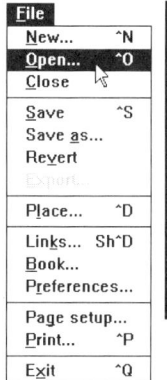

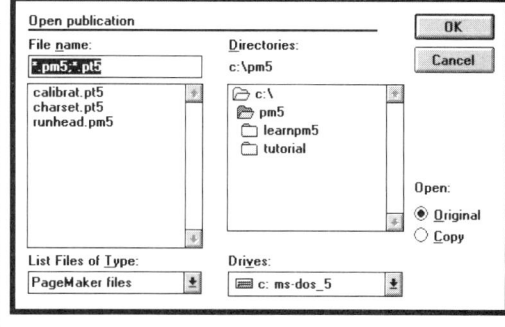

Chapter 2: Setting up a Publication

OPENING MULTIPLE PUBLICATIONS

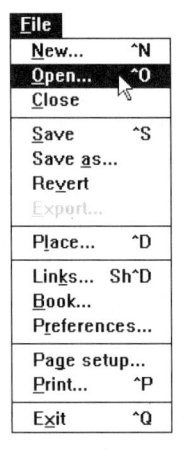

Figure 3. If you already have an existing publication open and you wish to open another, select *Open* from the **File** menu. (Select *New* if you wish to create a new publication.)

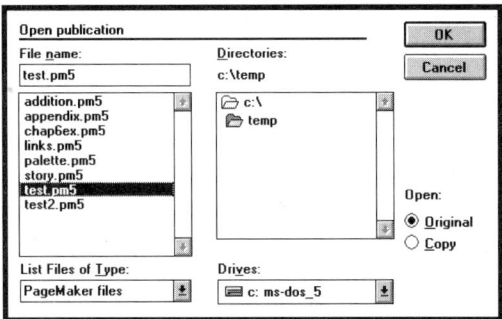

Figure 4. In the *Open publication* dialog box, find and select the file you wish to open and click on *OK*.

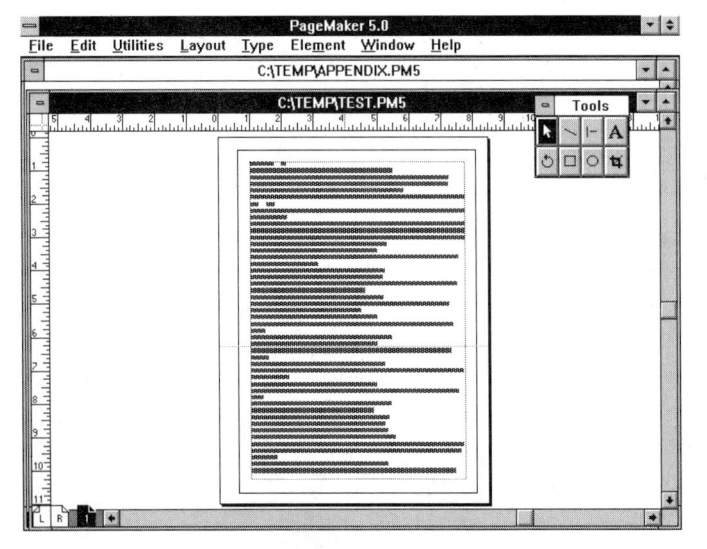

Figure 5. When the screen returns, you will see two windows. The window in front is the file you just opened and the window behind it is the file you previously opened.

You can open as many files as your computer's memory will allow, one on top of the other, by doing this.

16

Chapter 2: Setting up a Publication

ACCESSING MULTIPLE FILE WINDOWS

Figure 6. You can bring any file to the front in two ways, using the mouse and using the menu. You can click the mouse once on the exposed part of the file you wish to make active.

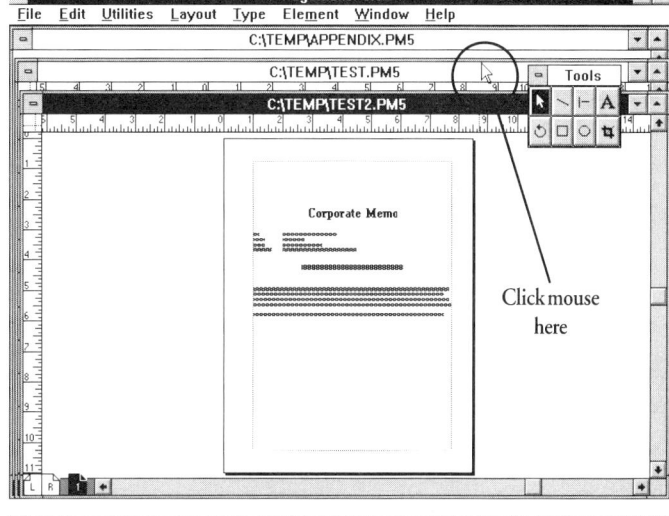

Click mouse here

Figure 7. The window you click on moves to the front of the other windows. Note that you can no longer see the file that was originally at the front.

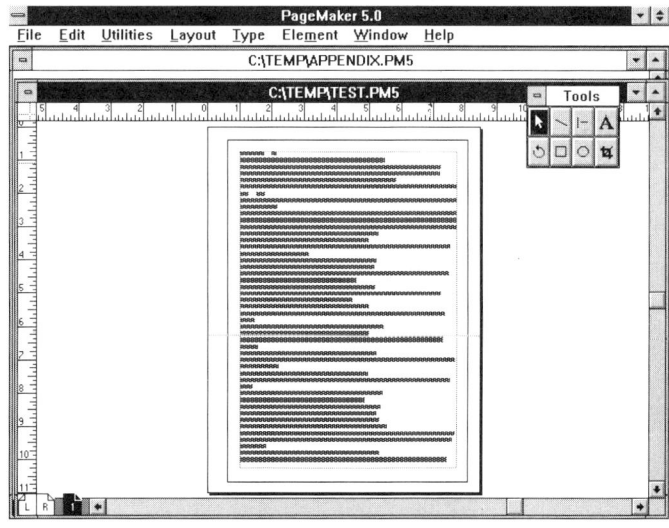

Figure 8. The second method is to move the files to the front using the **Window** menu. When you select this menu, all PageMaker files you have open will be listed in the menu. Select the file name that you wish to bring to the front.

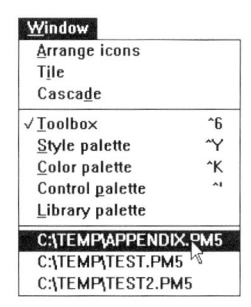

17

Chapter 2: Setting up a Publication

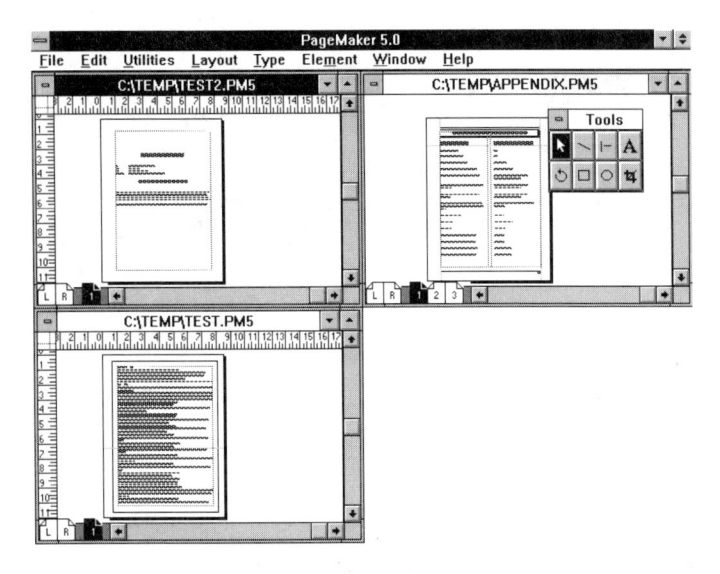

ARRANGING WINDOWS

Figure 9. Use the *Tile* command in the **Window** menu to arrange all the open publications on the screen.

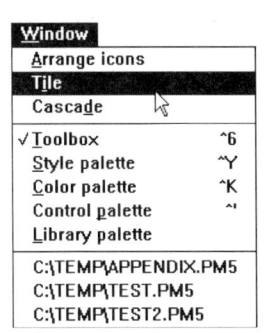

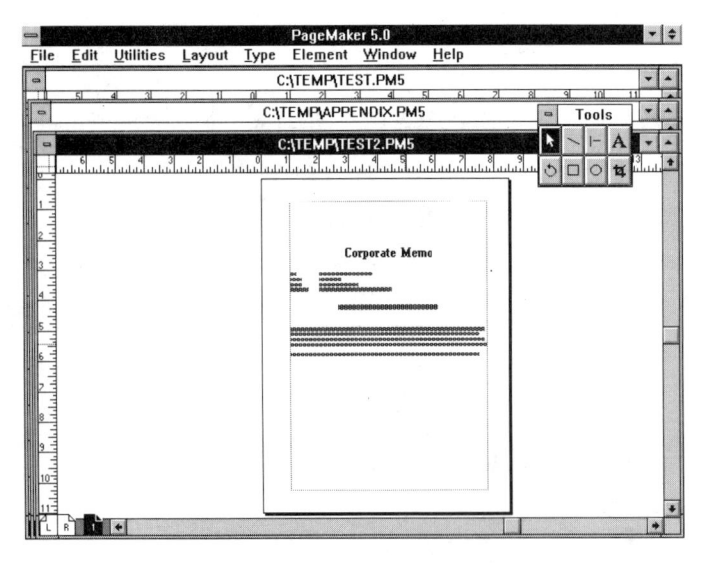

Figure 10. Use the *Cascade* command to overlay all the open publications, with just the title bars of the inactive publications showing.

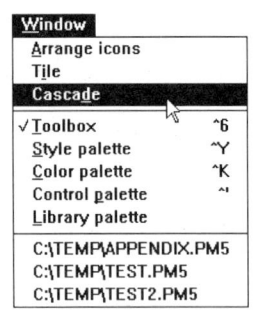

MINIMIZING AND MAXIMIZING PUBLICATION WINDOWS

Figure 11. You can use the minimize and maximize buttons to decrease or increase the size of the individual windows. Each window contains its own set of buttons. In this example, we clicked on the minimize button for each publication to minimize them all to icons.

The easiest way to restore a publication to its original size is to double-click on its icon with the mouse.

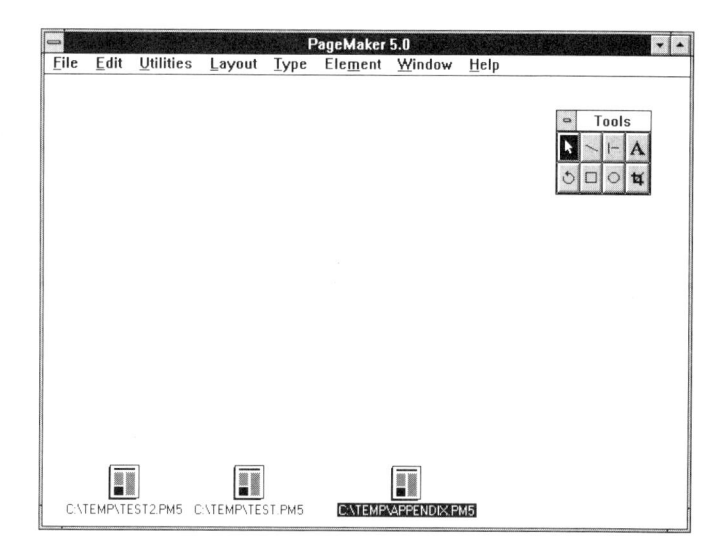

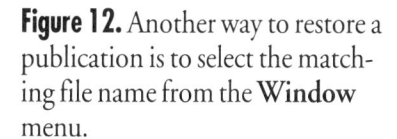

Figure 12. Another way to restore a publication is to select the matching file name from the **Window** menu.

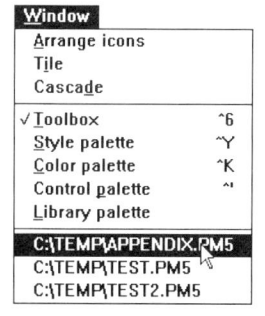

PLACING FILES

Figure 13. Use the *Place* command from the **File** menu to load all types of files into new and existing PageMaker publications—text and graphics. Selecting *Place* activates the *Place document* dialog box.

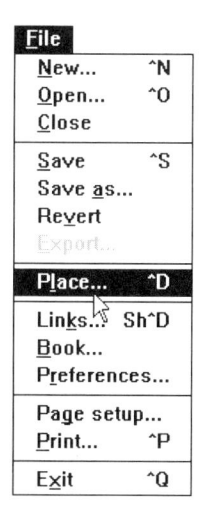

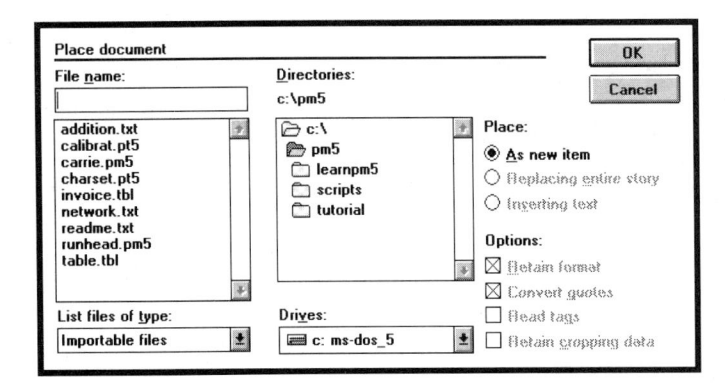

Figure 14. In the *Place document* dialog box you can move around your hard disk to find the necessary file, as is standard for all Windows software.

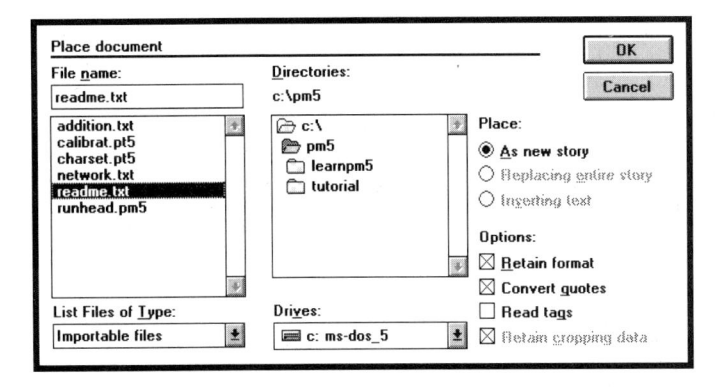

PLACING TEXT FILES

Figure 15. The *Place document* dialog box shows the options PageMaker gives you for placing text.

The options at the top-right are *As new story* (default setting for a new story), *Replacing entire story* (allows you to replace the selected story with the new text file) and *Inserting text* (allows you to insert a new text file at the insertion point).

The options at the bottom-right include *Retain format* (from your word processor), *Convert quotes* (turning straight quotes into typesetting quotes) and *Read tags* (discussed in Chapter 11, **Using Styles**). The *Retain cropping data* option is for imported graphics, and is explained in Chapter 6.

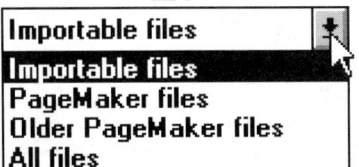

Figure 16. The *List Files of Type* option lets you list specific file types in the File list box so you can choose the type of files you want to see.

Chapter 2: Setting up a Publication

AUTO AND MANUAL TEXT FLOW

Figure 17. After clicking on a text file name and choosing *OK* in the *Place document* dialog box, you get a mouse cursor on screen in one of two modes:

— (a) Manual   — (b) Autoflow

(a) Manual text flow (default setting), or
(b) Autoflow.

Manual text flow allows you to load text into one column and then stop. Autoflow lets you load all text into as many columns or pages as you need, creating the pages as it goes.

Figure 18. Once the mouse cursor changes to a loaded text cursor as shown here, you can flow the text onto the page. Put the cursor where you want the text to start and click the mouse button once.

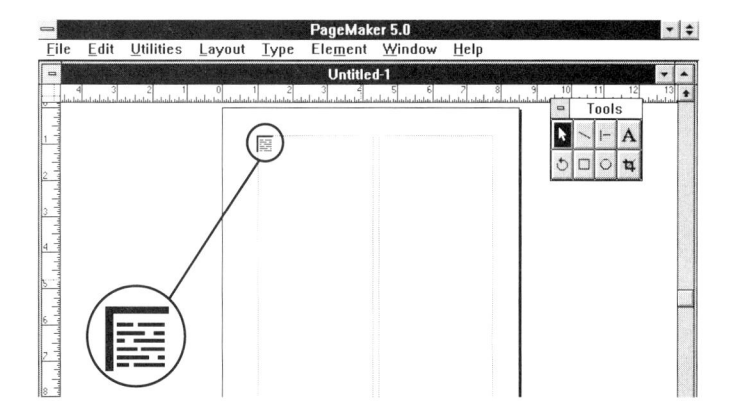

MANUAL TEXT FLOW

Figure 19. Manual text flow places the text in one column and then stops. If you have no text left to flow, the windowshade handle at the bottom is empty. In this figure it has a down-arrow in it, which means you have more text available.

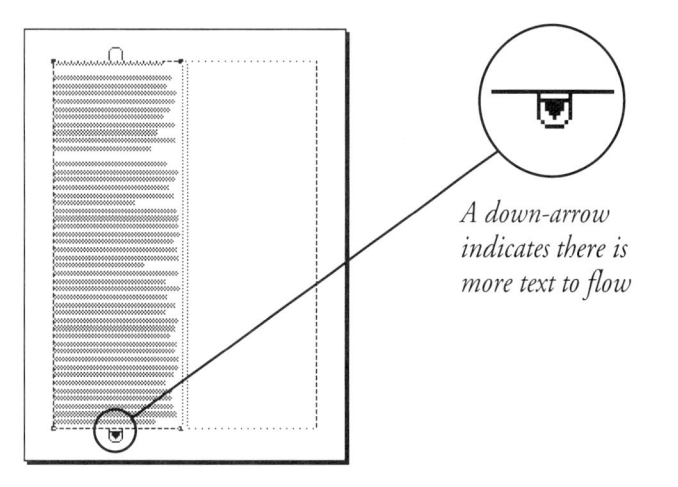

A down-arrow indicates there is more text to flow

21

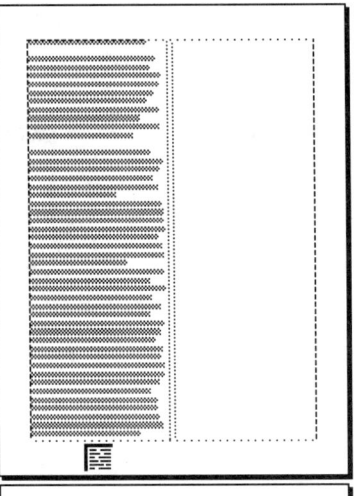

Figure 20. To continue flowing the text, click the mouse on the down-arrow symbol to re-activate the loaded text cursor.

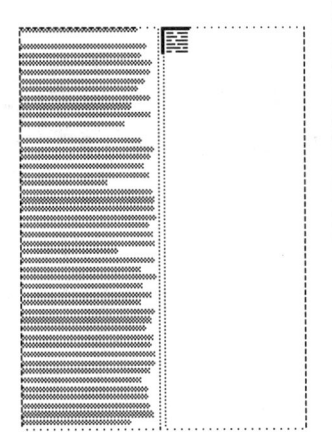

Figure 21. Position the loaded text cursor at the top of the next column (or wherever you wish to place the text), and click again. The text flows down this column and stops at the bottom (even if you have more text available).

Figure 22. Repeat the process outlined in the two figures above until text runs out. Click on the page number icons to "turn" the pages as needed or create new pages using *Insert pages* from the **Layout** menu. You can click on the page number icons with the loaded mouse cursor without losing the rest of the text.

You have finished placing the text file when the bottom window-shade handle is empty.

AUTOFLOW

Figure 23. Autoflow allows you to flow text across as many columns and pages as necessary to import the text file completely. Activate this mode by choosing *Autoflow* from the **Layout** menu. A tick alongside the *Autoflow* command indicates that you have turned automatic text flow on.

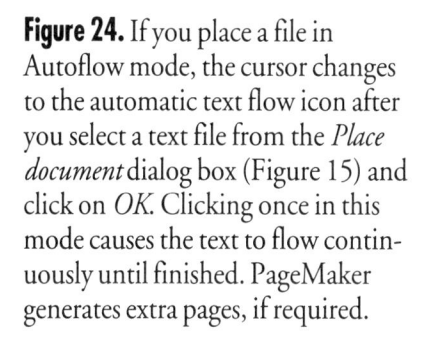

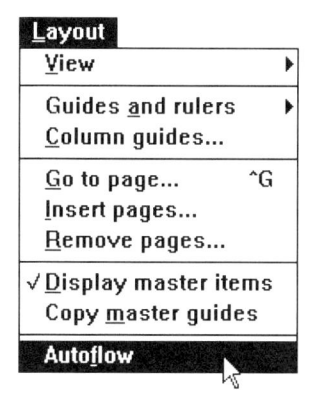

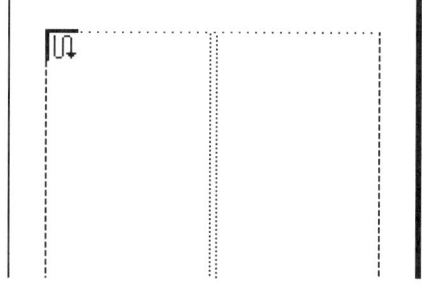

Figure 24. If you place a file in Autoflow mode, the cursor changes to the automatic text flow icon after you select a text file from the *Place document* dialog box (Figure 15) and click on *OK*. Clicking once in this mode causes the text to flow continuously until finished. PageMaker generates extra pages, if required.

Figure 25. Note that we have placed the text file using *Autoflow*, and PageMaker has automatically selected both text blocks.

To get semi-automatic text flow, hold down the Shift key before clicking the mouse cursor to place text in manual or automatic modes.

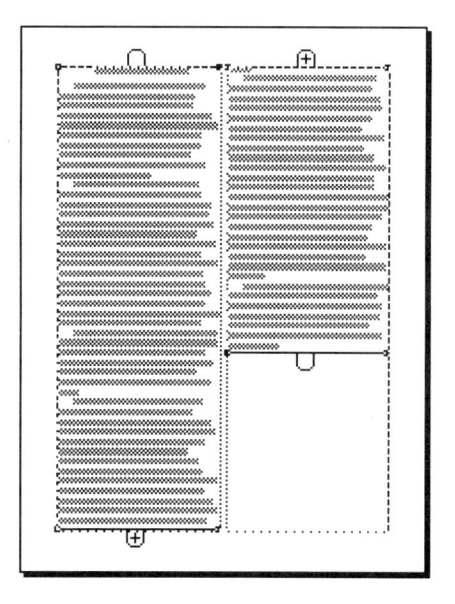

Figure 26. The cursor changes to the semi-automatic text flow icon as shown here. Text flows down the column and PageMaker automatically reloads the cursor to flow again, without your having to click on the bottom windowshade handle first (as discussed in Figure 20).

PLACING GRAPHICS

Figure 27. PageMaker can place a variety of graphic file types including: (a) *paint,* (b) *draw,* (c) *TIFF,* (d) *Encapsulated PostScript.* The different icons PageMaker displays for these different graphic types are shown here.

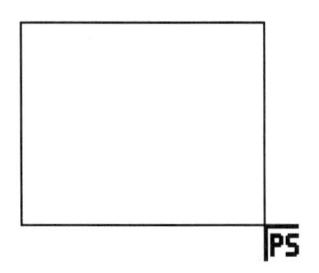

(a) Paint-type graphic (PCX, BMP, TIF, GEM)

(b) Draw-type graphic (EPS, WMF)

(c) TIFF graphic (TIF)

(d) Encapsulated PostScript graphic (EPS)

Figure 28. You can place graphics in the same way as text. Select the *Place* command, choose the graphic file, and place the cursor where you want the graphic to go, then click once.

Unfortunately, you don't know how big the graphic will be on the page when you place files this way. It is better to do what is shown here. Drag the mouse on the page until you have a box as big as you want the graphic to be and then release the mouse. The graphic appears only in the defined area. For more details on placing and proportionally resizing external graphics, see Chapter 7, **Imported Graphics.**

LIBRARY PALETTE

Use the Library palette to store, organize, search for and retrieve graphic and text files that you use often.

You can create several different object libraries and you can arrange each library by subject. For example you may wish to create a library containing EPS files only and then assign it a subject name—such as "animals." The library palette can display "thumbnail" images of the objects, and you can search the library based on keywords and other attributes you assigned to the objects.

Figure 29. Activate the Library palette through the *Library palette* command in the **Window** menu.

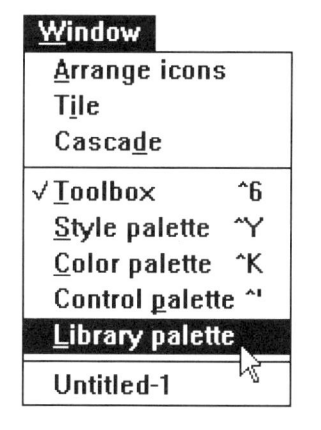

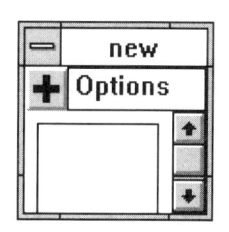

CREATING AND OPENING A LIBRARY

Figure 30. To create a library, click on the **Options** window to activate the menu and select *New library*. Similarly, to open an existing library select the *Open library* command. The dialog box that appears next is the same after selecting either command.

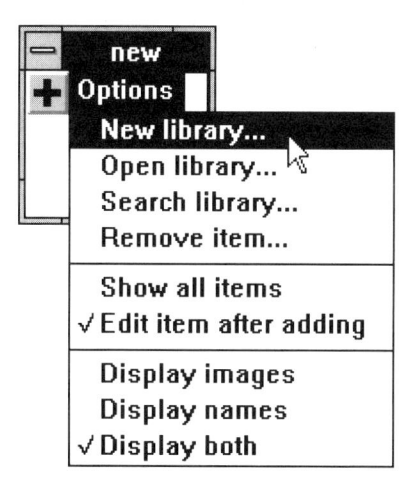

Chapter 2: Setting up a Publication

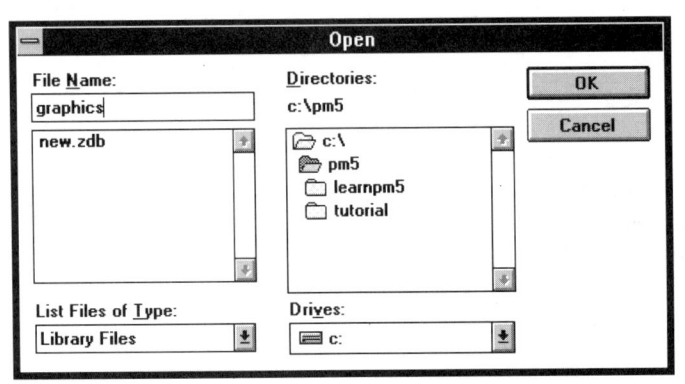

Figure 31. Give your new library a name, or if you wish to open an existing library double-click on the library file name. In this example, we are creating a library called "graphics."

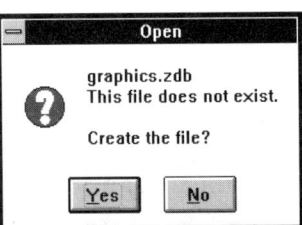

Figure 32. After you have selected *OK*, select *Yes* in the Prompt box to create the library file.

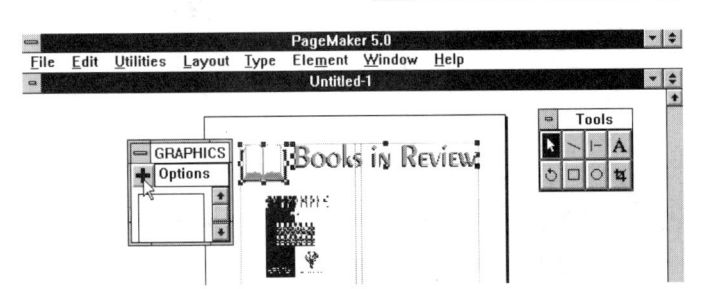

ADDING FILES TO A LIBRARY

Figure 33. To add files to the currently opened library, select one or more text or graphic objects on the page, then click on the + button on the Library palette.

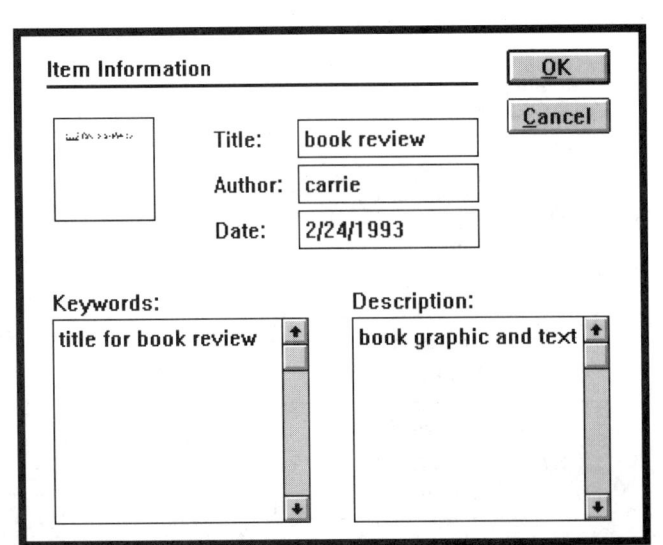

Figure 34. In the *Item Information* dialog box that appears, you can enter in a name for the item or items selected, as well as keywords and a description as additional information. When you select *OK*, you are returned to the screen.

You can also add items to the Library palette that you have copied to the clipboard. Copy the object and click on the + button.

Chapter 2: Setting up a Publication

Figure 35. The objects you have added to the library will be visible in the Library palette window if you have selected *Edit item after adding* from the **Options** menu previously. If you have added a number of items, you may need to scroll down the list.

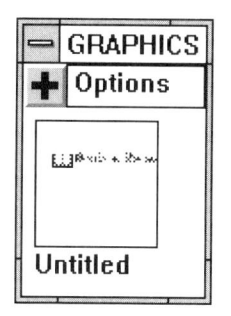

ADDING AND EDITING ITEM INFORMATION

If you wish to add or edit any information on an object already in the Library palette, double-click on this item in the Library palette window to reactivate the *Item Information* dialog box. You can then make any changes.

PLACING A LIBRARY PALETTE OBJECT ON THE PAGE

Figure 36. Select the object from the Library palette window with the mouse and drag the object onto the page. The mouse cursor changes shape. PageMaker places a copy of the object when you release the mouse at that location.

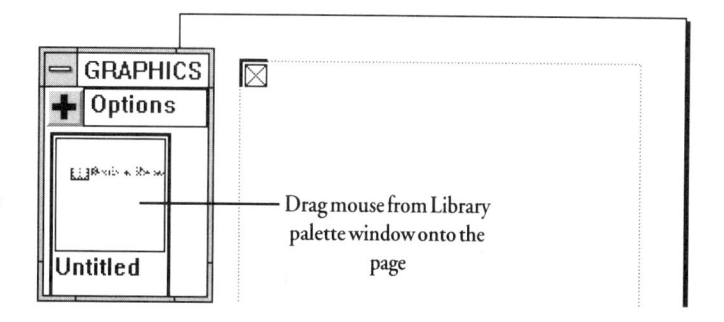

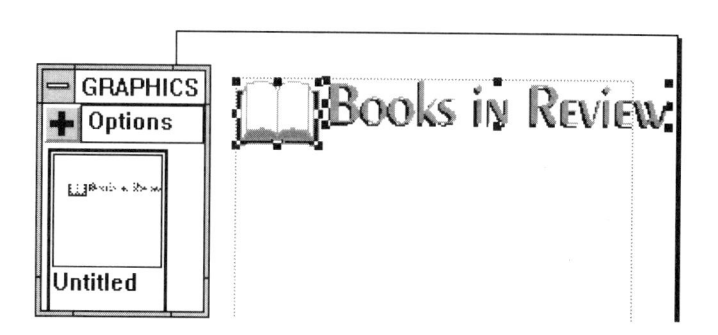

Drag mouse from Library palette window onto the page

27

Chapter 2: Setting up a Publication

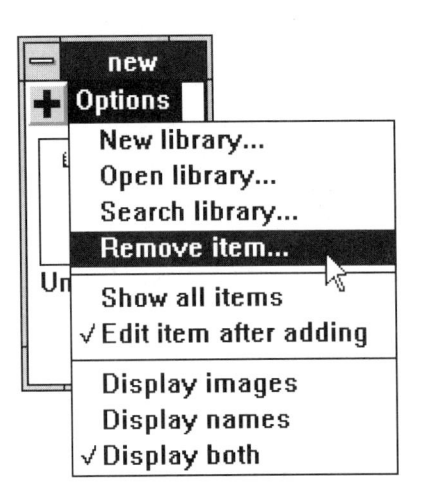

REMOVING ITEMS FROM A LIBRARY

Figure 37. To remove an item from a library, click on the item in the Library palette and then select *Remove item* from the **Options** menu.

SEARCHING FOR ITEMS

Figure 38. To search for a specific item that you have added to a library, select *Search library* from the **Options** menu. You can search by *keyword, Author* or *Name.* Leave any unwanted search option blank. Click on the *Search* button to start the search.

28

THE OPTIONS MENU

Figure 39. The *New library, Open library, Search library* and *Remove item* commands have all been described earlier in this section.

Click on the *Show all items* command to list all the items in the Library palette after you have conducted a search for specific items.

The *Edit item after adding* command ensures that the *Item Information* dialog box appears after you add an object to the library.

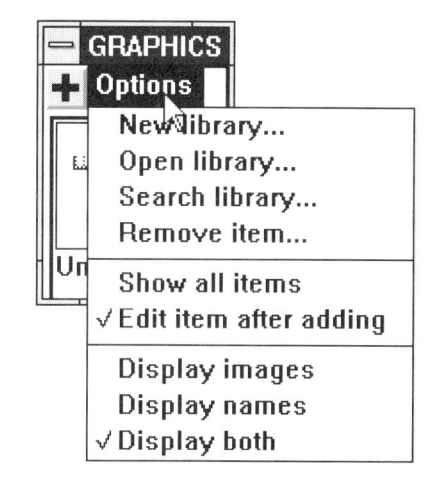

The last three commands, *Display images, Display names* and *Display both,* let you choose which way you display objects in the Library palette. These commands are self-explanatory.

CLOSING THE LIBRARY PALETTE

Either select *Library palette* in the **Window** menu or double-click on the Library palette system menu in its top left corner to close the Library palette.

COLUMN AND MARGIN GUIDES

Figure 40. You can adjust the number of columns using the *Column guides* command in the **Layout** menu. This activates the *Column guides* dialog box. In the example dialog box, we have changed the number of columns to 3. The maximum number of columns you can have is 40.

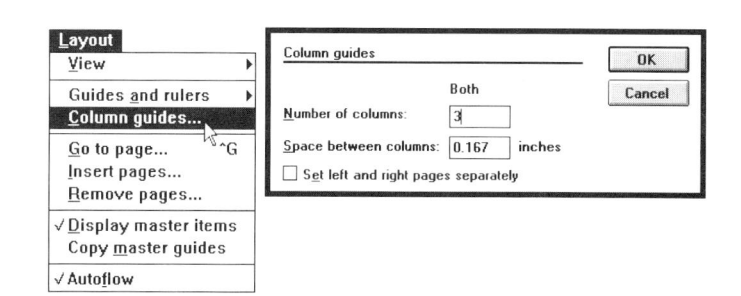

Figure 41. If you have already placed text on a page, changing the number of columns does not alter its layout. You must manually resize this text with the mouse, or delete and re-flow it onto the page. (See the **Resizing Text Blocks** section in Chapter 4 for more information.)

Note: You set up the margins in the *Page setup* dialog box as discussed earlier in this chapter.

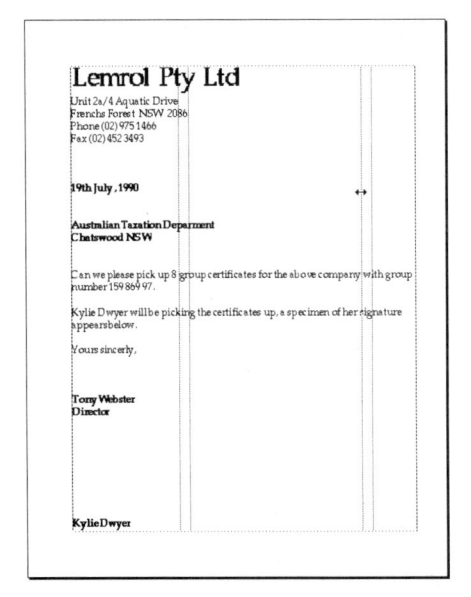

Figure 42. You can change margin and column guides on the screen. Position the mouse over the column guide or margin, so that the mouse changes to a double-headed arrow. Hold the mouse down and reposition the margin or column guide, then release the mouse.

Chapter 2: Setting up a Publication

SAVING PUBLICATIONS

Figure 43. You can save a PageMaker publication even before loading any text or graphics. You save the publication using the *Save* command in the **File** menu. The first time you *Save,* the *Save publication* dialog box appears, allowing you to name your document. Once you have named your document, the *Save* command will simply save to disk any new changes you have made to your publication.

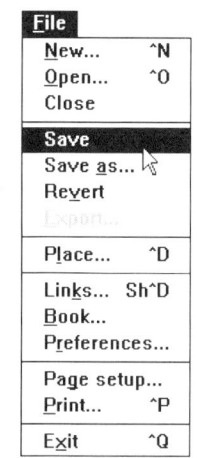

Figure 44. The *Save publication* dialog box allows you to type a name for the publication in the *File name* text box. As for all Windows applications, you can first choose the directory and disk in which to save the file.

THE SAVE AS COMMAND

Figure 45. If you are working on a large PageMaker publication, using the *Save* command periodically to save your changes will also save unnecessary elements, such as spelling corrections and deleted paragraphs. To compress the size of a publication, use the *Save as* command and give your file the same name just before you close the document.

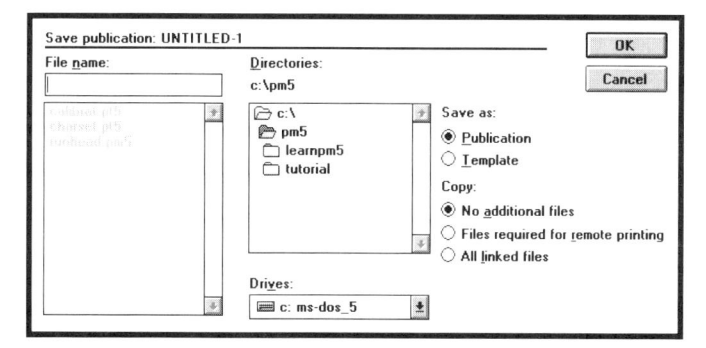

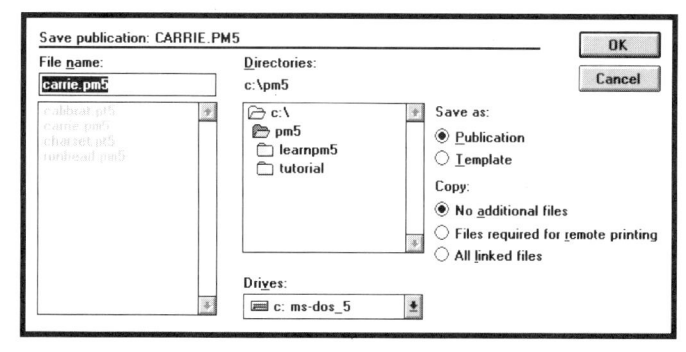

31

Chapter 2: Setting up a Publication

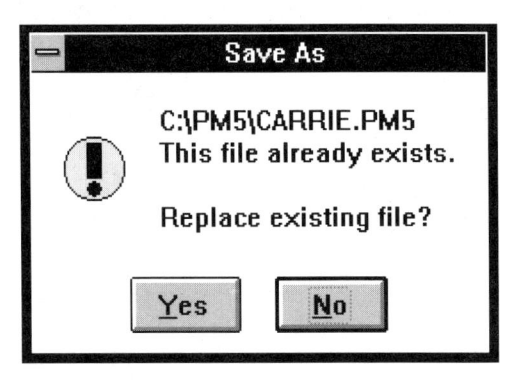

Figure 46. Type in the current name of the publication and select *OK*, and this alert box appears. Select *Yes* to overwrite the file.

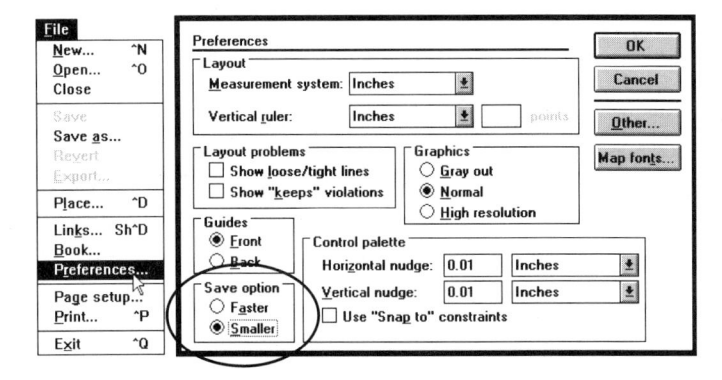

Figure 47. If you wish PageMaker to compress a file to its smallest size every time you save it, select the *Smaller* option in the *Preferences* dialog box. Keep in mind that this considerably slows down the time it takes to save.

You can also use the *Save as* command to create a copy of your publication. Just type a new name into the *File name* text box of Figure 44 and select *OK*.

32

LINKING FILES 3

LINK OPTIONS

PageMaker lets you link files you have placed so you can update imported text and graphics quickly and easily when you change the original file. PageMaker's linking, hotlinking, and OLE (object linking and embedding) allows you to create different types of links from within PageMaker. With hotlinking you can open the program you created the original document in from within PageMaker, edit the object and update your publication. You can use OLE to import objects created in programs that don't directly support PageMaker-compatible formats (such as CorelDRAW! files).

Figure 1. This table describes the different types of links that are available in PageMaker, and why you use them.

Link Type	Description	Function
Linking	Using the Place command will automatically import files that are linked. This is the Default setting for placing files in PageMaker. All files are linked to their original, external file.	For placing files that originate from a program that does not support OLE or for using a generic graphics format such as TIFF. You can edit the original files in their original program, and then update these files in PageMaker. You can do this automatically or manually, through the Links dialog box.
HotLinking	Creates a direct link between PageMaker and the following programs only: Freehand 3, Persuasion 2, PhotoStyler 1 and Table Editor 2. Any files created in these programs are automatically HotLinked when you place the file.	Hotlinks update your publication whenever you save changes to the original document.
OLE Linking	Used primarily for graphic objects. OLE linking allows you to edit the original file in the original program which automatically updates in PageMaker when you save it. OLE linked text cannot be edited in PageMaker. The original program must be an OLE server (i.e. supports OLE).	It is useful to OLE link graphic objects that you use more than once in a publication. When you edit the original file and save it, all occurrences of the graphic file are updated, even across multiple publications. OLE linking can be used to paste a graphic that is in a non-compatible PageMaker format.
OLE Embedding	Used primarily for graphic objects. OLE Embedded objects are not linked as such, but PageMaker contains all information required to edit the object. It is not necessary to keep the original file stored on the hard disk once the object has been inserted. OLE Embedded text cannot be edited in PageMaker. The original program must be an OLE server (i.e. supports OLE).	OLE Embedding is useful for graphic files used once in a publication. The original program can be activated by double-clicking on the graphic. Any changes made and saved are updated in the open publication. OLE Embedding can be used to paste a graphic that is in a non-compatible PageMaker format.

LINKING FILES

Figure 2. By default, PageMaker automatically links imported text and graphics to their original external files. This allows you to update these publications if you modify the external files.

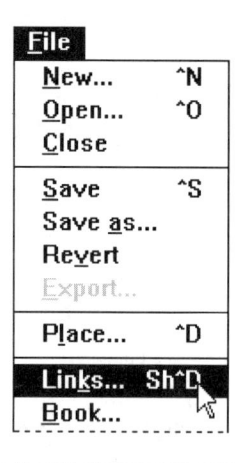

Figure 3. The *Links* command from the **File** menu gives you access to the *Links* dialog box (Figure 4).

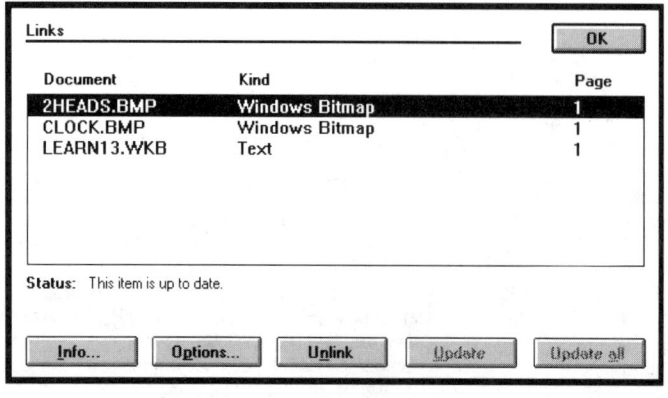

Figure 4. Selecting a file from the *Links* dialog box gives the current file status. The *Update* and *Update all* buttons update single linked elements or all publication files, respectively. The right-most column displays page number or other additional information.

Chapter 3: Linking Files

The *Unlink* button allows you to sever the link between the selected file and its original. See Figures 5 through 9 for descriptions of the *Link info* and *Link options* buttons.

Figure 5. You can activate the *Link info* dialog box through the *Link info* button shown in Figure 4 or by selecting a graphic or text block and choosing *Link info* from the **Element** menu.

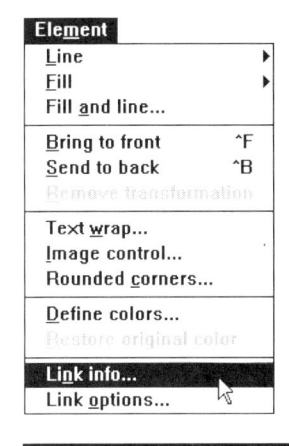

Figure 6. The *Link info* dialog box lets you update or re-establish a link between text or graphic elements and external files. You may have to re-establish a link if you move or rename the external file. All you need to do is select the new or moved file and click on the *Link* button.

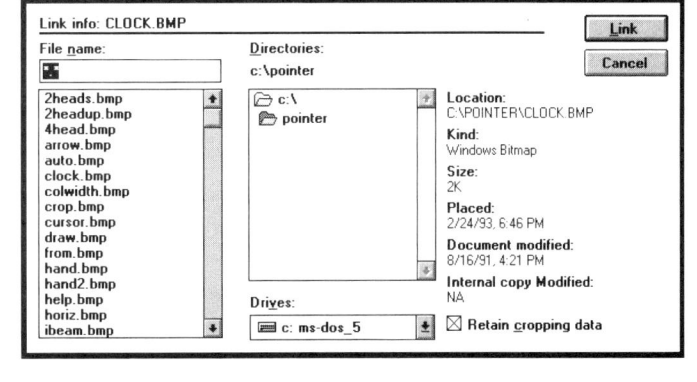

Figure 7. You get to the *Link options* dialog box through the *Link options* button shown in Figure 4, or by selecting *Link options* from the **Element** menu (if you selected a linked element).

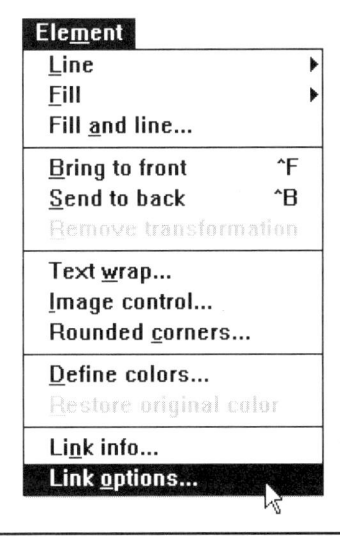

35

Chapter 3: Linking Files

Figure 8. The *Link options* dialog box gives you three options that gives you control over how linked files are updated. (These options are self-explanatory.)

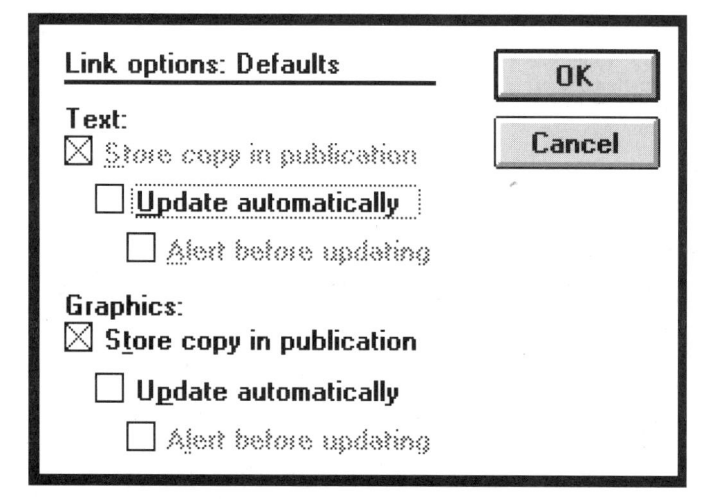

Figure 9. The *Link options* command in the **Element** menu activates the *Link options: Defaults* dialog box when you have nothing selected or you have no publications open. Use this dialog box to set default values.

OTHER LINK COMMANDS

PASTE LINK COMMAND

Figure 10. Use the *Paste link* command to paste a graphic as an OLE-linked object. You can also do this with the *Paste link* button in the *Paste special* dialog box (Figure 11). You must save the external program file before copying it to the clipboard or you will not be able to select *Paste link* in PageMaker, or, if you did not create the graphic in an OLE-supporting program, you will not be able to access this command.

Object created and saved in OLE program and copied to clipboard

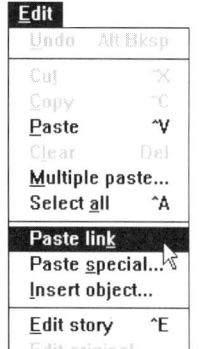

OLE-linked object in PageMaker

36

Chapter 3: Linking Files

PASTE SPECIAL COMMAND

Figure 11. Use the *Paste special* command to activate the *Paste special* dialog box. Often when you cut or copy an object to the Windows clipboard, the object is stored in more than one format. When you use the *Paste* command to insert an object, PageMaker will take the format that displays the truest image.

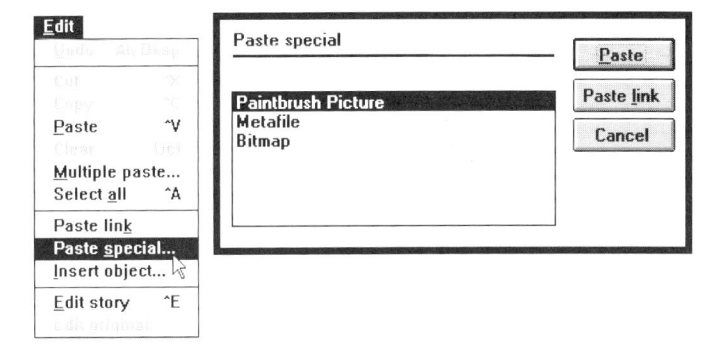

In the *Paste special* dialog box, you can select whichever format you like. The highest quality format is listed first. The *Paste* button in the *Paste special* dialog box pastes the selected format without linking it to the external file. The *Paste link* button establishes a link to the external file and you use it in the same way that you use the *Paste link* command (see Figure 10).

INSERT OBJECT COMMAND

Figure 12. Activate the *Insert object* dialog box by selecting *Insert object* in the **Edit** menu. Double-click on the object type you wish to create and the OLE-compatible program opens.

When you have finished creating the element, select *Update* or *Exit & return to PageMaker* from the **File** menu of the program that you are in. This inserts the element you have created into PageMaker as an OLE-embedded object.

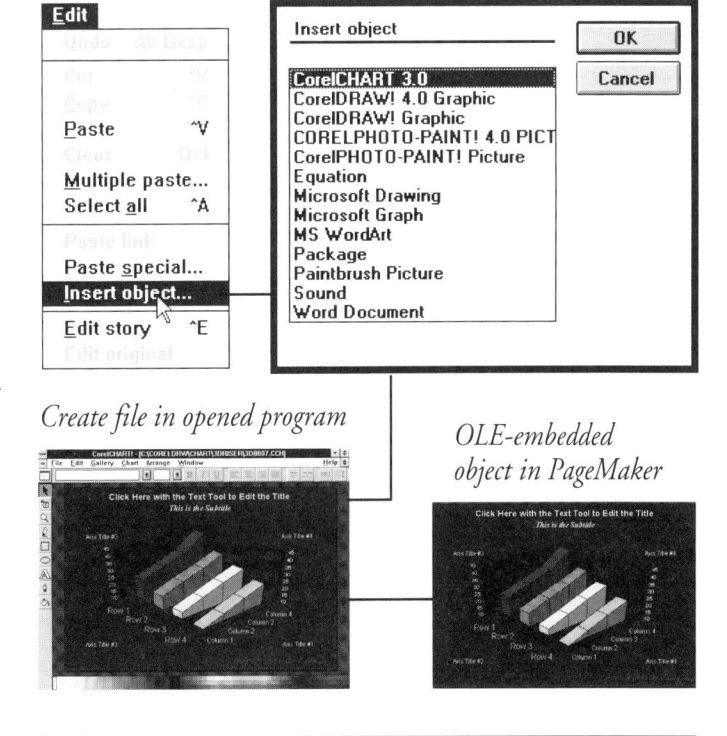

Create file in opened program

OLE-embedded object in PageMaker

37

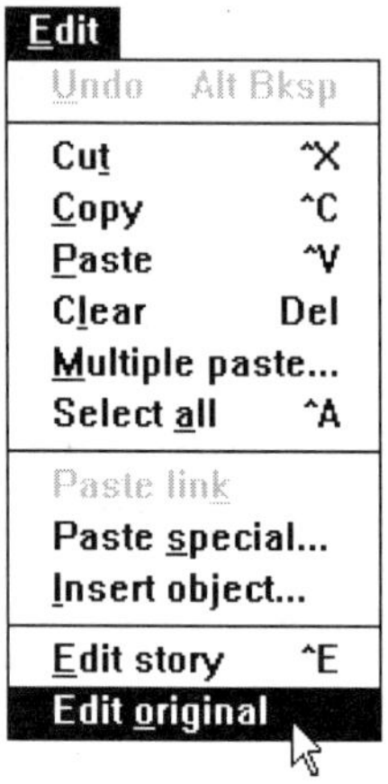

EDIT ORIGINAL COMMAND

Figure 13. Use the *Edit original* command to open the original program you used to create the selected object. You can then edit the object and save the file, which automatically updates the object in your PageMaker publication.

If you have selected an OLE linked or embedded object, the *Edit original* command changes to reflect the type of object you have selected.

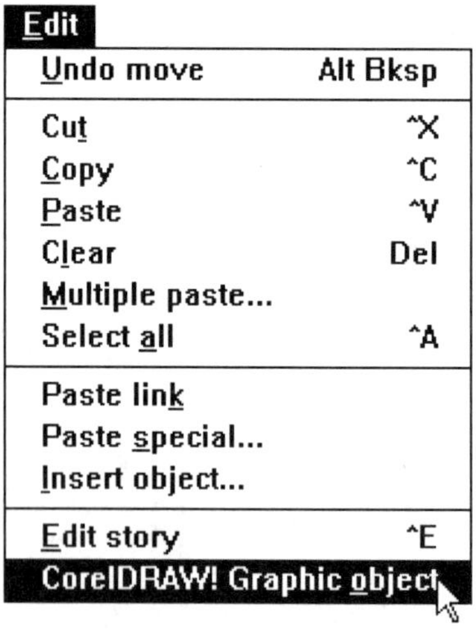

Figure 14. In the example, we have selected a CorelDRAW! graphic and the command *CorelDRAW! Graphic object* appears in the **Edit** menu.

Figure 15. After selecting the *Corel-DRAW! Graphic object* command, CorelDRAW! opens with the graphic you selected in PageMaker active.

Alternatively, to open the original program, double-click on the object.

Selected object in PageMaker

Opened file in original program

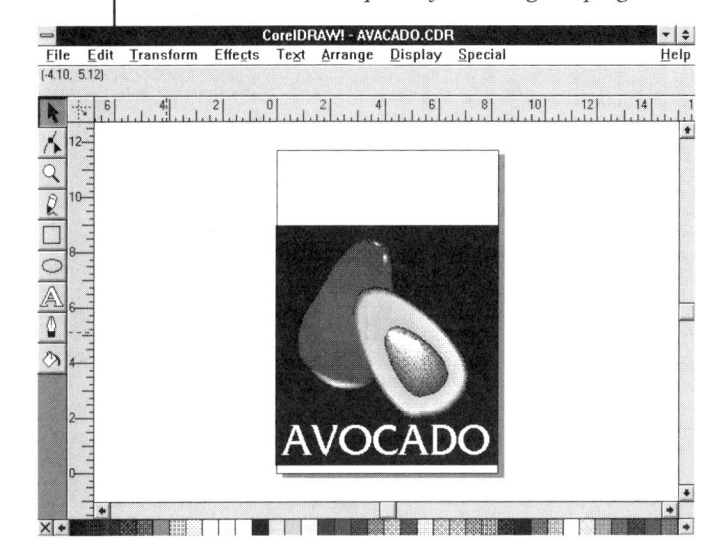

TEXT 4

GENERAL EDITING

It is possible to edit text in PageMaker in either normal layout mode, or in Story editor mode. Editing in story editor mode is the easier of the two methods. We discuss this method later on in this chapter from Figures 75 through 87. We briefly look first at editing in layout mode, as it is still useful for small text changes and for viewing the layout.

You can delete and insert text in PageMaker just as you would in a word processor. First insert the text tool cursor in the text. If you want to delete text to the left press the Backspace key. If you want to insert text simply type in the text. You can move the text insertion point in your document up, down, right or left by using the arrow keys on the keyboard. Alternatively, you can create a new insertion point by moving the mouse to a new location and clicking.

Figure 1. To copy or delete large blocks of text, you need to highlight the text first. You can do this in a number of ways. One way is to simply hold the mouse button down and move it over a section of text. When you release the mouse button you have selected the text, which is shown as white on a black background (reverse video).

The quick brown fox jumps over the lazy dog. The quick brown fox jumps over a lazy dog. The quick brown fox jumps over the lazy dog. The quick brown fox jumps over the lazy dog.

Figure 2. Double-clicking on a word automatically selects it. If you then hold the Shift key down and click the mouse button on consecutive words, you will continue to highlight text a word at a time. The same procedure applies to paragraphs, but initially you need to triple-click.

The quick brown fox jumps over the lazy dog. The quick brown fox jumps over a lazy dog. The quick brown fox jumps over the lazy dog. The quick brown fox jumps over the lazy dog.

Chapter 4: Text

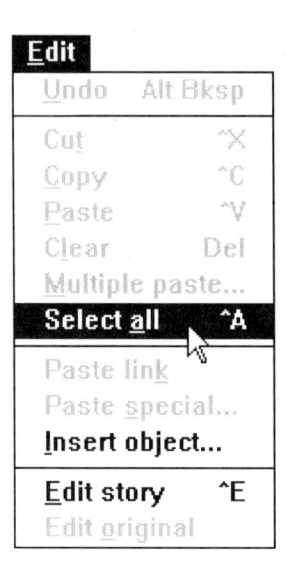

Figure 3. There are two other ways you can select the text. Click the cursor anywhere in the text and choose *Select all* from the **Edit** menu. Alternatively, click at the beginning of the text, move to the end of the text block, hold down the Shift key and click again. This will select everything in between these two points.

For the rest of the chapter, when we refer to selecting or highlighting text, you can use any of the methods we have discussed.

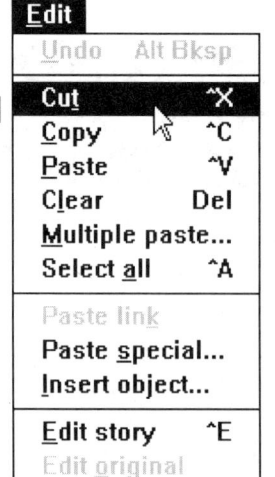

CUT, COPY, AND PASTE COMMANDS

Figure 4. To remove text from a page, first highlight the text you wish to delete. Select the *Cut* command from the **Edit** menu. This command removes the text from the page and makes a copy of it to the Windows clipboard.

Highlight the text, and then choose the Cut command.

Figure 4. To remove text from a page, first highlight the text you wish to delete. Select the *Cut* command from the **Edit** menu. This command removes the text from the page and makes a copy of it to the Windows clipboard.

The Cut command has removed the highlighted text from the screen.

Figure 4. | Select the *Cut* command from the **Edit** menu. This command removes the text from the page and makes a copy of it to the Windows clipboard.

Chapter 4: Text

Figure 5. To copy selected text to the Windows clipboard without removing it from the page, select the *Copy* command from the **Edit** menu.

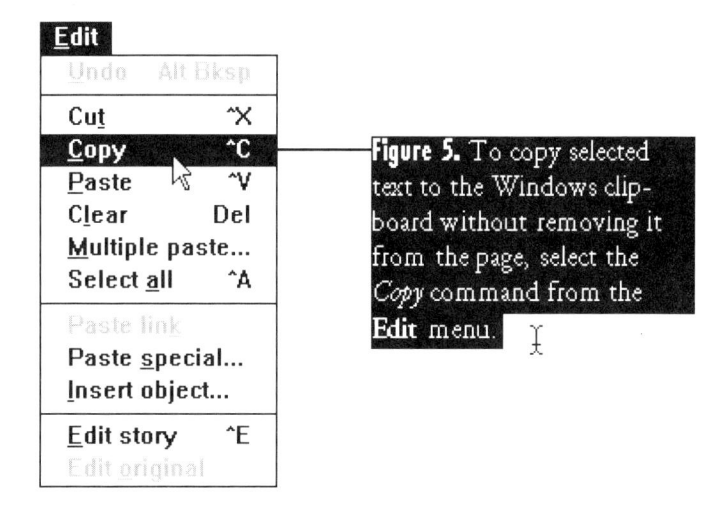

Figure 6. To paste text that you have cut or copied to the clipboard, click on the page where you would like the text to be pasted. Select the *Paste* command from the **Edit** menu, and your text automatically appears on the page. In this example the text copied in Figure 5 is pasted on to the text in Figure 6.

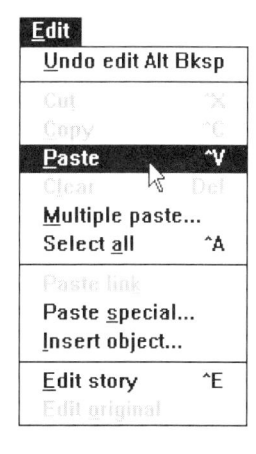

Figure 7. You can also cut and copy text by selecting a text block with the pointer tool before selecting the *Cut* or *Copy* command. To paste the text back onto the page, you can keep the pointer tool selected before selecting *Paste*, or you can click on the page to insert the text within another text block.

43

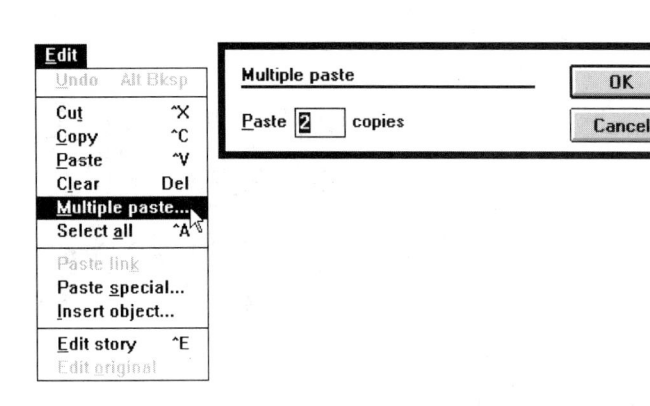

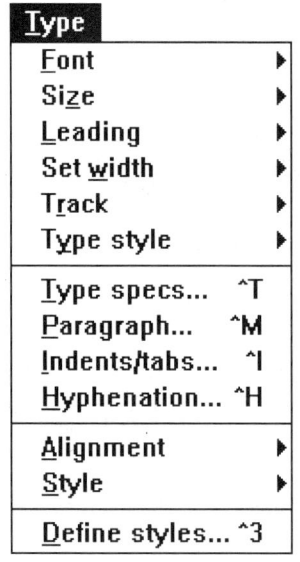

MULTIPLE PASTE COMMAND

Figure 8. Use the *Multiple paste* command to paste more than one copy at a time of your cut or copied text. If you selected the text with the text tool, the pasted text will appear at the insertion point.

THE TYPE MENU

Figure 9. The Type menu is one of the menus within PageMaker 5 that has a series of sub-menus available. Each command with the ▶ symbol to the right causes a sub-menu to appear. When it is selected, a sub-menu lets you quickly select a command as you don't have to activate a dialog box.

If you select any commands in the sub-menu without first highlighting text or with the pointer tool selected (except for *Define styles*), you will be setting the text defaults for the publication. If you highlight the text first, then you affect only this text.

Chapter 4: Text

Figure 10. The *Font* command displays the fonts you can select. This includes all the PostScript printer fonts and any additional downloadable fonts you have added to your system.

Depending on how many fonts you have loaded on your machine, you might not have enough room on your menu to display all the fonts.

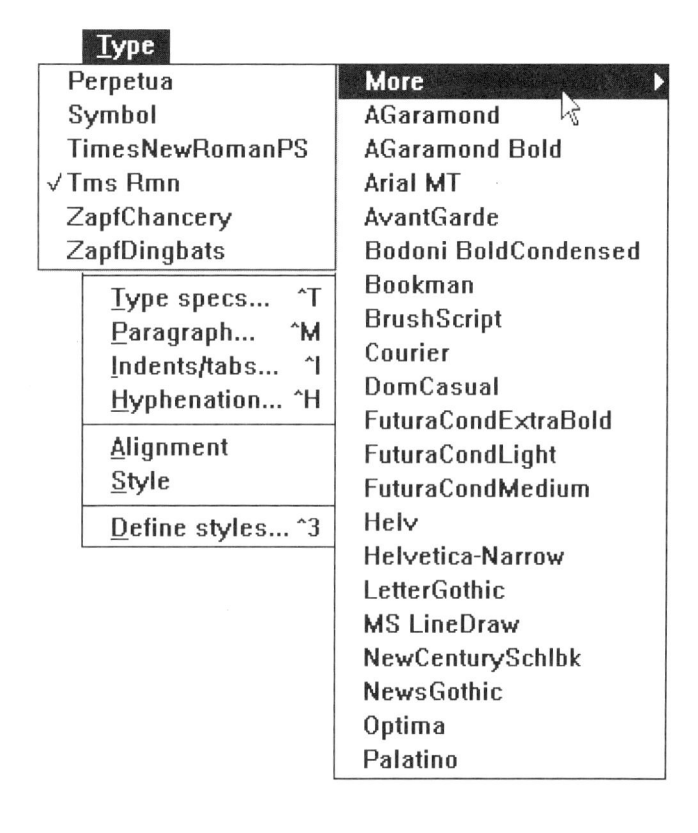

Figure 11. Selecting the *Size* command invokes a sub-menu as shown. Not all point sizes are available from within this sub-menu. Choosing *Other*, at the top, allows you to key in any point size between 4 and 650 points in 0.1 point increments.

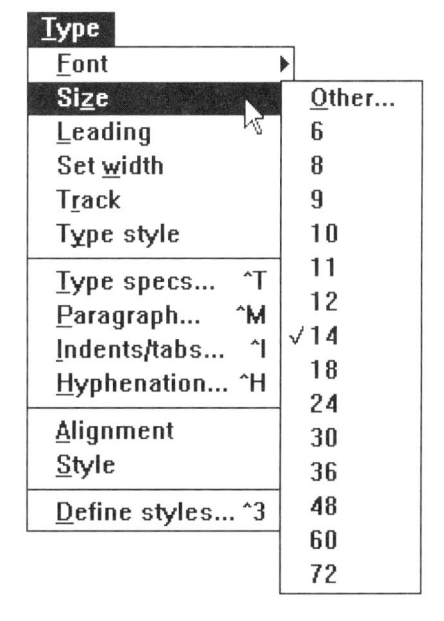

45

Chapter 4: Text

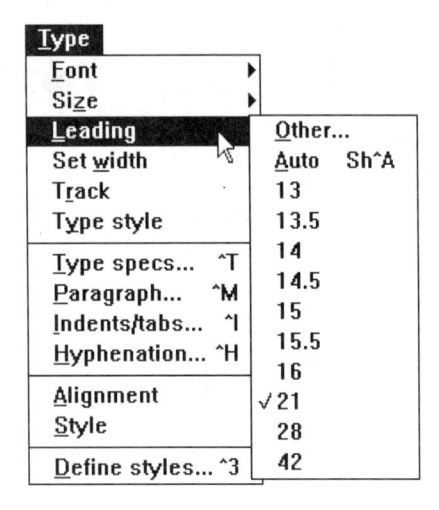

LEADING IS THE SPACE BETWEEN LINES OF TEXT

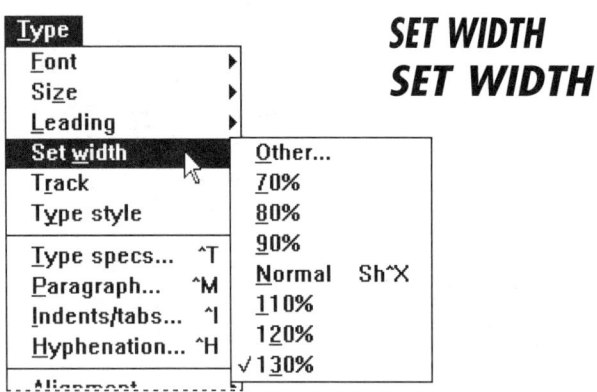

Figure 12. This is the sub-menu for *Leading*; leading is the vertical spacing between text. Choose any of the values shown or select *Other* to add your own value. *Other* lets you to choose a value from 0 to 1300 points in 0.1 point increments. *Auto*, by default, is set to 120% of the text point size (in the *Paragraph specifications* dialog box).

The text in this figure has had the leading increased to 21.

SET WIDTH
SET WIDTH

Figure 13. The *Set width* command controls the width of characters from 5% to 250% in 0.1% increments. Again, choose *Other* if you want a specific value that is not included in the sub-menu. This option allows you to condense or expand each character of any font.

Compare the two examples in this figure. The top text is set at *Normal* while the text below has been set to *130%*.

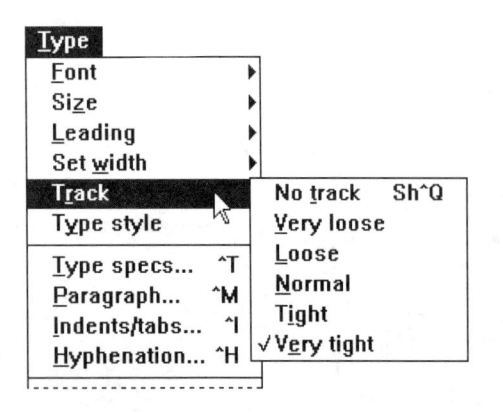

TRACK
TRACK

Figure 14. The *Track* command has its own sub-menu as shown. Use tracking to adjust the spacing between characters and words. As you can see in the sub-menu you have five levels of tracking, from very loose to very tight. Compare the two examples in this figure. The top text is *Normal* while other text is *Very tight*.

Chapter 4: Text

Figure 15. You can make simple style changes to the text with the *Type style* command. You can see what's available in this sub-menu. You can apply more than one style to selected text, but you must re-activate the *Type style* sub-menu for each additional style.

TYPE SPECIFICATIONS

Figure 16. The *Type specs* command combines all the choices of the six commands above it in the **Type** menu, plus additional features. This command and its associated dialog box (Figure 17) let you apply multiple commands at one time to highlighted text.

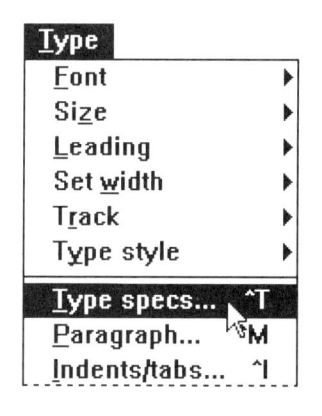

Figure 17. The *Type specifications* dialog box contains *Font*, *Size*, *Leading*, *Set width*, and *Track* options. They provide similar drop-down sub-menus to those described above in Figures 10 through 15. The *Type style* selections at the bottom of the box are the same as those in the *Type style* sub-menu (Figure 15). Figures 18 through 20 show the other options you have in this dialog box.

47

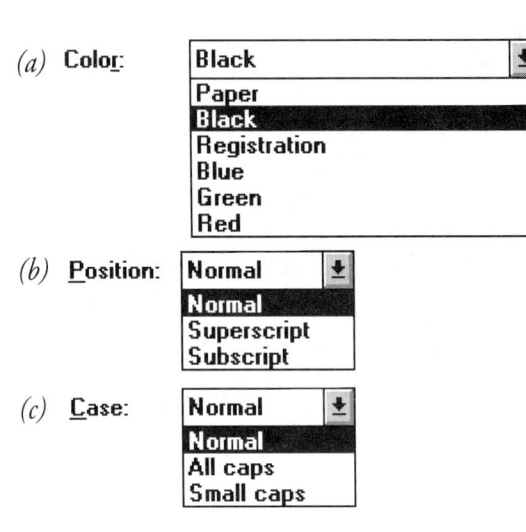

Figure 18. Three additional drop-down lists from the *Type specifications* dialog box are shown here. You can apply *Color* to text as shown in (a). (See Chapter 12, **Using Color** for more information on color.) The *Position* list (b) lets you super/subscript characters. The *Case* list (c) allows you to convert text to ALL CAPS or SMALL CAPS.

Figure 19. Clicking on *Options* in the *Type specifications* dialog box activates the *Type Options* dialog box. Here you can adjust the size of small caps and super/subscript characters, super/subscript positions, as well as the baseline position of highlighted text.

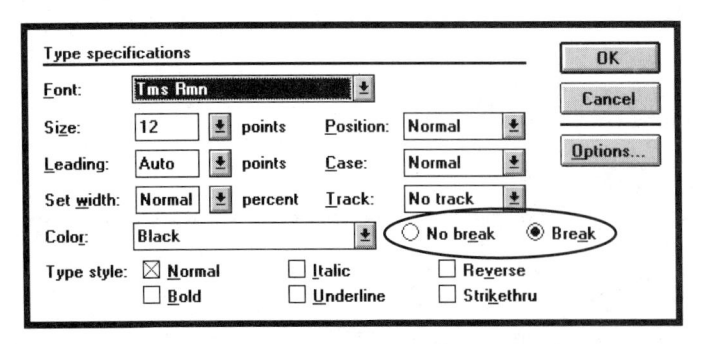

Figure 20. The *No break* option prevents selected text from wrapping from one line to the next. You can use *No break* to force PageMaker to keep words on one line. The *Break* option uses Page-Maker's normal rules for flowing text from one line to another.

PARAGRAPH SPECIFICATIONS

Figure 21. Activate the *Paragraph* specifications dialog box by choosing the *Paragraph* command. This dialog box contains a range of options that allow you to affect whole paragraphs rather than individual words. The options in this dialog box affect the selected text or the text containing the insertion point.

INDENTS AND PARAGRAPH SPACE

Figure 22. In the *Paragraph specifications* dialog box, the five options at the top are *Indents* (*Left* applies to the entire paragraph; *First* applies to the first line only; and *Right* applies to the right of the entire paragraph), and *Paragraph space* (controls the amount of space before and after your paragraph).

ALIGNMENT

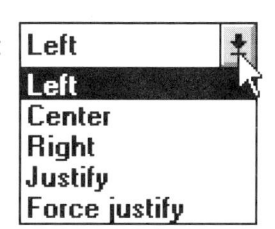

Figure 23. Activate this drop-down list by clicking or holding the mouse down on the arrow to the right of the *Alignment* box. This list is identical to the one activated by the *Alignment* command in the **Type** menu. You can change the alignment of the whole paragraph by selecting a different option.

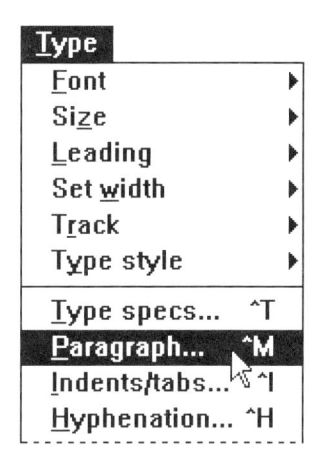

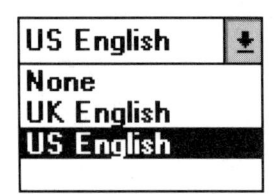

Figure 24. PageMaker uses the *Dictionary* when checking spelling and hyphenation. You activate it by holding or clicking the mouse down on the arrow to the right of the currently displayed dictionary. Select your choice from the drop-down list that appears, if any others are available.

OPTIONS

The *Keep lines together* option in the Paragraph specifications dialog box ensures that a selected paragraph is not separated by a page or column break.

The *Column break before* option ensures that the selected paragraph begins a new column.

The *Page break before* option ensures the selected paragraph begins a new page.

When you select the *Include in table of contents* option, the selected text is added to your table of contents. For more information on this command, see Chapter 15, **Creating Tables of Contents.**

Keep with next x lines makes sure that a selected paragraph moves with 1 to 3 lines of the next paragraph. This stops subheadings from appearing on their own at the bottom of a column.

Use the *Widow control* option to set how many lines at the end of a paragraph start a new page or column. You have the option of leaving 1 to 3 lines here.

The *Orphan control* command works in a similar way to the *Widow control* command. The difference is that *Orphan control* decides how many lines at the start of a paragraph remain at the bottom of a column or page. To ensure consistency throughout your document and to save time, you can preset these options before placing large documents.

PARAGRAPH RULES

Figure 25. The *Paragraph rules* dialog box appears after you click on *Rules* in the *Paragraph specifications* dialog box. These options let you place lines above and below your text. You can set the above and below rules separately, and you can have one without the other. You activate these rules by clicking inside the *Rule above paragraph* and the *Rule below paragraph* selection boxes.

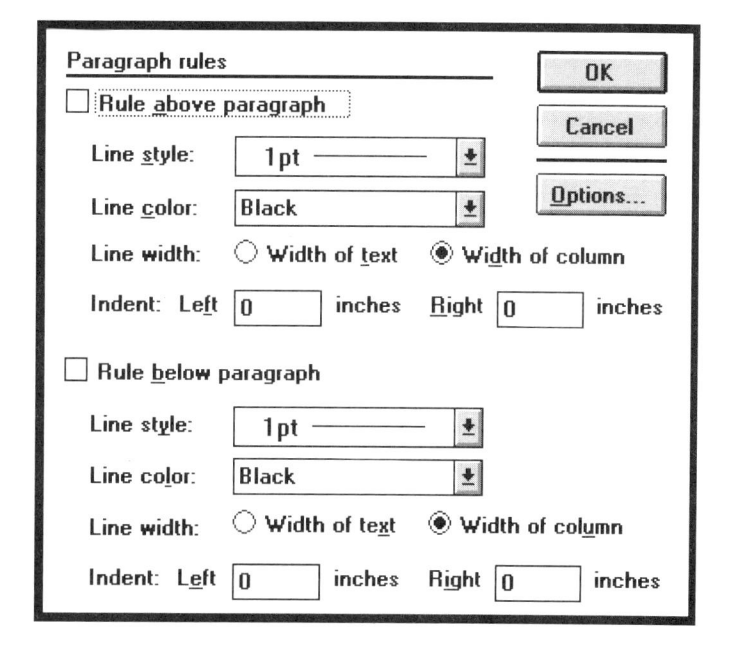

Figure 26. Click or hold the mouse down on the arrow to the right of the *Line style* box in the *Paragraph rules* dialog box. A drop-down list box appears. Use the mouse to select the line thickness you require.

Figure 27. If working with a color screen, you can apply a color to the lines above and below your text through the *Paragraph rules* dialog box. Use this drop-down list in the same way that you use the *Line style* drop-down list box.

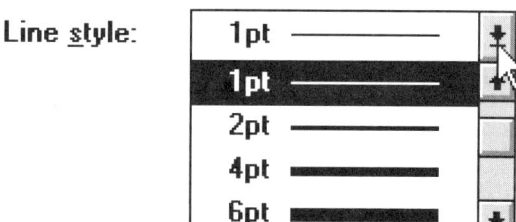

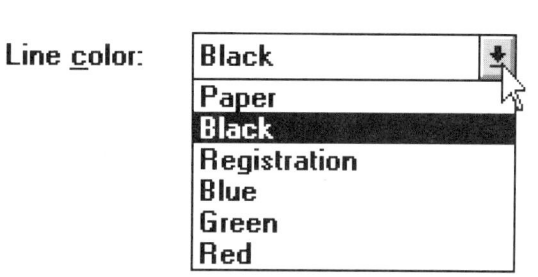

Chapter 4: Text

You have two choices in the *Line width* option. Choose either the *Width of text* or *Width of column* option.

You can apply indents to the rules if you do not want the rules to be exactly the width of the text or the column.

You have the same options for the *Rule below paragraph* as you do for the *Rule above paragraph*.

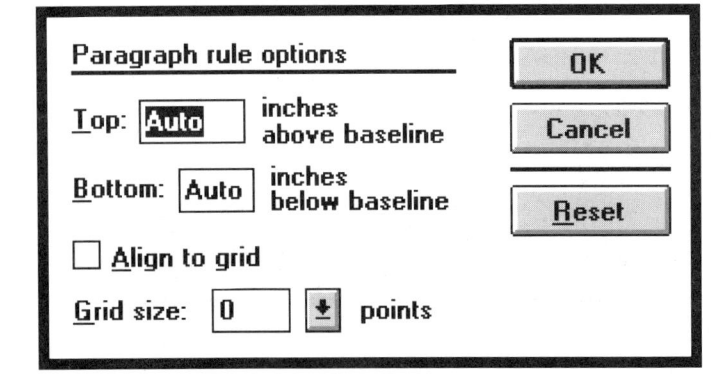

PARAGRAPH RULE OPTIONS

Figure 28. Activate the *Paragraph rule options* dialog box by clicking on the *Options* button in the *Paragraph rules* dialog box shown above. The *Top* and *Bottom* options allow you to position the rules relative to the text. Double-click in the relevant box and type in the desired value.

The *Align to grid* option in the *Paragraph rule options* dialog box ensures that the body text on your page aligns horizontally. When using this option, the grid size should reflect the leading size of the text. This option does not work when you have applied Autoleading to the text.

SPACING ATTRIBUTES

Figure 29. Activate the *Spacing attributes* dialog box by clicking on the *Spacing* button in the *Paragraph specifications* dialog box shown in Figure 22.

The *Word space* values in the *Spacing attributes* dialog box affect the spacing between your words. The percentages here are based on normal text. The possible settings for each option can range from 0% to 500%. Increasing or decreasing these figures increases or decreases the word spacing respectively.

Letter space affects the spacing between characters. The range available for *Minimum* and *Maximum* is -200% to +200%. The *Desired* figure should be somewhere between the minimum and maximum settings. Again, increasing and decreasing the settings here will change the letterspacing of the selected text.

Pair kerning varies the amount of space between two adjacent characters. By default, *Auto above x points* is selected.

The *Leading method* selection should nearly always be *Proportional*. You can use the *Top of caps* method for special design effects. Use the *Baseline* option when you wish to align leading from the baseline of the text — used in traditional typography.

The *Autoleading* option in the *Spacing attributes* dialog box represents a proportion of the point size. Changing this figure will affect the line spacing of the text.

INDENTS/TABS

Figure 30. Selecting the *Indents/tabs* command from the **Type** menu activates the *Indents/tabs* dialog box.

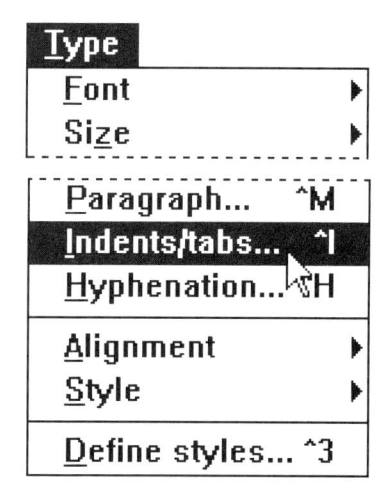

Chapter 4: Text

Figure 31. To start with, there are four tab options at the left of this dialog box. These are (a) left tab, (b) centered tab, (c) right tab and (d) decimal tab.

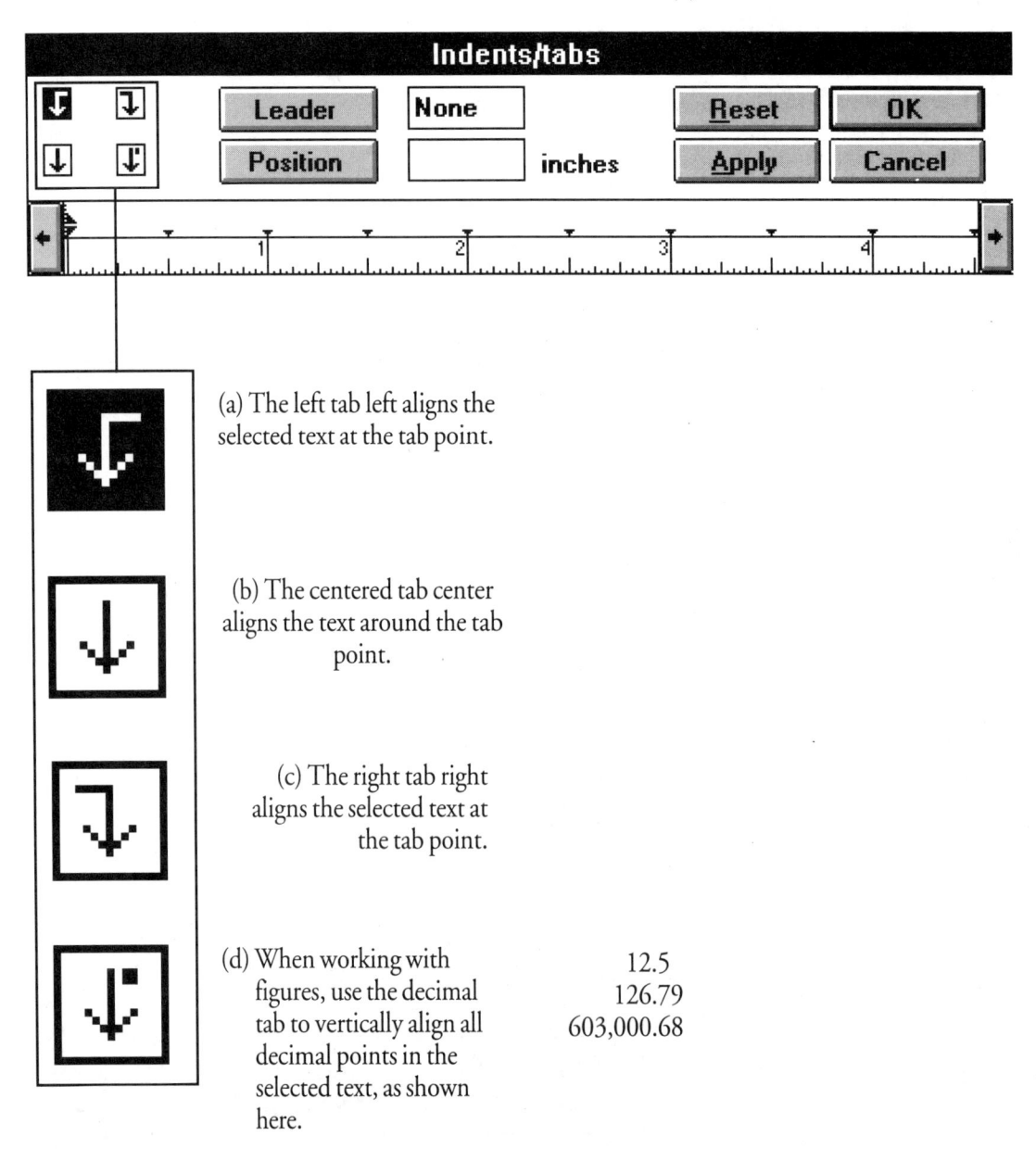

(a) The left tab left aligns the selected text at the tab point.

(b) The centered tab center aligns the text around the tab point.

(c) The right tab right aligns the selected text at the tab point.

(d) When working with figures, use the decimal tab to vertically align all decimal points in the selected text, as shown here.

```
     12.5
    126.79
 603,000.68
```

54

Figure 32. If you want a character repeated between tabs, such as the leader dots found in a table of contents, use the Leader option. The associated drop-down list, which you activate by clicking the mouse on the *Leader* button, gives you five options. The *Custom* option lets you type in your own preferred character to be used as your tab leader.

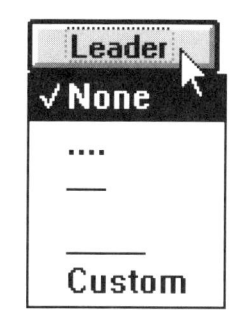

Figure 33. The *Position* option displays the position on the ruler of the currently selected tab. It also has a drop-down list that lets you add, delete, move and repeat tabs.

Figure 34. On activating the *Indents/tabs* dialog box, the zero point of the ruler indicates the beginning of the selected text or the beginning of the text block containing the insertion point.

You can move this dialog box around the page by holding the mouse down on the title bar and dragging it to a new position.

Figure 35. The ruler has two markers that start at the zero point. The top marker (▲) represents the first line indent of the selected paragraph. Moving this marker with the mouse will alter the position of the first line of your selected text.

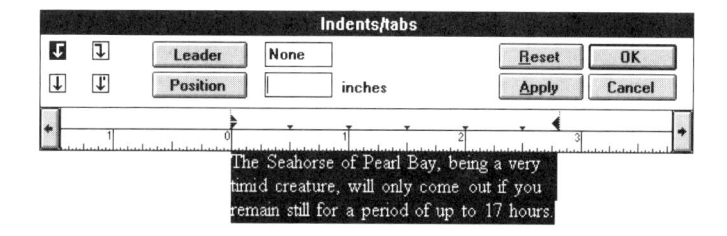

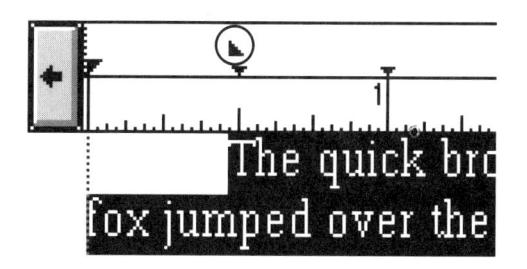

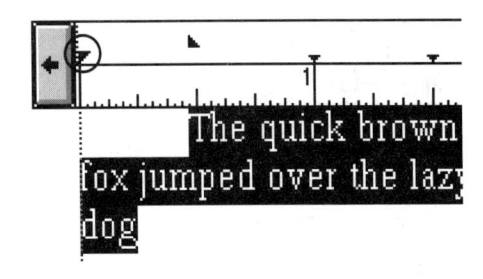

Figure 36. The bottom marker (▼) is the left indent of the whole paragraph, and all selected text will move to reflect the amount you have moved the marker with the mouse.

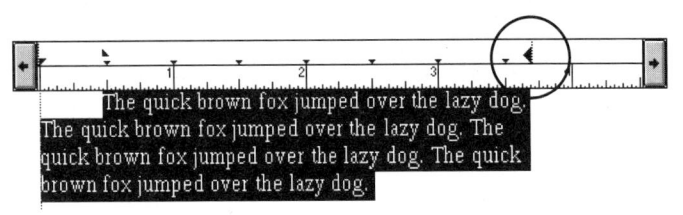

Figure 37. The right indent marker (◄) sits on the ruler at the right margin of the selected text block.

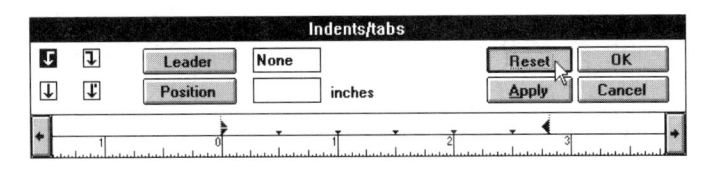

Figure 38. The *Reset* button in the Indent/tabs dialog box removes all tabs you have placed yourself and returns the dialog box to the default settings.

HYPHENATION

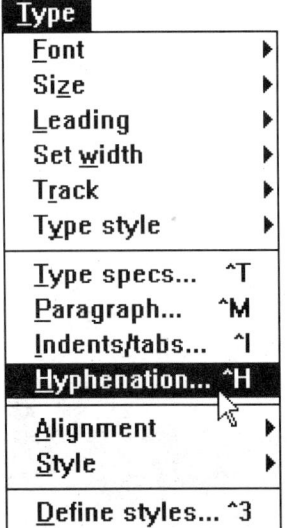

Figure 39. The next command in the **Type** menu is *Hyphenation*.

Figure 40. This command activates the *Hyphenation* dialog box. By default, the hyphenation is on.

If you select the *Manual only* choice, PageMaker hyphenates only where you have placed discretionary hyphens (Ctrl+-). The hyphen appears only when the manually hyphenated word falls at the end of a line. PageMaker splits it to fit the paragraph correctly.

If you select the *Manual plus dictionary* option, PageMaker uses all discretionary hyphens plus the hyphens that appear in PageMaker's dictionary.

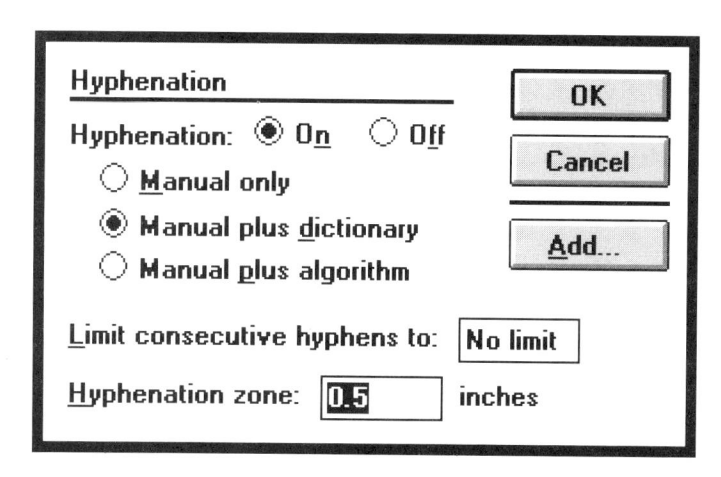

If you select the *Manual plus algorithm* option in the *Hyphenation* dialog box, PageMaker hyphenates any word whether it appears in the PageMaker dictionary or not. If a word falls at the end of a column, PageMaker hyphenates the word in what it calculates to be the most suitable place.

The *Limit consecutive hyphens to* option lets you set a maximum number of consecutive hyphens you would like to appear (from 1 to 255 or No limit) in the selected text.

The *Hyphenation zone* option affects the amount of space before hyphenation occurs. The larger the figure you place in this box (up to 2 inches), the less hyphens that occur.

Figure 41. Clicking on the *Add* option in the *Hyphenation* dialog box activates this dialog box. Here you can add words to your dictionary and select your preferred place of hyphenation.

Chapter 4: Text

You can also change the position of hyphens in words that already exist in the dictionary. Put one tilde (~) in a word where you would prefer to split the word. Add two tildes for your second choice and three for your third choice. For example: Hyph~en~~a~~~tion.

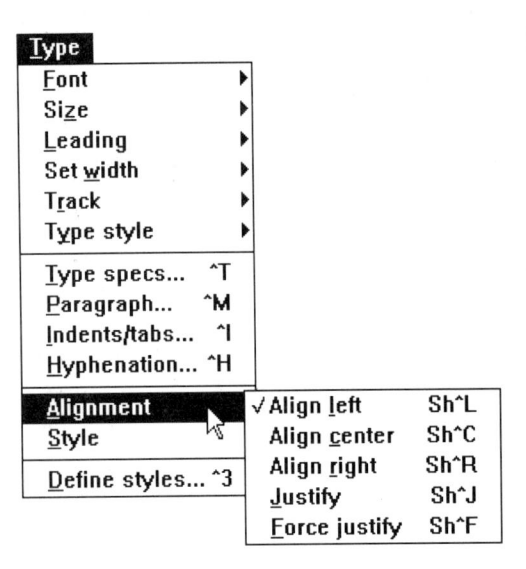

Figure 42. You have the same alignment choices in the *Alignment* sub-menu as you do in the *Paragraph specifications* dialog box (see Figure 23).

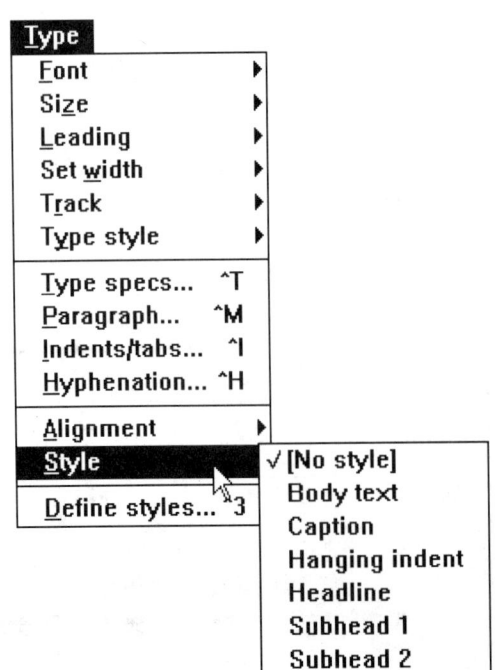

Figure 43. The *Style* and *Define styles* commands are explained in Chapter 11, **Using Styles**.

58

Chapter 4: Text

EXPORTING TEXT

You can export text from PageMaker to a file through the *Export* command in the **File** menu.

Figure 44. Before choosing the *Export* command, highlight the text that you would like to export. If you wish to export the whole story, insert the text cursor anywhere in the text.

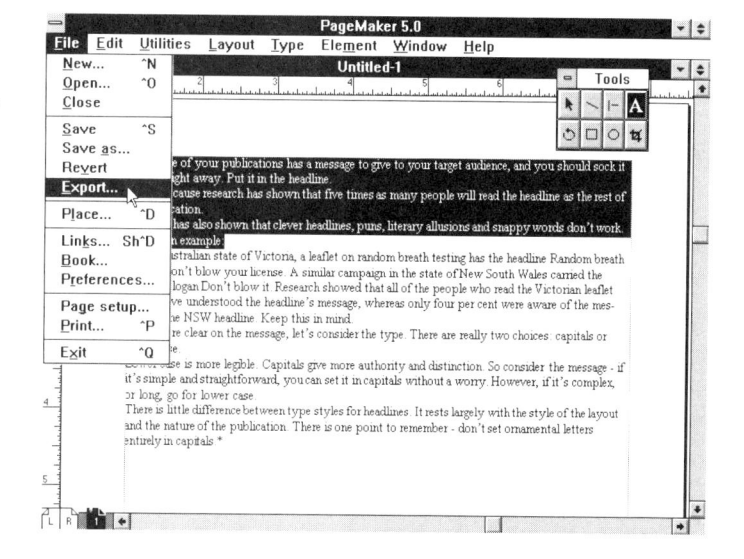

Figure 45. In the *Export document* dialog box, give the file a name and select the drive or directory where you want to save it.

You can either export the entire story or just the selected text.

Select *Export tags* if you also want to export the styles you created for your text in PageMaker.

When you export a file, the *File format* drop-down list in the *Export document* dialog box lets you select the format from the export filters you installed. Click on the format you require. After you have set up the *Export document* dialog box, click on *OK*.

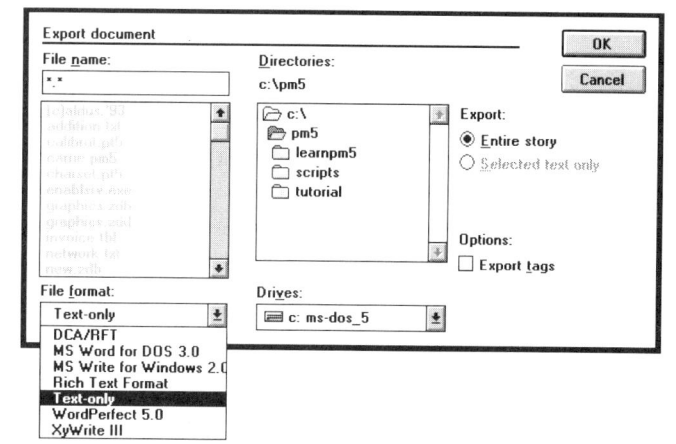

59

Chapter 4: Text

THE CONTROL PALETTE AND TEXT

You can use the Control palette as a quick way of formatting text and applying styles, as an alternative to using the menu commands in the **Type** menu. Nearly every option in the Control palette has an equivalent menu command. See the section on the *Type specs* command earlier in the chapter for more information.

Figure 46. You activate the Control palette (above) through the *Window* menu.

Figure 47. This (below) is how the Control palette looks on screen when you have nothing selected and the pointer tool is active. The X and Y co-ordinates indicate the position of the mouse.

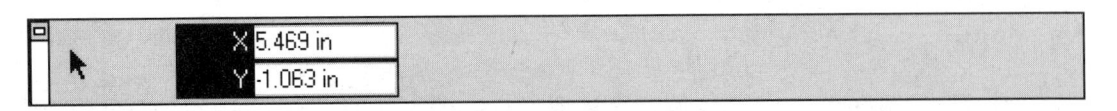

60

Chapter 4: Text

THE TEXT PALETTE

CHARACTER VIEW

Figure 48. When you select the text tool, the Control palette changes to the one shown below—the Text palette. PageMaker uses Character view by default. You use Character view to apply text attributes to selected text.

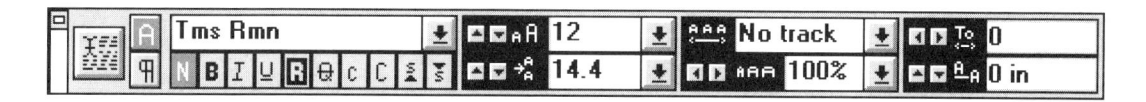

Figure 49. In this figure, we have labeled the different parts of the Text palette in *Character view.*

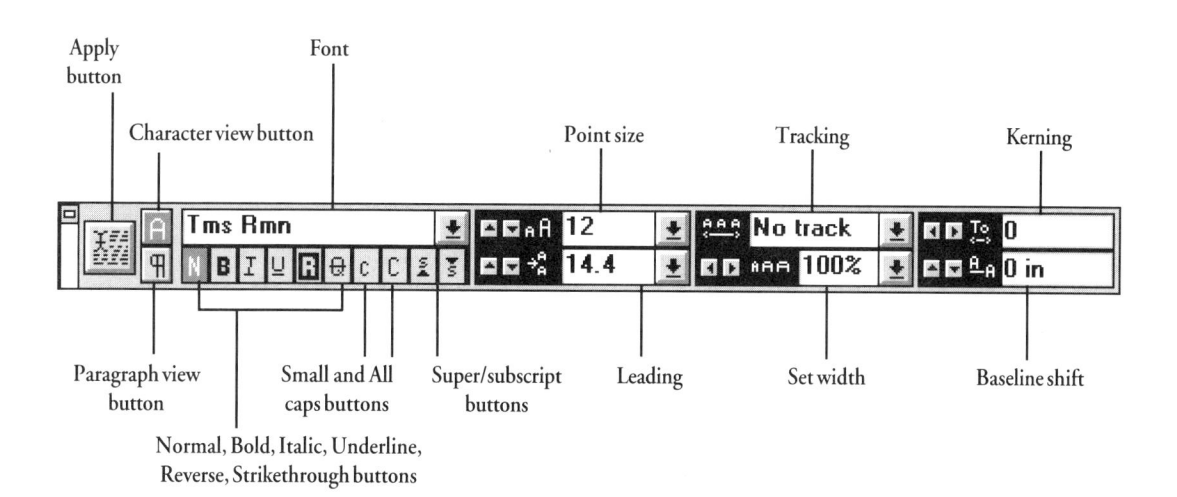

Apply button
Font
Character view button
Point size
Tracking
Kerning
Paragraph view button
Small and All caps buttons
Super/subscript buttons
Leading
Set width
Baseline shift
Normal, Bold, Italic, Underline, Reverse, Strikethrough buttons

61

Chapter 4: Text

APPLY BUTTON

Figure 50. Use the *Apply* button in the Control palette to display changes you have made to selected text using the Control palette. (Some changes appear automatically.)

Pressing the Tab key moves you to the next option in the Control palette.

PALETTE VIEW BUTTONS

Figure 51. Click on the appropriate button to switch between Character view and Paragraph view.

FONT

Figure 52. Use this drop-down list to change the font of selected text. Click on the down arrow to display the drop-down list and click on the desired font.

TYPE STYLE, CASE, AND SUB/SUPERSCRIPT BUTTONS

Figure 53. Use these buttons to change the style of highlighted text. To turn a style off, click on the button of the relevant type style. (Do not confuse these styles with paragraph styles.)

POINT SIZE OPTION

Figure 54. The *Point size* edit box lets you either change the point size from the drop-down list, or type the size into the edit box to change the size of highlighted text.

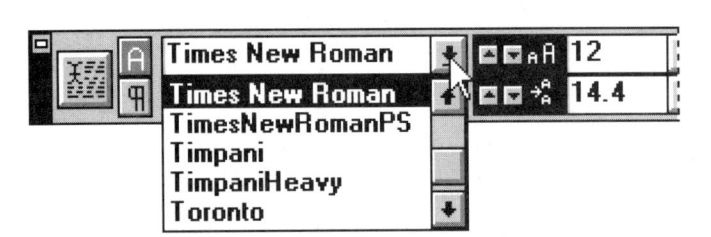

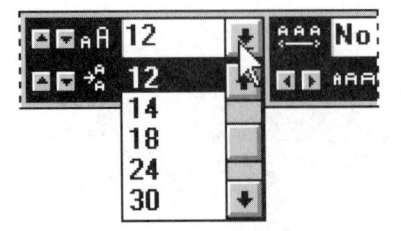

The nudge buttons to the left allow you to increase or decrease the point size by 0.1 of a point. Holding down the Ctrl key while clicking on a nudge button increases or decreases the point size by 1 point. You can set the nudge amount in the *Preferences* dialog box.

LEADING OPTION

Figure 55. The *Leading* edit box allows you to set the leading value for highlighted text. Choose from the drop-down list or type a value into the edit box. Use the nudge buttons to increase or decrease the leading size by 0.1 of a point.

Holding down the Ctrl key while clicking on a nudge button increases or decreases the leading by 1 point.

TRACKING OPTION

Figure 56. Use the *Tracking* option to set the tracking (letter space) for selected text.

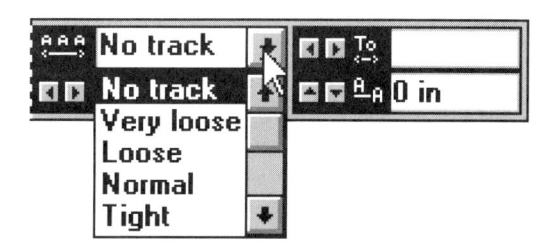

SET WIDTH OPTION

Figure 57. Use the *Set width* option to change the horizontal width of the selected characters. Use the nudge buttons to increase or decrease the width by 1%. Holding down the Ctrl key while clicking on a nudge button increases or decreases the width by 10%.

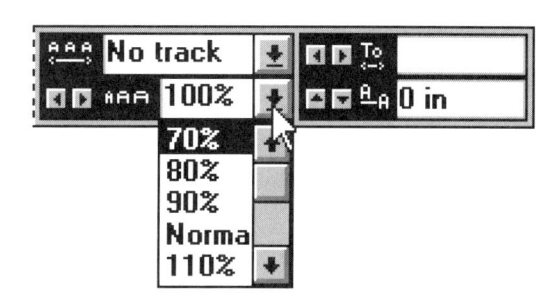

KERNING OPTION

Figure 58. Change the *Kerning* option to modify the space between the letters of highlighted text. Use the nudge buttons to increase or decrease the space by 0.01 em. Holding down the Ctrl key while clicking on a nudge button increases or decreases the space by 0.1 em.

BASELINE OPTION

Figure 59. You can modify the baseline of highlighted text by changing this option. The default unit of measure used for the baseline is the unit of measure used for the vertical ruler (specified in the Preferences dialog box). Use the nudge buttons to increase or decrease baseline by the nudge amount specified in Preferences. Holding down the Ctrl key while clicking on a nudge button increases or decreases the baseline by 10 times that amount.

PARAGRAPH VIEW

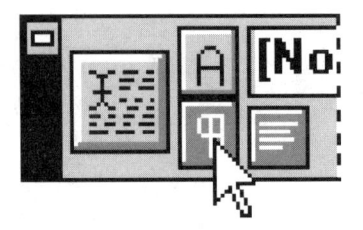

Figure 60. When you click on the *Paragraph view* button, the Control palette changes.

Chapter 4: Text

Figure 61. You use *Paragraph view* to apply paragraph styles to text. You can also modify and create styles in *Paragraph* view (see Chapter 11, **Using Styles** for more information).

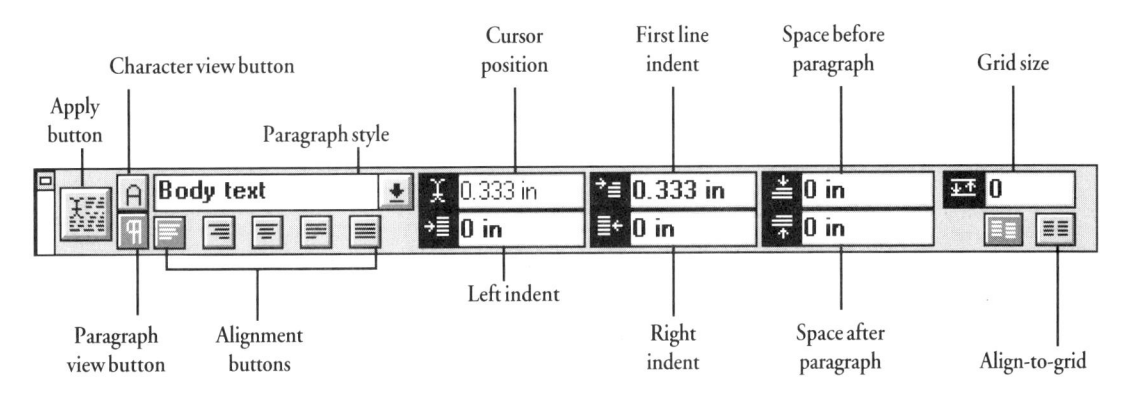

[Labeled diagram of Paragraph view palette with the following labels: Apply button, Character view button, Paragraph style, Cursor position, First line indent, Space before paragraph, Grid size, Paragraph view button, Alignment buttons, Left indent, Right indent, Space after paragraph, Align-to-grid. Values shown: Body text, 0.333 in, 0.333 in, 0 in, 0, 0 in, 0 in, 0 in.]

APPLY BUTTON

See Figure 50 in this chapter.

PALETTE VIEW BUTTONS

See Figure 51 in this chapter.

PARAGRAPH STYLE

Figure 62. Use the *Paragraph style* drop-down list to apply a style to selected text. To create a new style, format some text with the attributes of the style you wish to create, select it, and type a new style name in the edit box (see Chapter 11, **Using Styles** for more information).

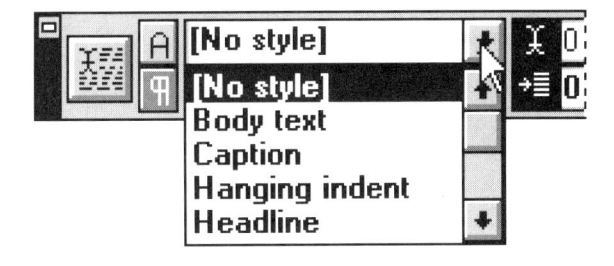

[Drop-down list showing: [No style], [No style], Body text, Caption, Hanging indent, Headline]

65

Chapter 4: Text

ALIGNMENT BUTTONS

Figure 63. Use the *Alignment* buttons to change the justification of highlighted text.

CURSOR POSITION INDICATOR

Figure 64. The *Cursor position* indicator displays the horizontal position of the cursor on the page in relation to the left side of the text block, as opposed to rulers or margins.

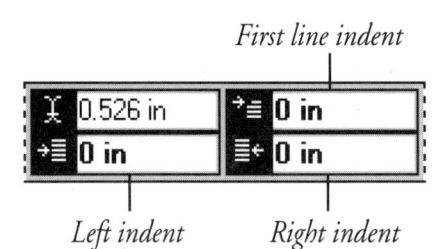

INDENT OPTIONS

First line indent

Left indent   *Right indent*

Figure 65. You can insert values in the *Indent* option edit boxes to apply left, right and first-line indents to highlighted text. Indents are measured from the left and right sides of the text block.

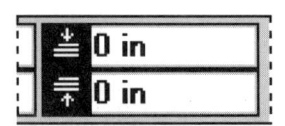

SPACE BEFORE AND SPACE AFTER OPTIONS

Figure 66. Use the *Space before* and *Space after* edit boxes to insert space above and below highlighted paragraphs.

GRID SIZE OPTION

Figure 67. The value you type in the *Grid size* edit box relates to the text grid size when you use the Align-to-grid option. The leading value of your text is the best value to key into this option, in this case 13.

Chapter 4: Text

ALIGN-TO-GRID OPTION

Figure 68. If you have set your vertical ruler measurement to points, you can use the *Align-to-grid* option to ensure that adjacent columns of text remain aligned. Click on the right button to turn the grid align feature on.

USING THE CONTROL PALETTE

Figure 69. You can apply any options in the Control palette simply by highlighting some text and changing an option. You will notice that after you highlight some text and click on an option in the Control palette (as shown here) that the highlighted text becomes surrounded by a box rather than remaining highlighted. Here we are changing the font of the selected text from Times Roman to Futura Condensed Medium.

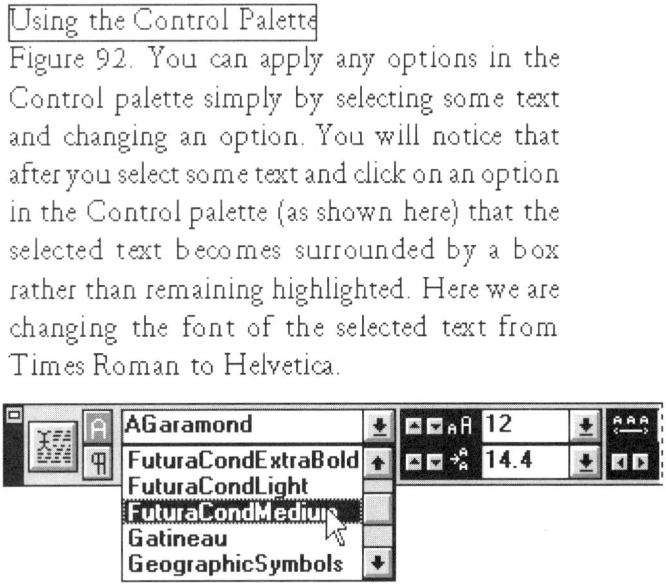

Using the Control Palette

Figure 92. You can apply any options in the Control palette simply by selecting some text and changing an option. You will notice that after you select some text and click on an option in the Control palette (as shown here) that the selected text becomes surrounded by a box rather than remaining highlighted. Here we are changing the font of the selected text from Times Roman to Helvetica.

Figure 70. The changes occur immediately, and are reflected in the text and in the Control palette.

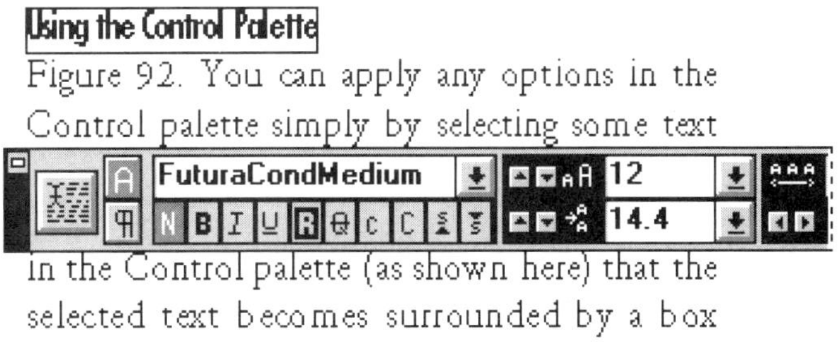

Using the Control Palette

Figure 92. You can apply any options in the Control palette simply by selecting some text in the Control palette (as shown here) that the selected text becomes surrounded by a box

Chapter 4: Text

Using the Control Palette

Figure 92. You can apply any options in the Control palette simply by selecting some text and changing an option. You will notice that after you select some text and click on an option in the Control palette (as shown here) that the selected text becomes surrounded by a box

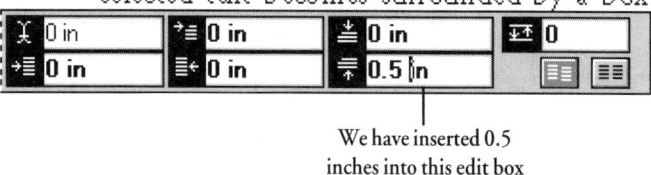

We have inserted 0.5 inches into this edit box

Figure 71. In this figure, we have switched to *Paragraph view*, and have inserted space in the edit box of the *Space after* option to apply to the selected text. As in this case, some options which require you to type in a value do not affect the text automatically.

Using the Control Palette

Figure 92. You can apply any options in the Control palette simply by selecting some text and changing an option. You will notice that

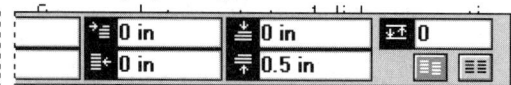

rather than remaining highlighted. Here we are changing the font of the selected text from Times Roman to Helvetica.

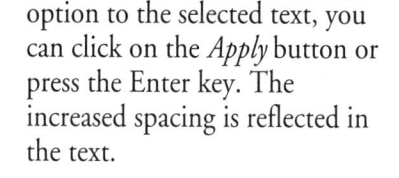

Figure 72. To apply the changed option to the selected text, you can click on the *Apply* button or press the Enter key. The increased spacing is reflected in the text.

Figure 73. Use the nudge buttons by clicking on a right, a left, an up or a down button to increase or decrease the value in the connected edit box. Nudge buttons occur in pairs of up and down and left and right. As with all the other options, you must have some text selected before you can make any change.

Chapter 4: Text

Figure 74. This table displays a number of keyboard shortcuts and their results.

Keyboard shortcut	Result
Ctrl+'	Displays or hides Control palette.
Tab/Shift+Tab	Moves to next option/moves to previous option.
Enter/Tab	Applies change to selected text.
Spacebar	Turns the current button on or off.

STORY EDITOR

Figure 75. Story editor, which provides the word processing features in PageMaker 5, places a separate text window on top of PageMaker's *Layout* view. The menus are slightly different within Story editor. PageMaker displays all text in a story in one continuous block. You can scroll through the text if you cannot see it all. You can resize and move the story window around the screen if you need to.

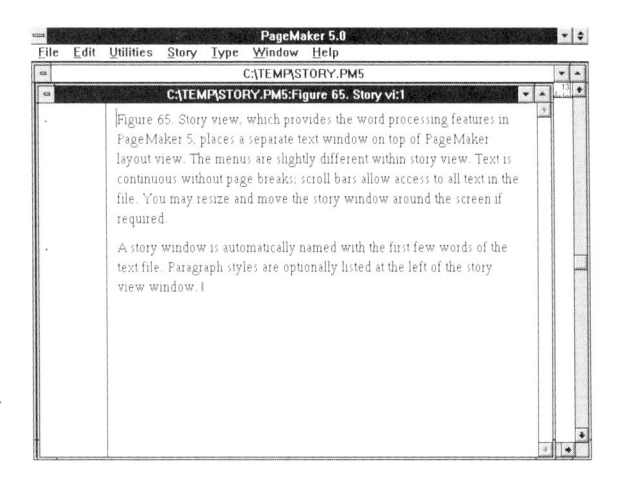

PageMaker automatically names a story window with the first few words of the text file. You can list paragraph styles at the left of the Story editor window by choosing *Display style names* from the **Story** menu.

Figure 76. You can access Story editor in a variety of ways. Clicking the text cursor in a story and choosing *Edit story* from the **Edit** menu is one way. You can also triple-click on a text block with the pointer tool.

The difference between a story and a text block is that a story is a combination of text blocks that are threaded together as part of the same text file. A text block that you select with the pointer tool may only be a part of a story.

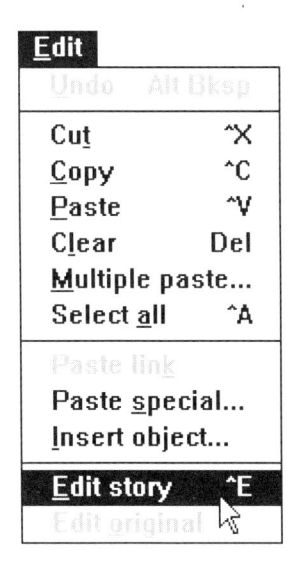

Chapter 4: Text

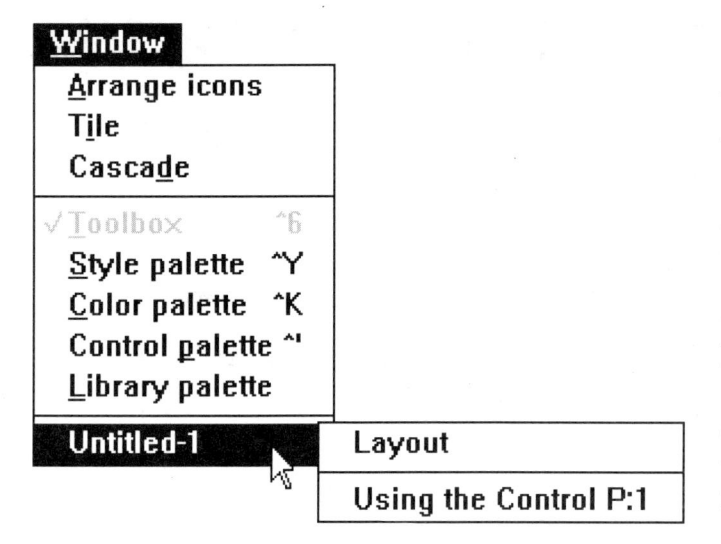

Figure 77. To move between *Story editor* and *Layout* view, use the **Window** menu to select the window you want to view. You can also triple-click with the pointer tool on text to move automatically into story view. Clicking on an exposed part of an open story window also moves you into Story editor view.

If you have no text on screen, select the *Edit story* command and the story window appears ready for you to enter a new story.

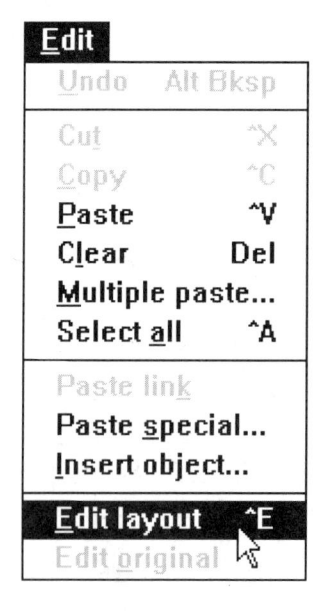

Figure 78. To return to *Layout* view from Story editor you can double-click on the Control menu box in the story window, choose *Close story* from the **Story** menu, choose *Edit layout* from the **Edit** menu, or click on an exposed portion of the *Layout* view publication. The latter two options keep the Story editor window open but it moves behind the layout window.

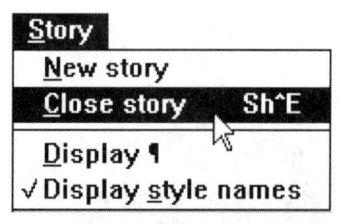

Figure 79. If you have not yet placed your story (e.g. if you activated Story editor to type in a text file), PageMaker will give you the option of placing this text or discarding it when you select the *Close story* command.

70

Chapter 4: Text

Figure 80. The *Find* command from the **Utilities** menu in Story editor allows you to search for text while in story view.

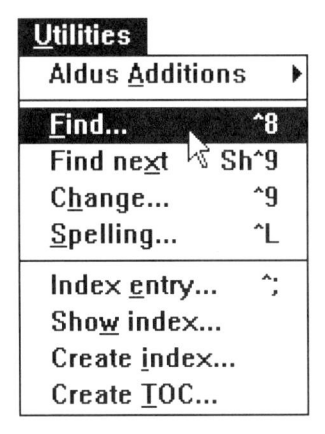

Figure 81. The *Find* dialog box allows you to insert the text for which to search. You can search selected text, the current story, all stories, or even all publications. The *Attributes* button activates a further dialog box where you can select to search for a certain paragraph styles, font, size or type style.

To close this or any similar dialog box in Story editor, double-click on the system menu in the top-left corner of the dialog box or click outside the dialog box.

Figure 82. Use the *Change* command from the **Utilities** menu in Story editor to search for and replace found text with new text.

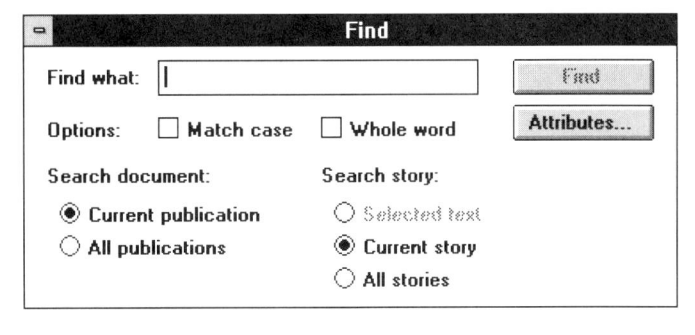

71

Chapter 4: Text

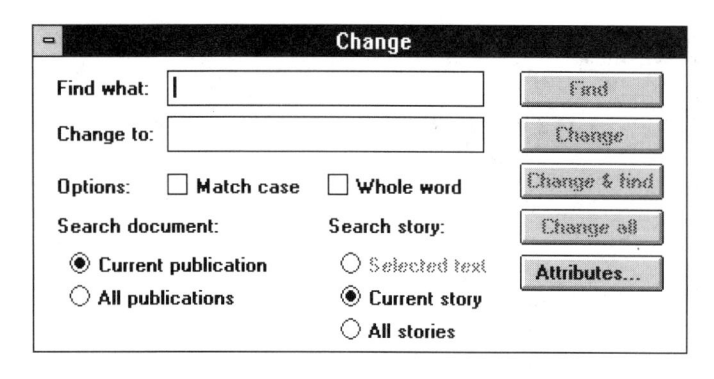

Figure 83. Insert the appropriate text in the *Find what* and *Change to* edit boxes. The *Match case* option allows you to search for words in upper and lower case combinations, exactly as you have typed them. The *Whole word* option allows you to search for the whole word as you have typed it, and not as part of another word.

You have a number of choices throughout this process which include *Find, Change, Change & find* and *Change all*. If you want to search for formatting features applied to text, and replace these attributes with others, click on the *Attributes* button.

Figure 84. You can check the spelling of your text in Story editor by choosing the *Spelling* command from the **Utilities** menu.

Figure 85. Click on *Start* in the *Spelling* dialog box to commence the spell check. When PageMaker detects a word that isn't in its dictionary, it displays it in the dialog box, as well as possible alternatives in the bottom rectangle (if you have the *Alternate spellings* option selected).

The *Show duplicates* option detects any duplicated words next to each other. When PageMaker detects an error, you can select a PageMaker suggestion, key in your own correct spelling, or ignore the selected error altogether by using the *Ignore* button that appears.

The *Place* command from the **File** menu allows you to import text and graphics into the story window.

Figure 86. The *Import to Story* dialog box allows you to choose the file you wish to import.

You have the option of importing graphics as inline graphics only in Story editor. These graphics will not appear as graphics in Story editor, but as small markers. See Chapter 7 for more information on inline and independent graphics.

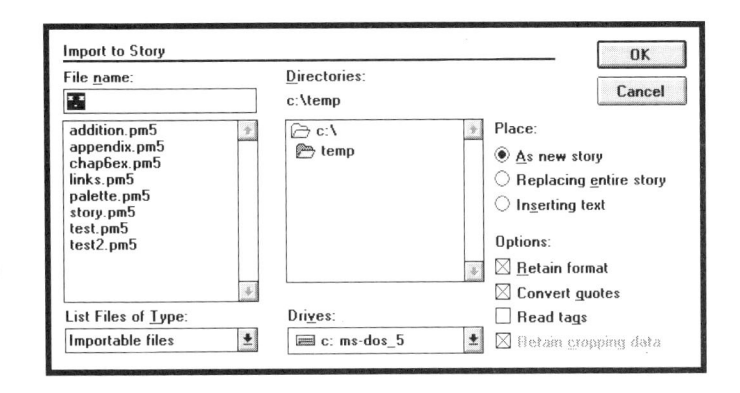

STORY EDITOR AND THE CONTROL PALETTE

Figure 87. You can use the Control palette in Story editor exactly as you do in layout view (see Figures 70 through 97 for information on the Control palette). You will not, however, see most of the changes until you switch back to *Layout* view.

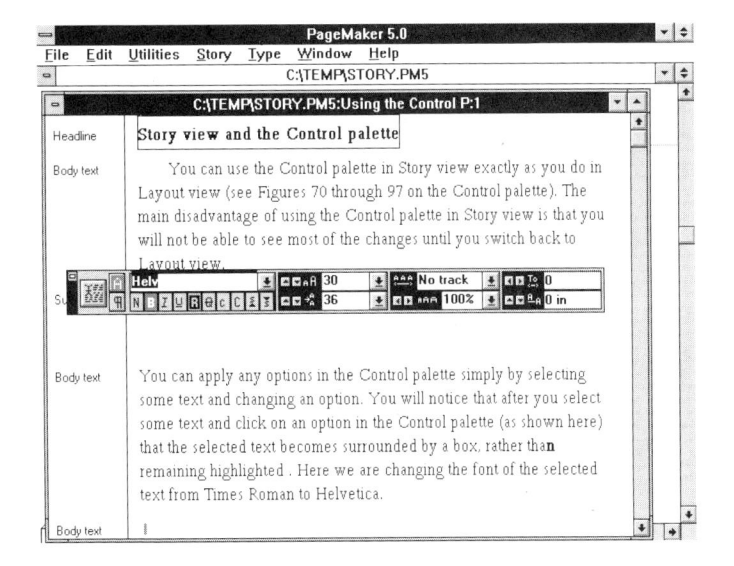

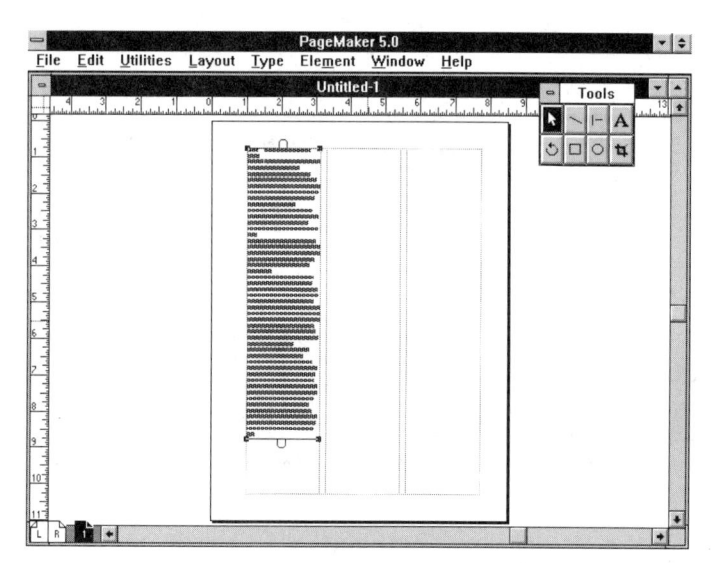

Manipulating Text Blocks

MOVING TEXT BLOCKS

Figure 88. When PageMaker loads text into a publication it does so in what are called text blocks. You can manipulate these text blocks using the pointer tool in a variety of ways. This figure shows text placed into one column of a three-column page.

You will now look at different ways to manipulate this text block.

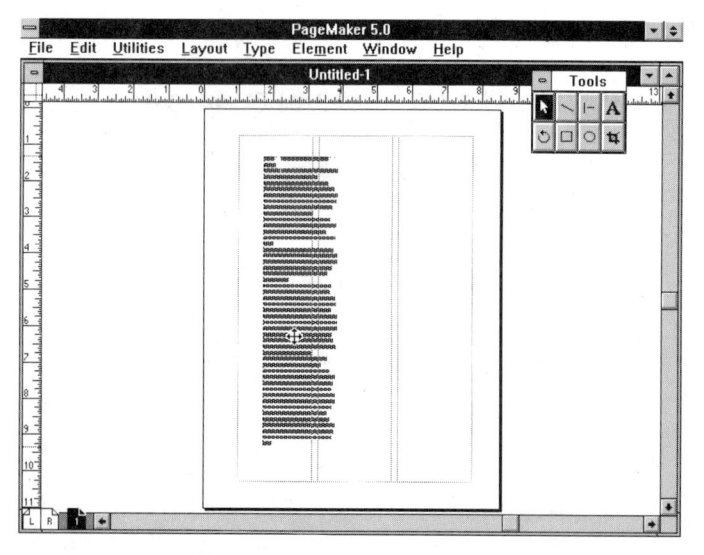

Figure 89. Using the pointer tool, you can hold the mouse down on the text block and move it anywhere on the page. In this figure, we held the mouse down on the block for a few seconds and then moved the mouse to the right. This results in the text block moving. You release the mouse when the text block is in the desired position.

If we had held our mouse down on the block and immediately moved it, only a boxed outline of the text would move. The result, however, is the same—you move the text block to a new location.

RESIZING TEXT BLOCKS

Figure 90. As well as repositioning text blocks, you can also adjust the size horizontally, vertically and diagonally. This figure shows the various handles of a selected text block that you use for resizing

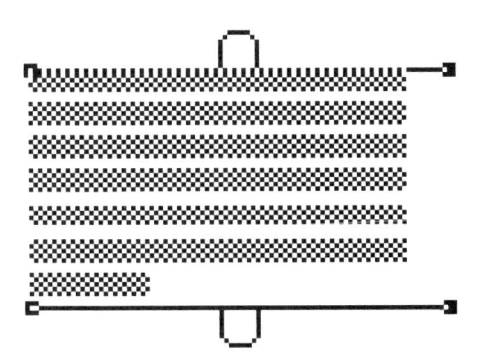

Figure 91. The corner squares of the selected text block allow you to resize a block in any direction. You simply grab the corner handle with the mouse pointer tool, and move it in any direction you like. You can resize the text block horizontally, vertically and diagonally using this method. If you enlarge the text block, additional text (assuming more text is available) appears.

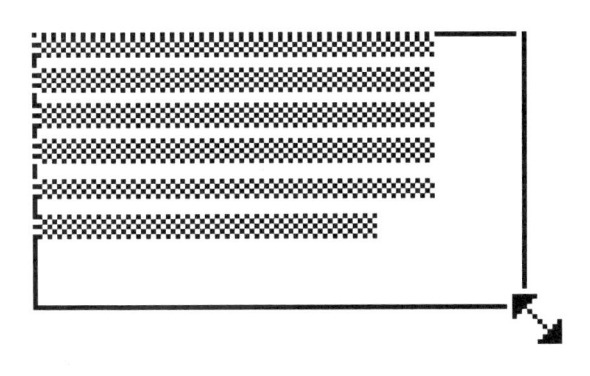

Figure 92. If a selected text block appears with windowshade handle that has a ▼ symbol in it, then more text is available to flow onto the page. Holding the mouse down on this handle with the pointer tool active and pulling it downwards resizes the block vertically and reveals the text that belongs to this particular text block.

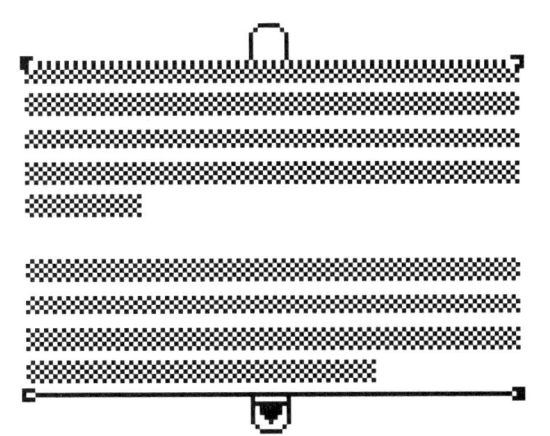

ADJUSTING TEXT BLOCKS

(a) (b)

Move this handle up

Figure 93. Here there is a text block that was placed in column one (a). No further text is contained in this story. If you wish to break this text block into three parts and place parts of it in columns 2 and 3 as well, select the block with the pointer tool and move the bottom windowshade handle up to approximately one-third down the second column (b).

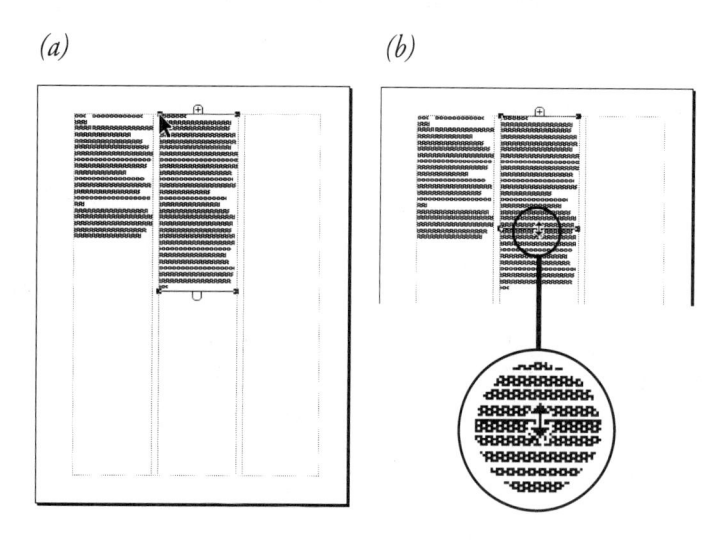

(a) (b)

Figure 94. Click once on the bottom windowshade handle in Figure 93(b) and place the loaded text cursor at the top of the middle column. Click at the top of the middle column to place the text (a). Now drag the bottom windowshade handle and drag it up. Release it at approximately one-third of the way up the column (b).

Figure 95. Click once on the bottom windowshade handle from Figure 94(b) and place the loaded text cursor at the top of column three (a). Click here to place the text down this column (b). You have now broken the text into three separate blocks.

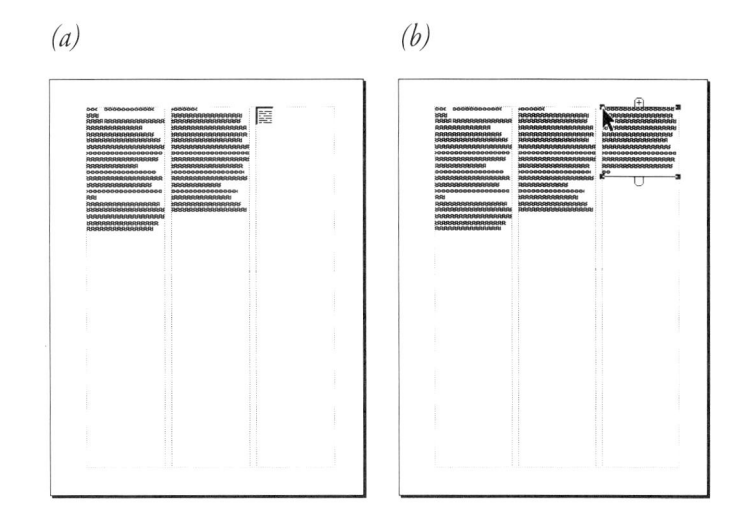

(a)   *(b)*

CAN YOU LOSE TEXT?

When you are manipulating and placing text, you cannot lose text that is part of a text block, unless you delete it. You can manipulate text blocks in PageMaker in a variety of ways. For example, you could remove the middle text block of Figure 95 by simply grabbing the bottom windowshade handle and pulling it right up to the top. Then, if you click anywhere on the page you will remove this block without losing text. The text from the middle block flows into column three. The size of the block in column three will change to accommodate the extra text.

So far, you have seen the manipulation of text blocks which are all part of the same story. Sometimes you may need to take some text from the original text block and make it an independent text block. This is called *unthreading* text. The reverse process, *threading* text, is when you join independent text blocks to create one text block.

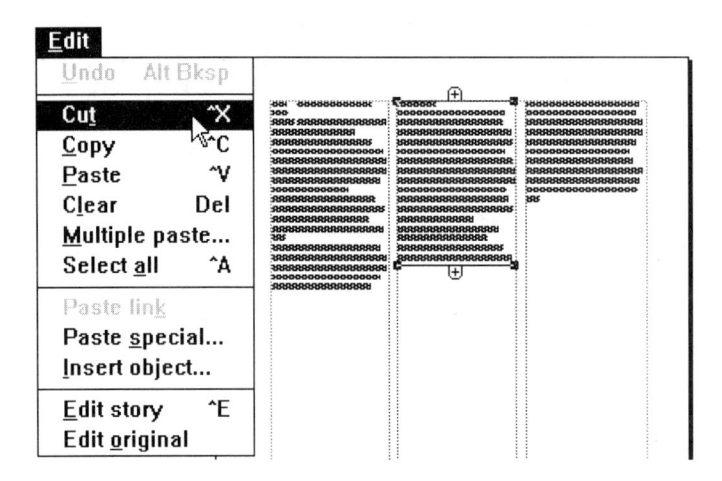

UNTHREADING TEXT

Figure 96. Let's say you want to unthread the text block in the middle column of this figure. Select it with the pointer tool and choose *Cut* from the **Edit** menu.

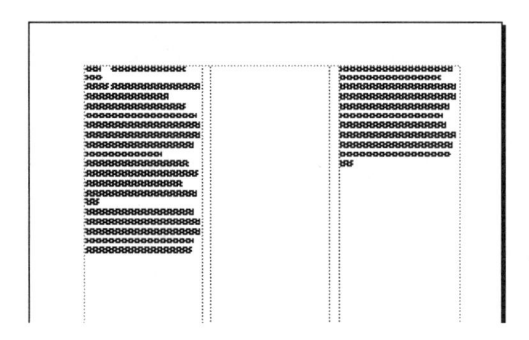

Figure 97. The selected text block is removed from the page.

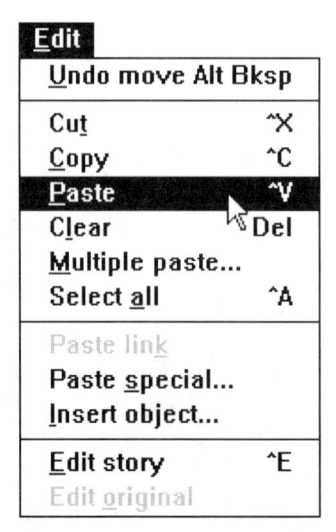

Figure 98. To bring the deleted text block back as a separate independent story, select *Paste* from the **Edit** menu.

Figure 99. The *Paste* command puts the text block back into the middle column. However, this text block is no longer part of the original story. The empty windowshade handles at both the top and bottom of the middle text block indicate this. You can change, edit, and modify the block without affecting the other two columns. You will probably notice that PageMaker pastes the text block back slightly offset to its original position.

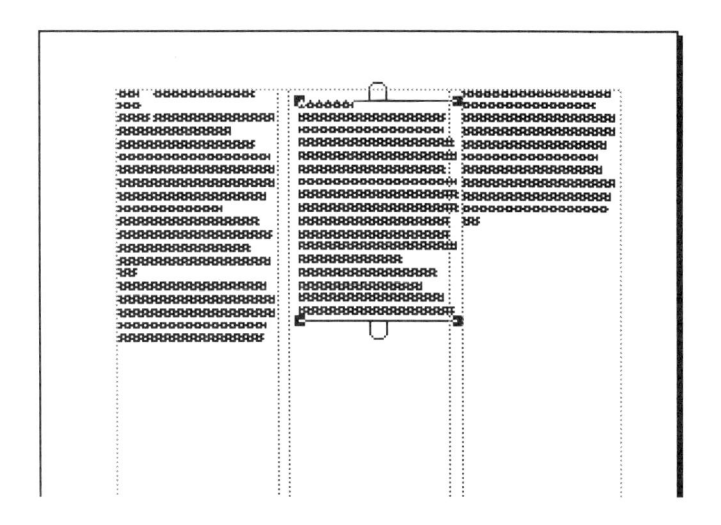

THREADING TEXT

Figure 100. To rethread the text block of Figure 99 back into the original story, select this block with the pointer tool and choose *Cut* from the **Edit** menu.

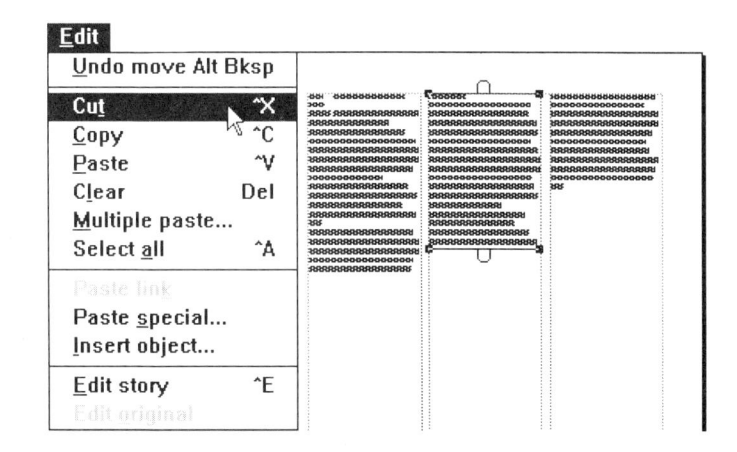

Figure 101. You have removed the text block from the page. Next, select the text tool and click an insertion point within the text wherever you wish the deleted text block to appear.

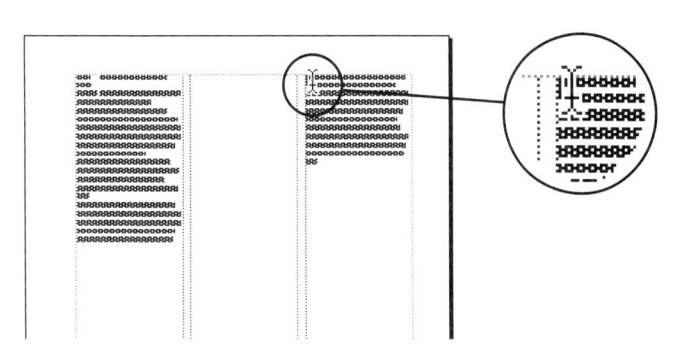

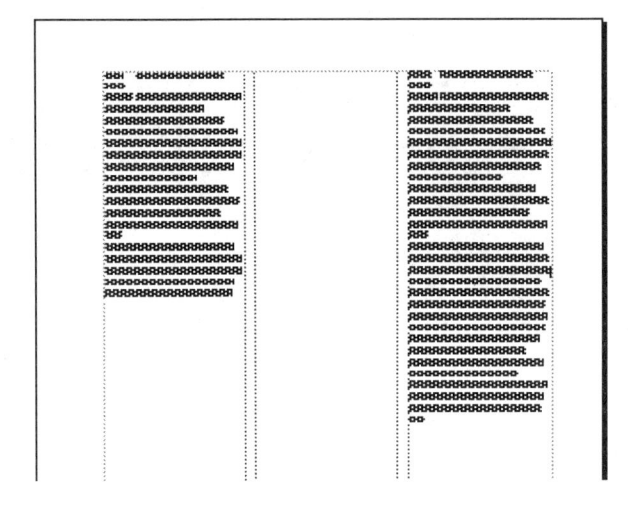

Figure 102. Now choose *Paste* from the **Edit** menu to insert the text back into the original text block.

TRANSFORMING TEXT

You can rotate, skew and reflect selected text blocks using the rotation tool and the Control palette. These features are described in this section.

ROTATING TEXT

THE CONTROL PALETTE

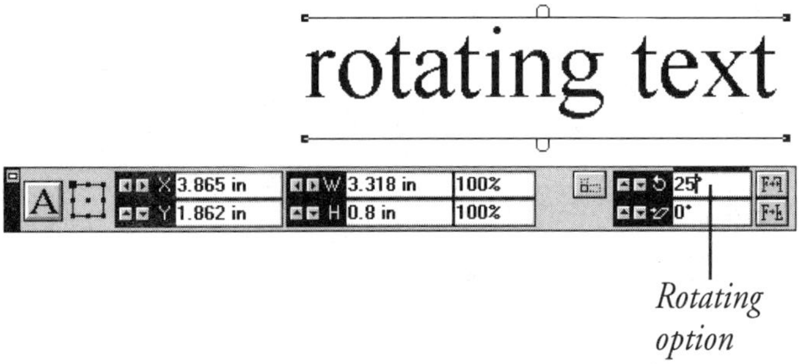

Figure 103. You can rotate text in PageMaker by 360 degrees at 0.01 degree intervals. Select *Control palette* from the **Window** menu to activate the Control palette. Select the text block with the pointer tool and select a reference point in the *Proxy*. This determines from which point you will rotate the selected object. Type a value into the *Rotation* edit box (in this case 25°) and click on the Apply button.

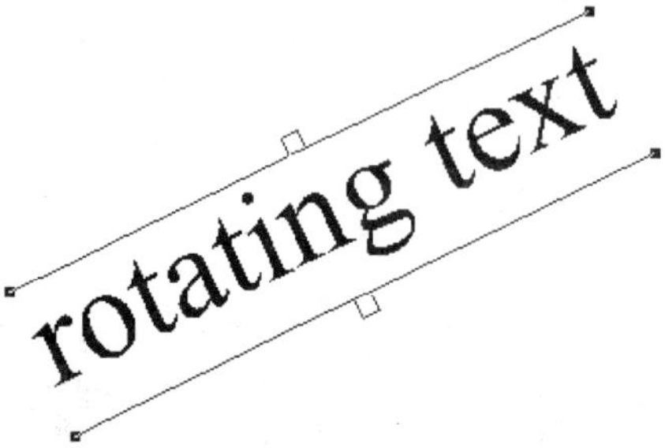

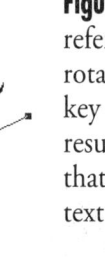

Rotating option

Figure 104. Once you select a reference point and insert a rotation value, press the Enter key to make the changes. The results can be seen here. Note that you can also rotate longer text blocks in this fashion.

Chapter 4: Text

USING THE ROTATION TOOL

Figure 105. Select the text block with the pointer tool, then activate the rotation tool.

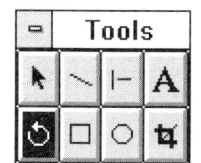

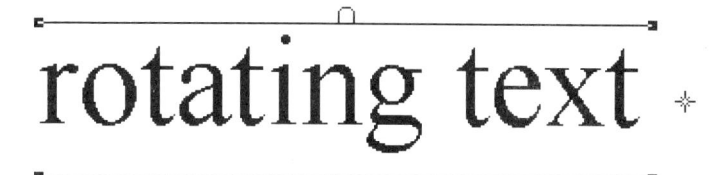

Figure 106. Position the starburst cursor on the text block or anywhere on the page. Drag it in the opposite direction to which you wish to rotate the text. The rotation lever that appears gives you control over the amount of rotation. The further you drag the starburst cursor away from the fixed point, the more control you have.

Use the Shift key while you are rotating the object to constrain the rotation to 45 degree angles.

Figure 107. When you release the mouse, the rotated text will reformat on the screen as seen here. If you have the Control palette on screen while you are rotating an object, the total amount of rotation is reflected in the *Rotating* option edit box, even if you have rotated the object more than once.

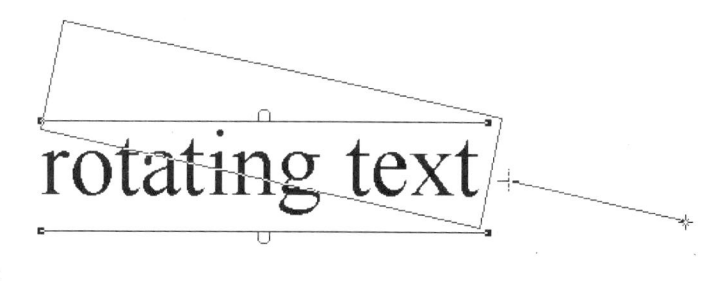

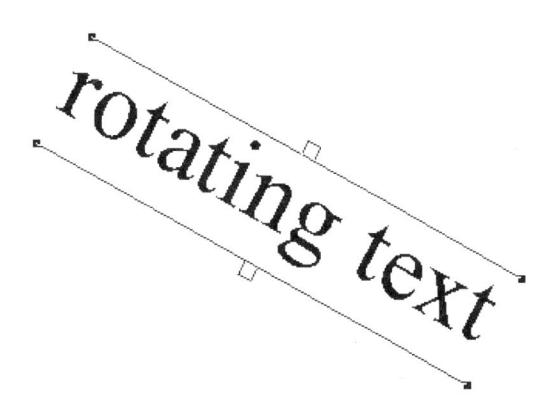

81

SKEWING TEXT

Use the Control palette to skew text horizontally by + or - 85 degrees at 0.1 degree increments.

Figure 108. To skew a text block, first select it with the pointer tool.

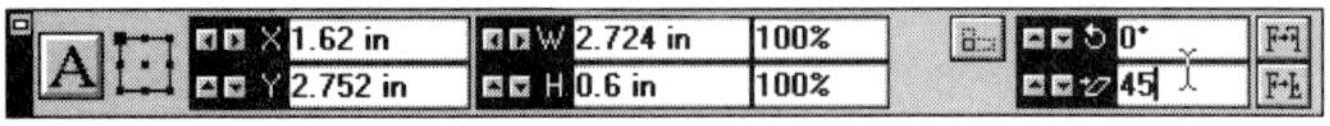

Figure 109. Select a reference point on the *Proxy*. The equivalent point of the selected text block remains stationary when you skew the text. (If you click twice on a reference point, it becomes a resizing reference point, which looks like a two-way or a four-way arrow. The equivalent point of the selected text block moves in this case, as you skew it.)

 Specify a skewing angle in the *Skewing* option edit box in the Control palette. A positive angle moves the top edge to the right and a negative angle moves it to the left.

Figure 110. Press the Enter key or click on the *Apply* button to view the skewing changes.

REFLECTING TEXT

Figure 111. Use the Control palette to reflect text or other objects. First, select the text block with the pointer tool. Then, select a point on the *Proxy* and click on one of the reflecting buttons in the Control Palette.

Horizontal reflection

Vertical reflection

Figure 112. Clicking on one of the reflecting options affects the selected text immediately.

Note: Reflecting an object horizontally is the same as reflecting it vertically and rotating it 180 degrees. When you do this, PageMaker adds 180 degrees to the object's rotation value in the Control palette.

REMOVING TRANSFORMATIONS

Figure 113. To restore any transformed object (rotated, reflected or skewed) to its original state, select the object and select *Remove transformation* from the **Element** menu.

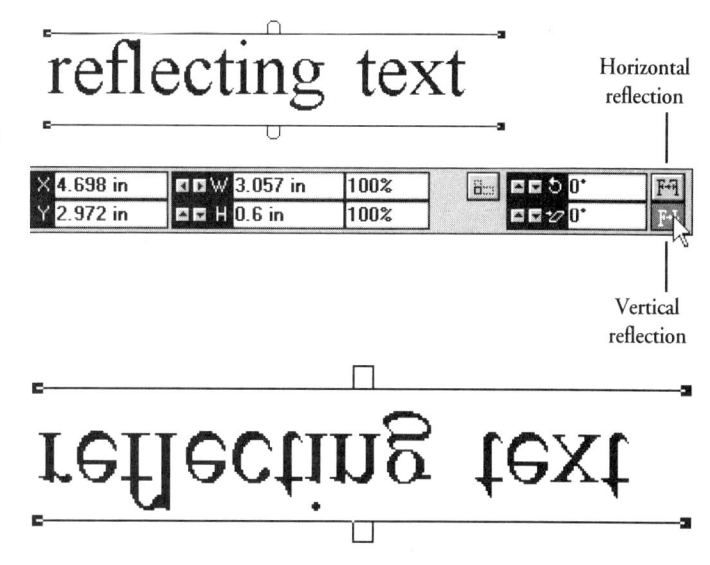

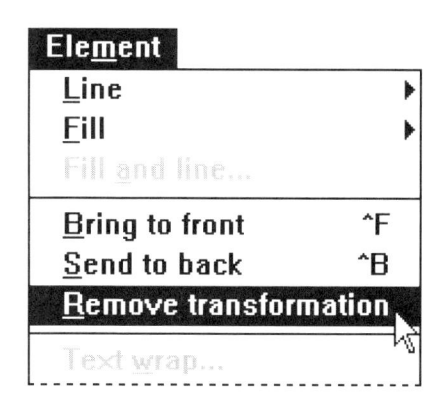

MASTER PAGES 5

MASTER PAGE CONCEPT

Every PageMaker publication has a master page. The master page stores information that you want to appear on every page of a publication. How the master page or pages are set up is determined by how you define your document in the *Page setup* dialog box; a double-sided document has two master pages, a single-sided document only one.

Figure 1. The L and R icons to the left of the numbered publication page icons represent the master pages. If PageMaker is set up as a single-sided document, only the R icon shows.

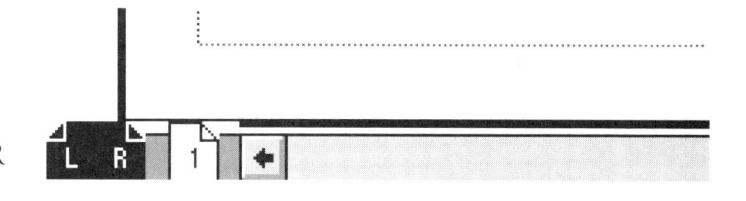

Figure 2. The left and right master pages are identical to all other PageMaker pages, except for some important considerations. First, you cannot print the contents of the master pages directly. Second, anything (text or graphics) you include on a master page appears on all other pages in your publication. This is useful if you have items such as headers, footers, or a company logo that you wish to include on every page in your document.

Simply put these objects on the left or right master page and they appear, unless you turn them off, on every left or right page in your publication.

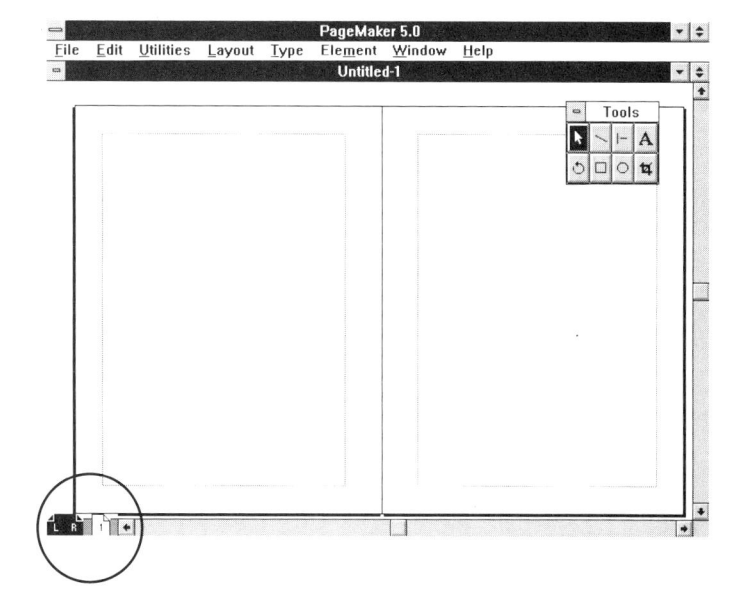

Chapter 5: Master Pages

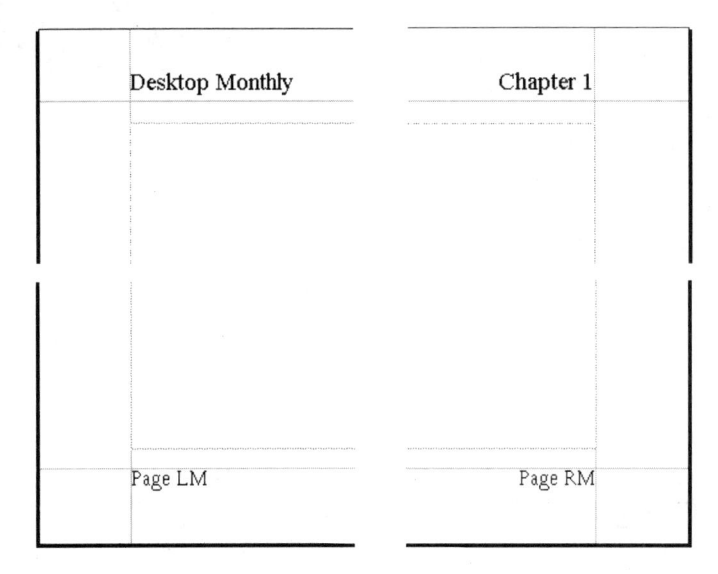

AUTOMATIC PAGE NUMBERING

Figure 3. Here we have enlarged the four corners of the left and right master pages. The top left and right corners include a header each, and the bottom left and right corners include a page number as a footer. You insert the page number on the master pages by pressing Ctrl+Shift+3 with the insertion point at the required locations. The page numbers, appearing as LM and RM on the left and right master pages, automatically update to reflect the correct number on every page. The headers, like the page number, will also appear on every page.

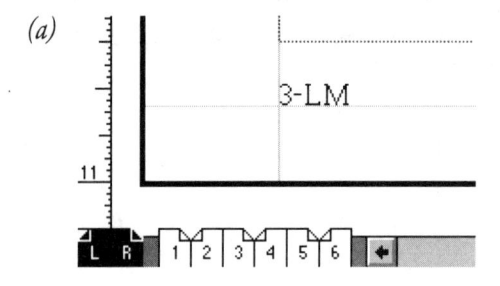

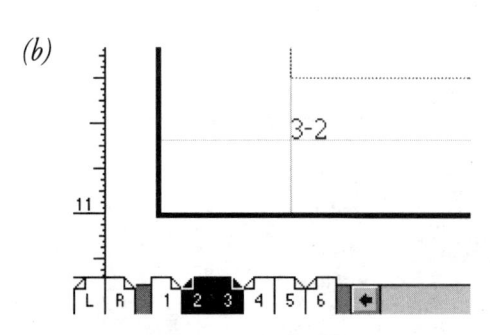

Figure 4. It is also possible to place fixed wording on the master page in front of the page number. This fixed wording, in our case "3" (for denoting part of Chapter 3), will now appear on every page as part of the page numbering system.
(a) The fixed character "3" on the master page denotes the whole publication is Chapter 3.
(b) Page 2 of the publication reflects the numbering format as "3-2", being page 2 of Chapter 3.

Figure 5. The automatic page number that appears on a page is the same as the number inside the icon representing that page that appears in the bottom left-hand corner of the screen. You can alter the actual page number, as shown here, by adjusting the *Start page #* box in the *Page setup* dialog box from the **File** menu.

Figure 6. The *Page numbering* box, which you get by clicking on the *Numbers* button in the *Page setup* dialog box, gives you a choice of numbering systems. You may choose from the different options shown in this dialog box.

GUIDES ON MASTER PAGES

Figure 7. Apart from headers, footers and page numbers, you can use the master pages to set up column guides, ruler guides and other constant information, such as a company logo.

Here we have set up, through the *Column guides* command, three columns on both master pages. In addition, we have included one vertical and two horizontal ruler guides per page, two headers and one footer per page, and a logo. These will now appear on all pages of the publication (unless you turn them off on a particular page).

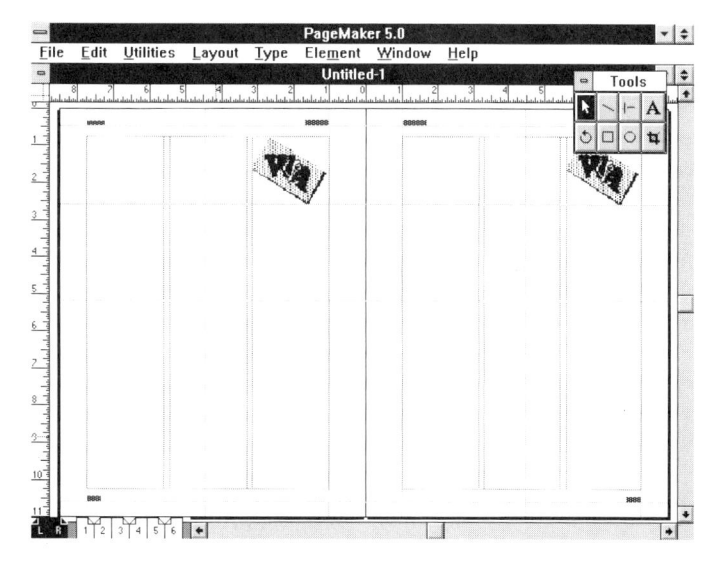

Chapter 5: Master Pages

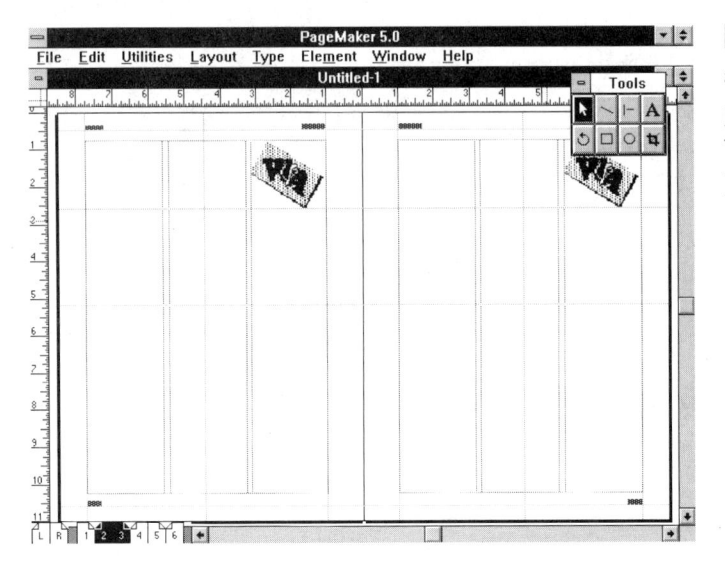

Figure 8. This figure shows pages 2 and 3. All items from the master pages are now showing exactly as we positioned them on the master pages.

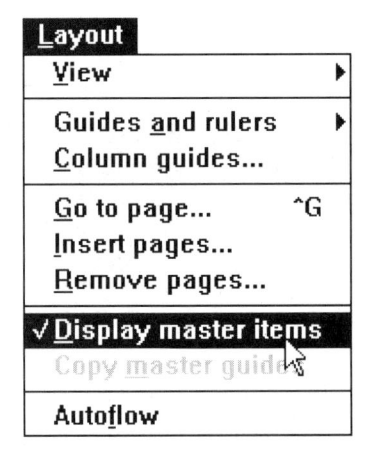

REMOVING MASTER PAGE ITEMS

Figure 9. You cannot select or delete text and graphics created on master pages in the normal way. You can select and manipulate master page text and graphics only on the master pages. To delete all master page items from the currently active page or pages, select *Display master items* from the Page menu.

88

Chapter 5: Master Pages

Figure 10. After you deselect the *Display master items* command, the current pages do not have the master page items on them.

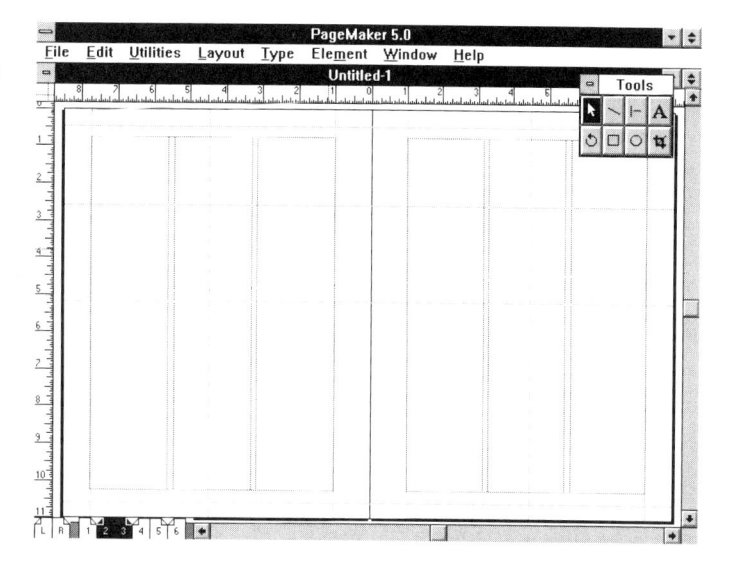

Figure 11. If you wish to delete only certain master page items on a particular page, simply draw a box with a paper fill over them. In this case, we have drawn a box over the top left header on page one, to stop it from printing. You can do this for any number of master page items you wish to hide. (To create a box to hide elements, apply *Fill: Paper* and *Line: None* from the **Element** menu to a selected rectangle.)

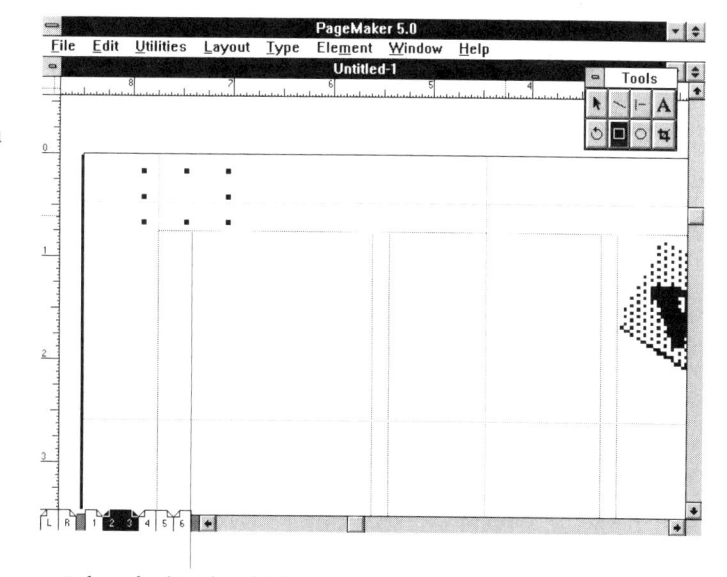

Selected white box hiding a master page item at the top left of page 2

89

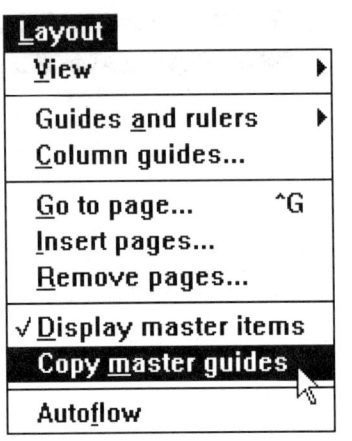

Figure 12. You can adjust column, ruler, and margin guides on any page, even though you may have created them on the master pages. If you wish to revert to the original non-printing guides as they appear on the master pages, choose *Copy master guides* from the **Page** menu.

CREATING GRAPHICS 6

THE DRAWING TOOLS

PageMaker's drawing tools in the toolbox let you draw graphic objects in PageMaker.

Figure 1. The toolbox has the drawing tools you use to create and manipulate internal graphics.

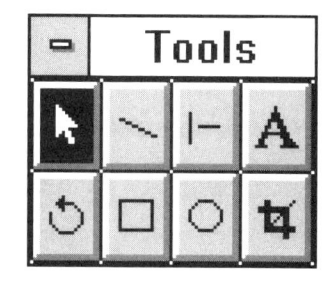

(a) Use the line tool to draw straight lines at any angle.

(b) Use the constrained line tool to draw lines at 45 degree angles.

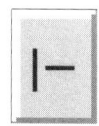

(c) Use the rotation tool to rotate objects on the page.

(d) Use the rectangle tool to draw squares and rectangles.

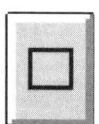

(e) Use the ellipse tool to draw circles and ellipses.

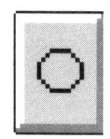

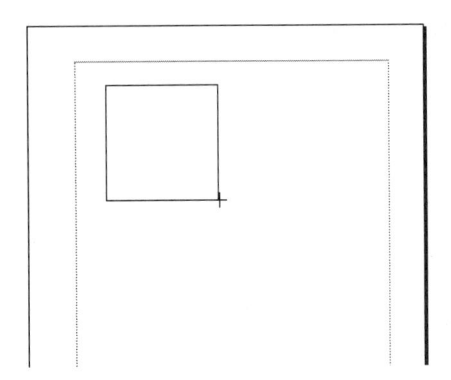

Drawing Graphics

Figure 2. To draw a graphic, select the appropriate tool, hold down the mouse and drag it across the page. You can drag in any direction.

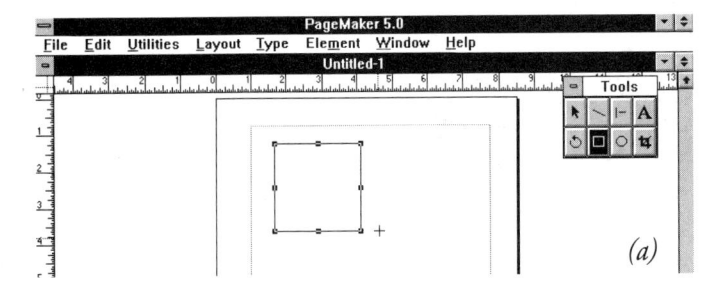

Figure 3. Release the mouse button when you finish. PageMaker automatically selects the graphic. (Note the eight small square dots or handles around the edge of the graphic shown in (a)). You can draw many types of different graphics in PageMaker (b).

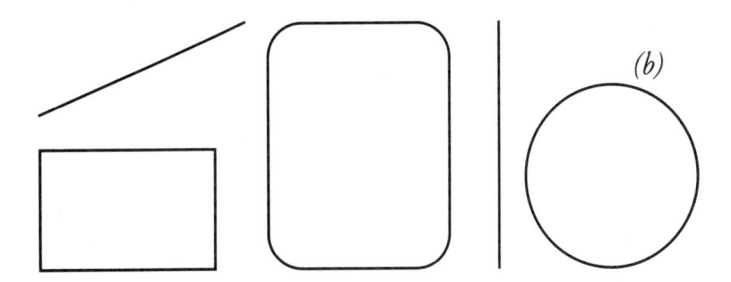

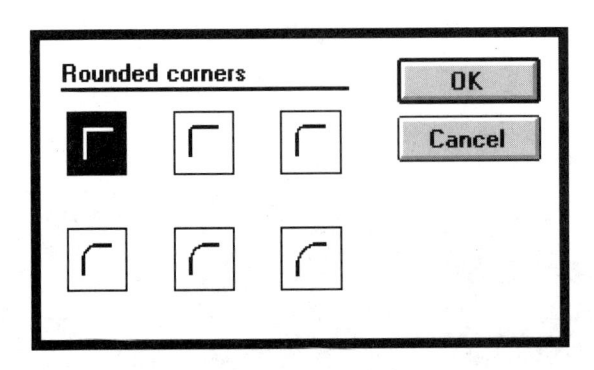

Figure 4. The *Rounded corners* dialog box (from the **Element** menu) gives you a choice of various radii for drawing rectangles or squares with the rectangle-drawing tool.

Chapter 6: Creating Graphics

Figure 5. Graphics are automatically selected after you have drawn them. If you choose another tool from the toolbox, this deselects the graphic. To re-select a graphic, click on its edge with the pointer tool or drag the mouse over the graphic with the pointer tool selected.

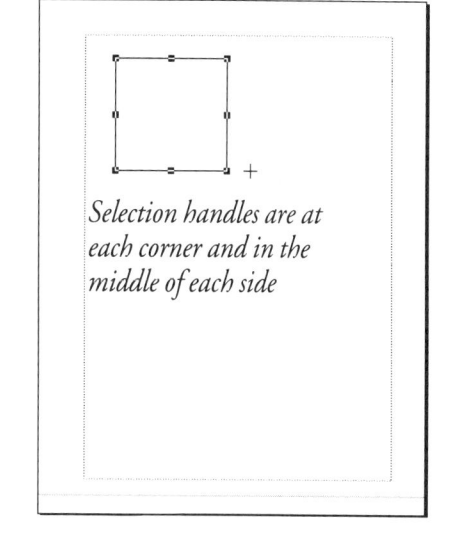

Selection handles are at each corner and in the middle of each side

SELECTING MULTIPLE GRAPHICS

Figure 6. You can select multiple graphics by selecting each graphic while pressing the Shift key or by choosing *Select all* from the **Edit** menu.

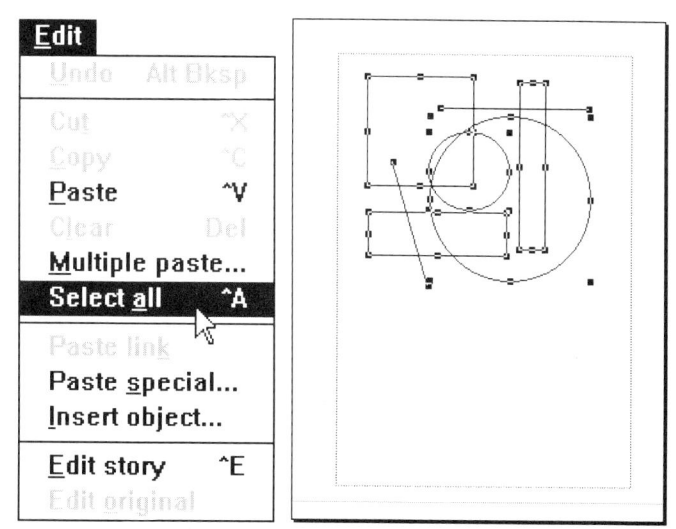

Figure 7. You can also drag a selection rectangle around all graphics with the pointer tool.

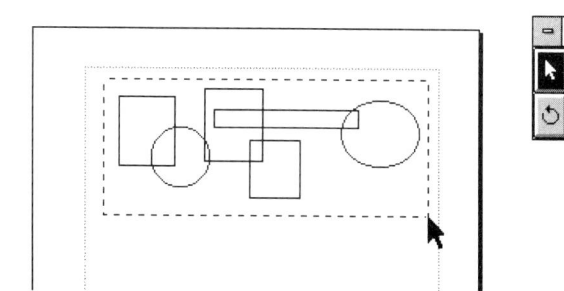

93

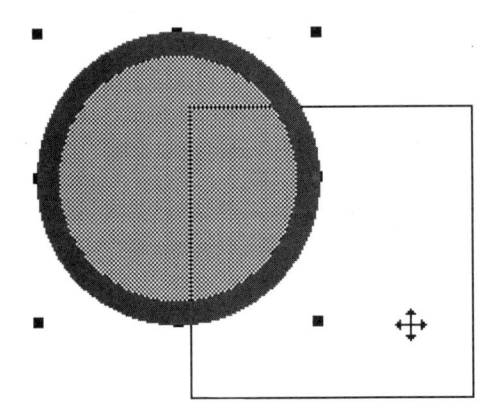

MOVING AND RESIZING GRAPHICS

Figure 8. To move a graphic, hold down the mouse button on the border of the graphic if it is hollow, or anywhere within the graphic if it has a fill pattern, and move the mouse. Note in this figure, the mouse changes to a four-headed arrow.

If you drag the graphic immediately, the original graphic stays in position and an outline or rectangle moves with the mouse, as the example shows in this figure. If you hold the mouse button down for a few seconds before dragging it, the actual object moves with the mouse.

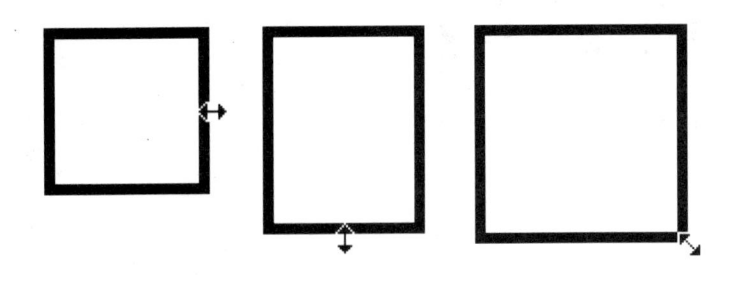

Figure 9. You can resize a selected graphic by grabbing one of the small black handles on its edge and dragging the mouse horizontally, vertically or diagonally.

See the section in this chapter on **The Control Palette and Graphics** for more information on moving and resizing graphics.

ALTERING THE APPEARANCE OF GRAPHICS

Figure 10. The **Element** menu includes *Line, Fill,* and *Fill and line* commands that you can use to change the appearance of graphics.

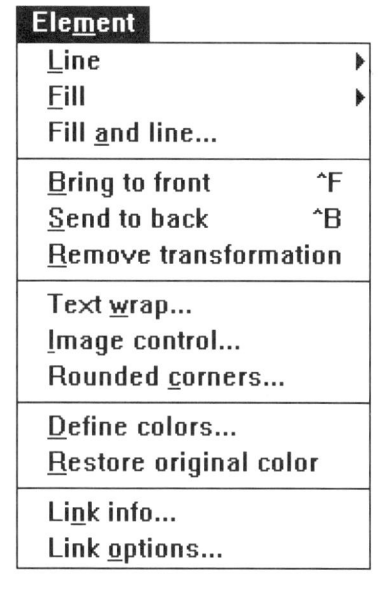

Figure 11. To use the *Line* command from the **Element** menu, choose a line thickness or style from the submenu.

In this figure, we are choosing a *4pt* line thickness.

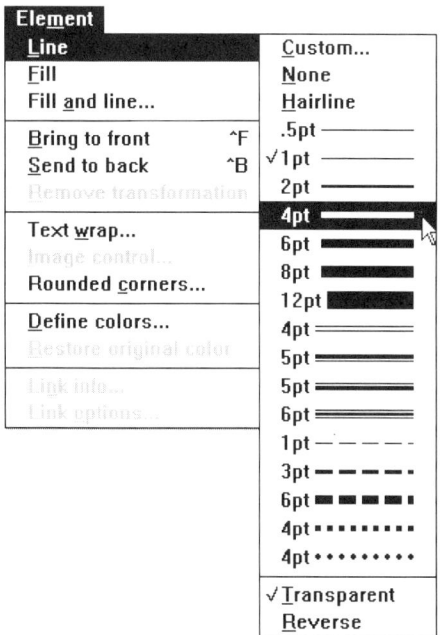

Chapter 6: Creating Graphics

95

Chapter 6: Creating Graphics

Figure 12. The graphic now adjusts to the new line thickness we selected in the previous figure.

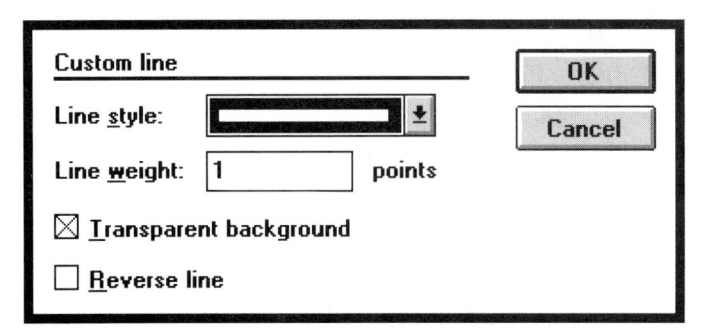

Figure 13. Choosing *Custom* from the *Line* sub-menu activates this dialog box. Here you can specify a line weight (thickness) from 0 to 800, and you can select a line style from the *Line style* drop-down list.

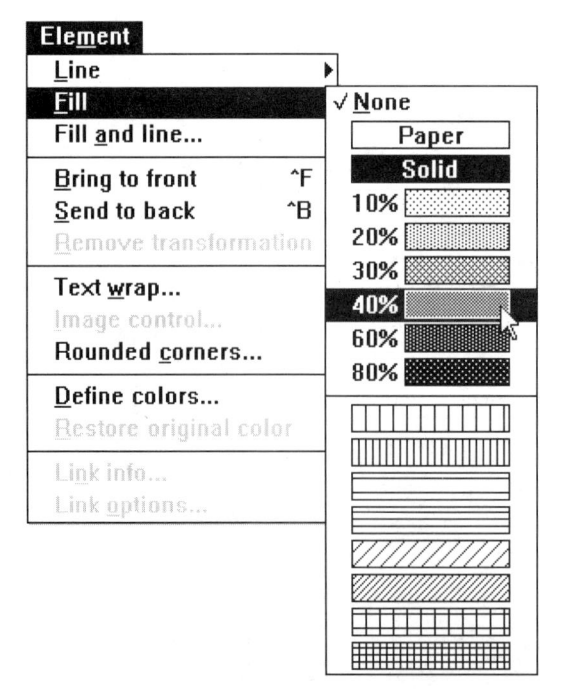

Figure 14. To change the fill of a graphic, select it, then go to the **Element** menu and choose the *Fill* command. When the sub-menu appears, select the fill pattern you want.

In this figure, we have chosen a 40% fill.

96

Chapter 6: Creating Graphics

Figure 15. The selected graphic reflects the new pattern or shade chosen in the previous graphic.

Figure 16. Select *Fill and line* from the **Element** menu to activate the *Fill and line* dialog box.

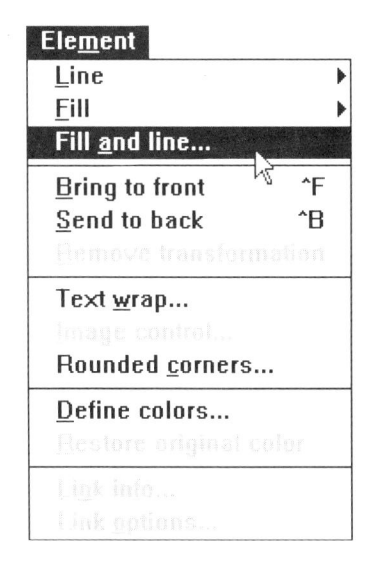

Figure 17. In this dialog box, you can select fill, line and color attributes together to apply to a selected graphic. Refer to Chapter 12 for information on the *Overprint* option. Use the *Reverse line* option to draw a white line on a colored or black background. If you have no graphic selected, the choices you make in this dialog box become the default settings.

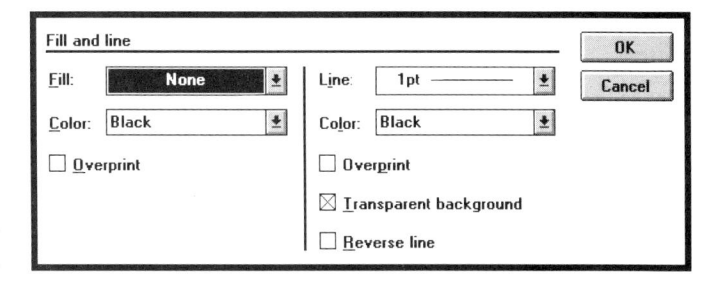

97

Chapter 6: Creating Graphics

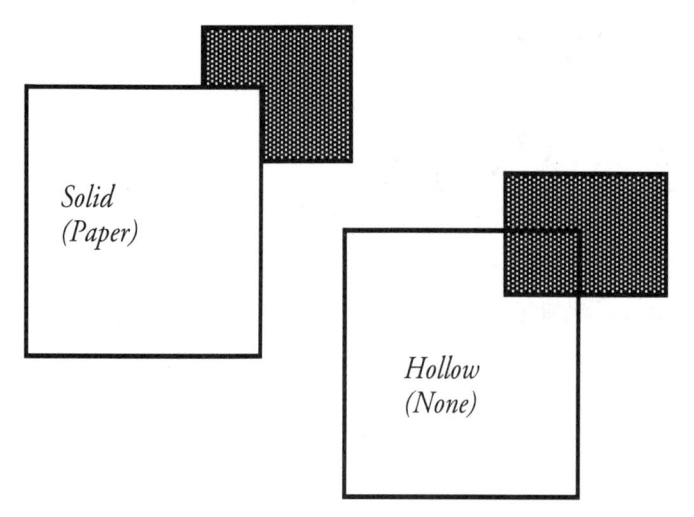

Figure 18. You can give a graphic on screen a hollow or a solid fill.

You apply a hollow fill by choosing *None* from the *Fill* sub-menu. You apply a solid fill by choosing *Solid* or *Paper* from the *Fill* sub-menu.

Solid (Paper)

Hollow (None)

LAYERING OF GRAPHICS

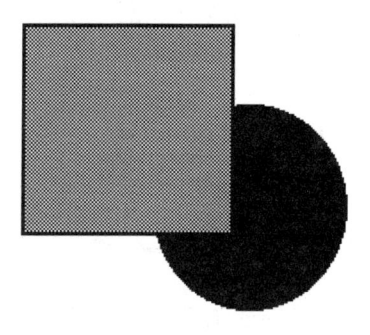

Figure 19. These two graphics overlap each other. The gray is on top and the black on the bottom. We now want to reverse this situation.

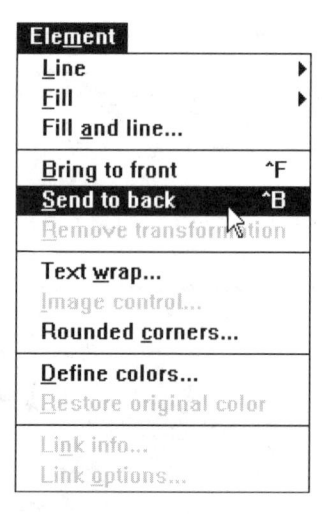

Figure 20. Select the top graphic and choose *Send to back* from the **Element** menu.

Chapter 6: Creating Graphics

Figure 21. PageMaker puts the black graphic on top.

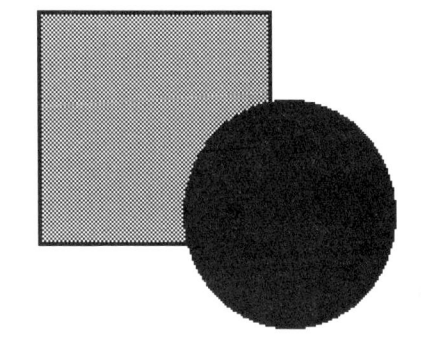

EDITING GRAPHICS

CUT, COPY, AND PASTE

Figure 22. In the **Edit** menu, *Cut* removes a selected graphic from the screen to the clipboard; *Copy* copies the selected graphic to the clipboard and leaves the original graphic on screen; *Paste* transfers whatever is in the clipboard back to the screen; *Clear* deletes a selected graphic from the screen without transferring it to the clipboard; *Multiple paste* positions and pastes a specified number of copies; and *Select all* selects all objects (graphics and text) on the screen.

MULTIPLE PASTE

Figure 23. Use the *Multiple paste* command from the **Edit** menu if you want to paste multiple copies of an object from the clipboard onto your publication page. In the *Multiple paste* dialog box, you can specify the number of pasted copies and where they will appear on the page.

We have specified 5 copies, with a 1 inch horizontal and vertical offset. See the results in the next figure.

99

Chapter 6: Creating Graphics

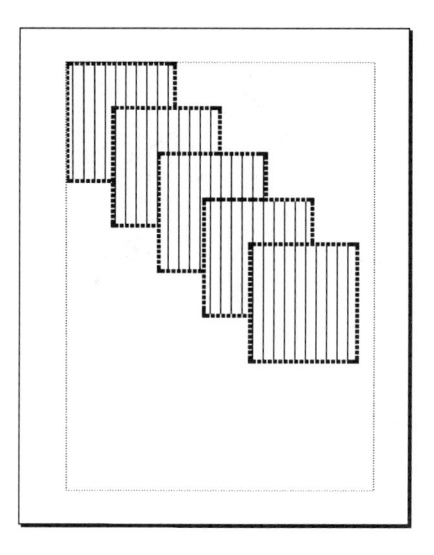

Figure 24. PageMaker has pasted the object copied to the clipboard as we defined in the *Multiple paste* dialog box.

To duplicate objects without the *Multiple paste* dialog box, press the Alt key while selecting the *Multiple paste* command. Objects are duplicated using the values you last entered for each option.

SETTING GRAPHIC DEFAULTS

Figure 25. Choosing the *Line* or *Fill* command from the **Element** menu with the pointer tool (with no graphic selected) causes the particular *Line* or *Fill* selection to be the new default setting. This means that every new graphic you draw on the page will have these line and fill settings as their attributes.

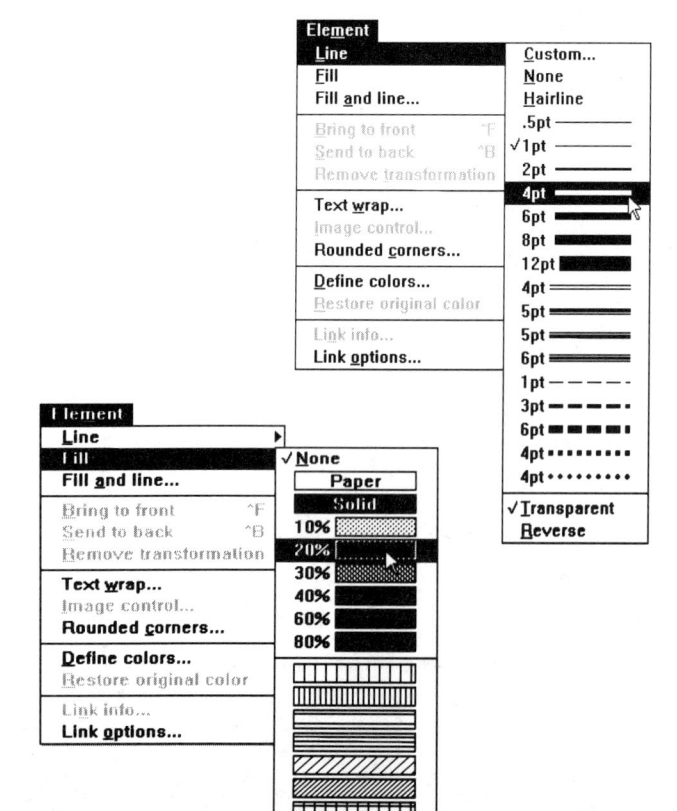

Chapter 6: Creating Graphics

Figure 26. You can also define the default settings in the *Fill and line* dialog box. As well as setting the default for the line and fill attributes, you can also specify a default color for the line and fill.

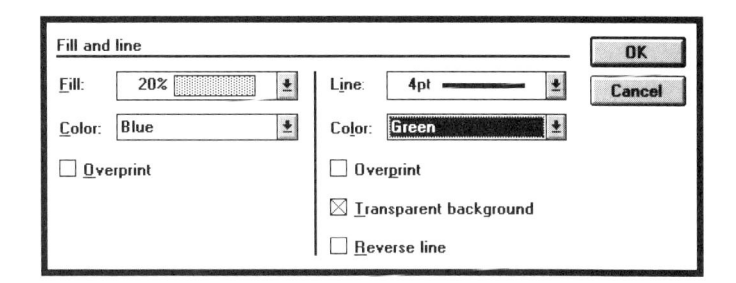

CONSTRAINING GRAPHICS

Figure 27. You can constrain graphics while drawing them by using the Shift key. When you press Shift with the rectangle or ellipse tool this constrains the object to a square or a circle, respectively. When you use the Shift key with the line tool, a line can be drawn at 45 degree intervals, which is the same as using the constrained line tool.

Square drawn with the Shift key held down

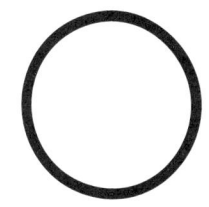

Circle drawn with the Shift key held down

THE ROTATION TOOL

Figure 28. Use the rotation tool to rotate selected graphics on the page. Select the graphic with the pointer tool and then select the rotation tool.

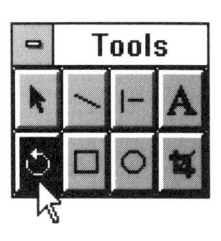

101

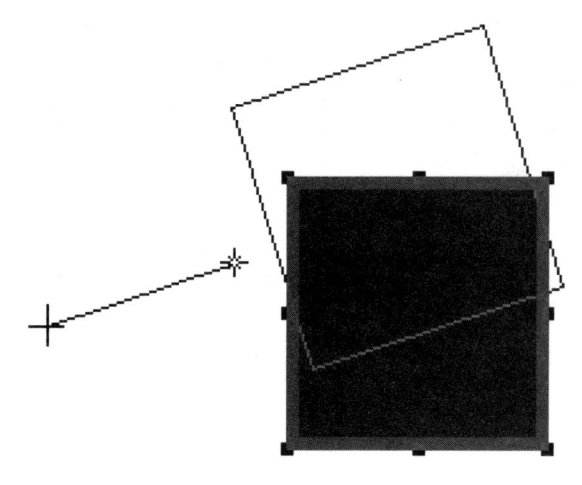

Figure 29. Position the starburst cursor within the graphic or anywhere on the page. This becomes the point around which the graphic rotates. Hold the mouse down and drag it in the direction you want to rotate the object.

The rotation lever helps you control the amount of rotation. The further you drag the mouse away from the graphic, the more control you have.

Hold down the Shift key while rotating the object to constrain the rotation to 45 degree increments.

Figure 30. Release the mouse when you have rotated the graphic to the desired position.

If the Control palette is on screen, it will display the total rotation in degrees of the selected graphic in the *Rotation* option edit box. See Figure 42 for more information.

THE CONTROL PALETTE AND GRAPHICS

You can use the Control palette as a quick, precise way of manipulating graphics as an alternative to using the toolbox or menu commands. If you would rather use the mouse to edit objects, the Control palette still displays an immediate response to any changes you make to a graphic in its edit boxes.

Chapter 6: Creating Graphics

Figure 31. Activate the Control palette through the **Window** menu. This is how the Control palette looks on screen when you have nothing selected. The X and Y coordinates change to reflect where you move the mouse.

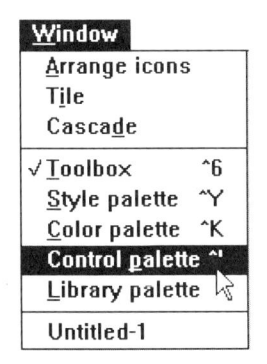

Window	
Arrange icons	
Tile	
Cascade	
✓ Toolbox	^6
Style palette	^Y
Color palette	^K
Control palette	**^'**
Library palette	
Untitled-1	

X -1.219 in
Y 7.563 in

Figure 32. When you select or draw a graphic, the Control palette changes as shown below. The first example shows the Control palette for ellipses and rectangles, and the second, graphics drawn with the line tools.

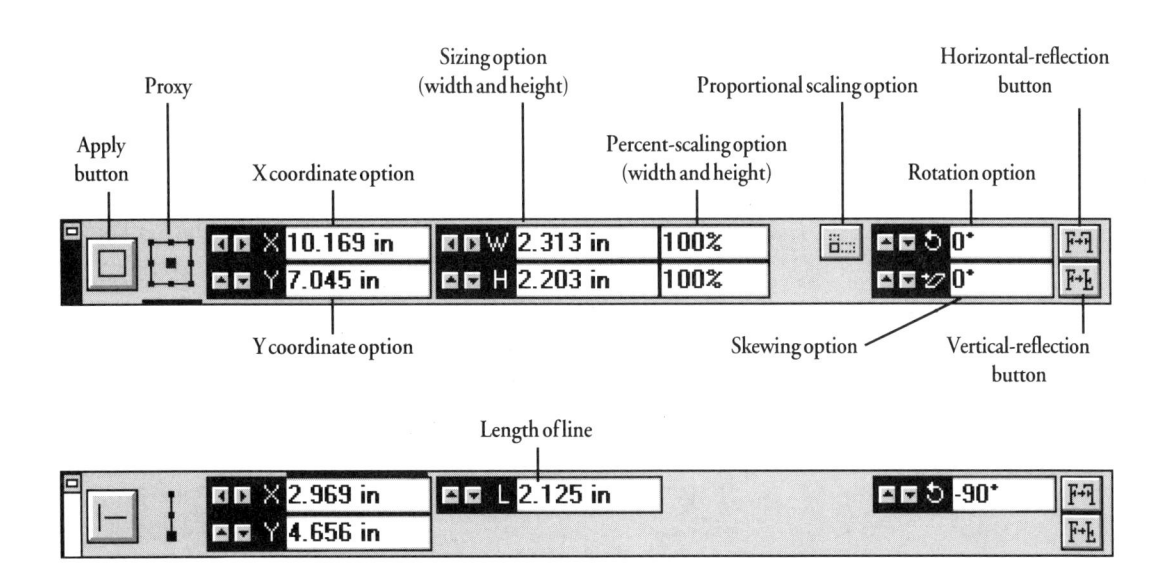

Apply button
Proxy
X coordinate option
Sizing option (width and height)
Percent-scaling option (width and height)
Proportional scaling option
Rotation option
Horizontal-reflection button

X 10.169 in   W 2.313 in   100%   0°
Y 7.045 in   H 2.203 in   100%   0°

Y coordinate option
Skewing option
Vertical-reflection button

Length of line

X 2.969 in   L 2.125 in   -90°
Y 4.656 in

103

Chapter 6: Creating Graphics

APPLY BUTTON

If the Apply button displays this icon, you have selected ...

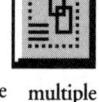

| a rectangle or square | an ellipse or circle | a line | a perpendicular line | multiple graphics |

Figure 33. Use the *Apply* button to display changes you have made to selected graphics with the Control palette. Note that the *Apply* button icon changes depending on what type of graphic object you select.

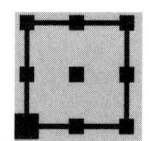

THE PROXY

Click on the bottom-left corner for a moving reference point

Double-click on the bottom-left corner for a resizing reference point

Double-click on the center point for a resizing reference point

Figure 34. Select a reference point in relation to the selected object by clicking on one of the black handles. This becomes the reference point for all objects you select until you choose a new reference point.

Note: When you resize a graphic with the mouse, the corresponding reference point on the proxy is selected automatically.

If you click on a reference point once, the selected point becomes a moving reference point, indicated by a larger black box. The corresponding point of the selected graphic remains stationary when you are modifying the graphic.

If you double-click on a reference point, it becomes a resizing reference point, indicated by a double-headed arrow, or a four-headed arrow on the center point. This corresponding point on the selected graphic moves when you are modifying the graphic. Pressing the spacebar toggles between a moving and a resizing reference point.

POSITION OPTION

Figure 35. You can modify the X and Y coordinates to both move and resize a selected object. For more information on resizing and moving objects, see Figures 38 through 41. Use the nudge buttons to increase or decrease the width or height by increments of 0.01 inch.

Holding down the Ctrl key while clicking on the nudge button increases or decreases values by increments of 0.1 inch.

SIZING AND PERCENTAGE SCALING OPTION

Figure 36. You can change the width and the height of a graphic by specifying values in the *W* and *H* edit boxes. See Figures 38 through 41 for more information. Use the nudge buttons to increase or decrease the width or height by increments of 0.01 inch.

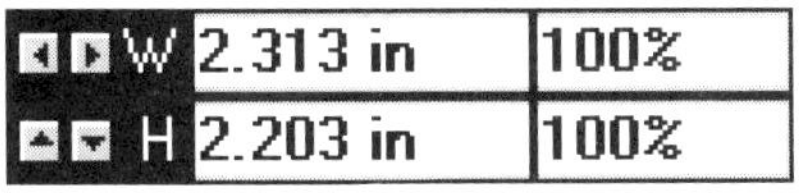

Holding down the Ctrl key while clicking on the nudge button increases or decreases the value by increments of 0.1 inch.

You can type in a percentage to increase or decrease the size of the selected object.

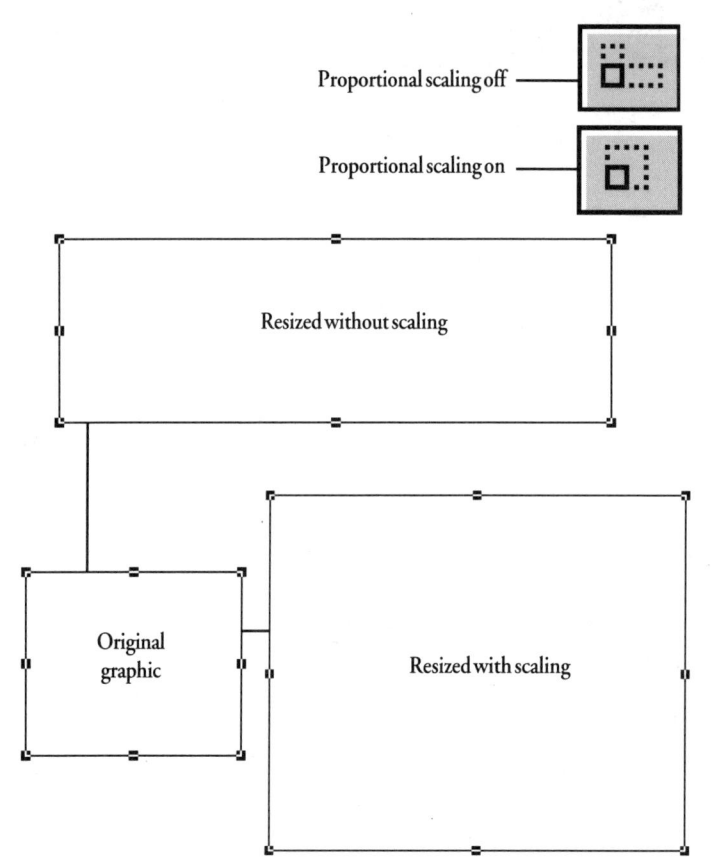

PROPORTIONAL SCALING OPTION

Figure 37. Click on this button to turn the proportional scaling on or off. If you have the scaling button turned on, when you change the height (for example) of a selected graphic using the *H* edit box, then PageMaker will also scale the width of the graphic proportionally to the original size. The scaling option does not affect a graphic if you resize it directly with the mouse.

Proportional scaling off

Proportional scaling on

Resized without scaling

Original graphic

Resized with scaling

TRANSFORMING GRAPHICS

MOVING AND RESIZING GRAPHICS

Figure 38. If you are using the Control palette to move an object, select the object and then select a reference point on the *Proxy*. Click on the reference point once for a fixed reference point (a). Change either the X or the Y value depending on where you want it to move and then press the Enter key.

Here, we have moved the rectangle 1 inch to the right (b).

You can also click on the nudge buttons to the left of the X and Y edit boxes to move the object in small increments. If you click on the graphic again you can use any of the directional arrow keys on the keyboard to move the selected graphic in increments of 0.01 inch in the direction of the chosen arrow.

Holding down the Ctrl key while clicking on the nudge button moves the graphic in increments of 0.1 inch.

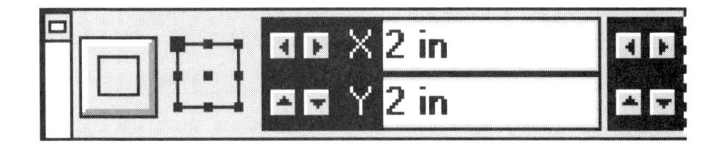

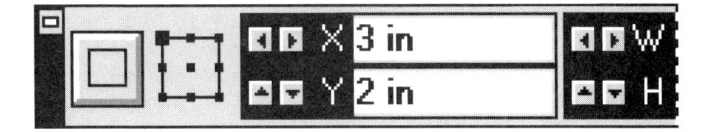

(a)

(b)

(a)

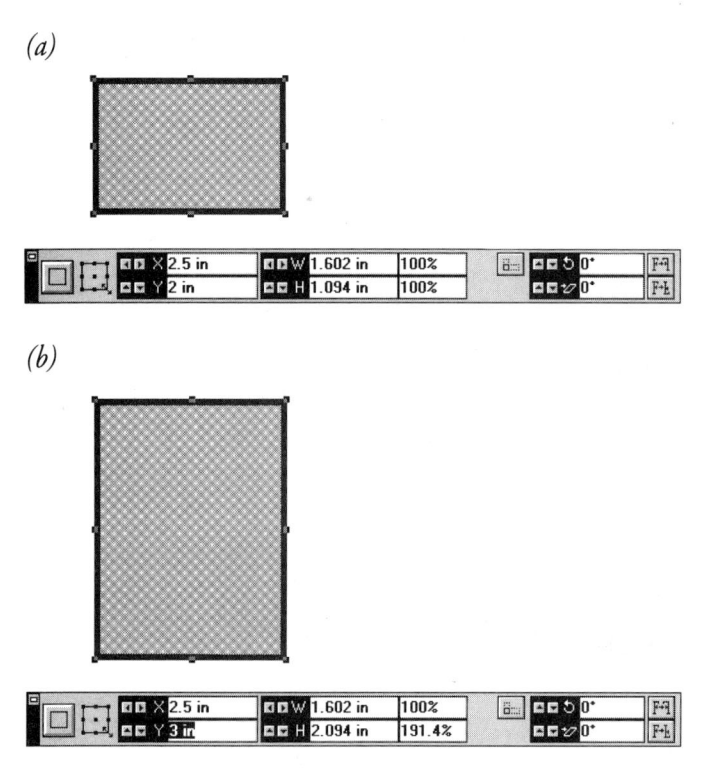

Figure 39. To resize an object using the Control palette, select the object with the pointer tool and click twice on a reference point in the *Proxy*. You may also like to alter the proportional scaling option (see Figure 37) as required (a).

(b)

When you change either the X or Y values, the object resizes accordingly. Here, we have resized the rectangle 1 inch taller by changing the Y value (b).

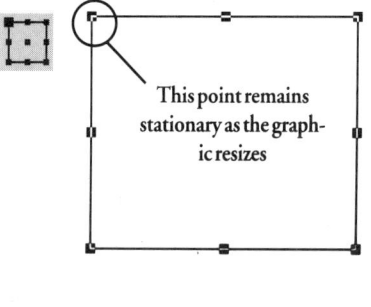

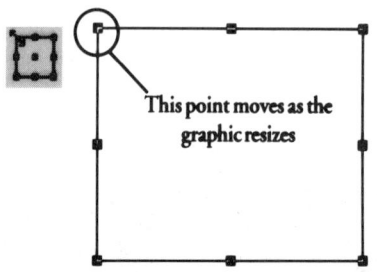

Figure 40. When you use the *W* and *H* edit boxes to resize a graphic, again you must select the graphic and then a reference point on the *Proxy*. If you click once on a reference point, the selected point remains stationary when you change a value.

If you click twice on a reference point, this point moves as the graphic resizes. You can insert new values into the *W* and *H* edit boxes and you can apply them by pressing the Enter key or clicking on the *Apply* button.

Chapter 6: Creating Graphics

Figure 41. A third way you can resize graphics using the Control palette is to use the *Percent-scaling* option. Select the required graphic and change the width and height value if proportional scaling is not turned on, or just the width or the height (if the scaling option is on). In this example we have turned proportional scaling on and changed the *H* value to 1 (a).

Press the Enter key or click on the *Apply* button to see the results. Because the proportional scaling option is on, the circle is proportionally scaled (b).

(a)

(b)

ROTATING GRAPHICS

Figure 42. You can rotate objects within PageMaker by 360 degrees at 0.01 degree intervals. Select the object with the pointer tool, choose a reference point on the *Proxy* (this determines the point that the object rotates around), and type a value into the *Rotation* option edit box (a).

After pressing the Enter key or clicking on the *Apply* button, the object rotates (b). For clockwise rotation, use - angles; for anti-clockwise rotation, use + angles.

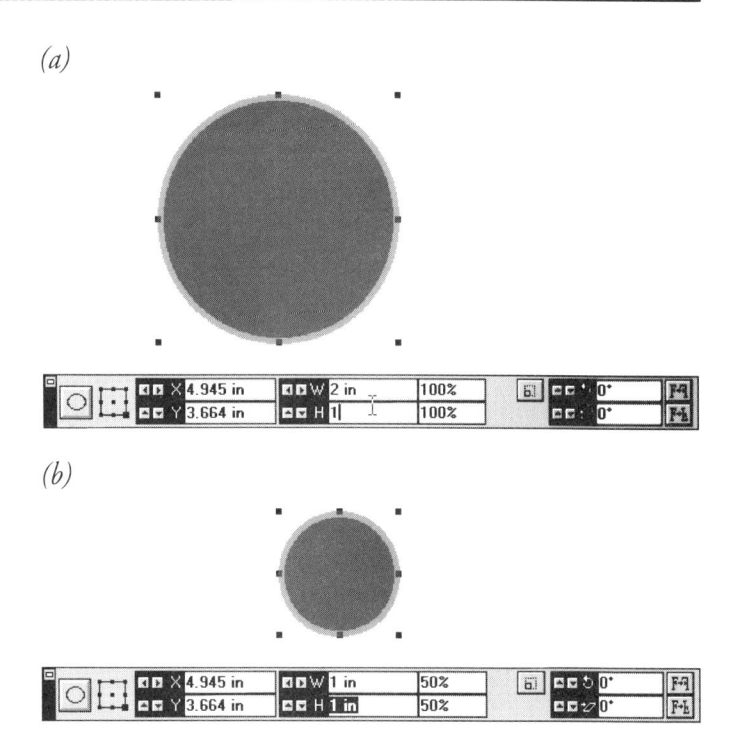

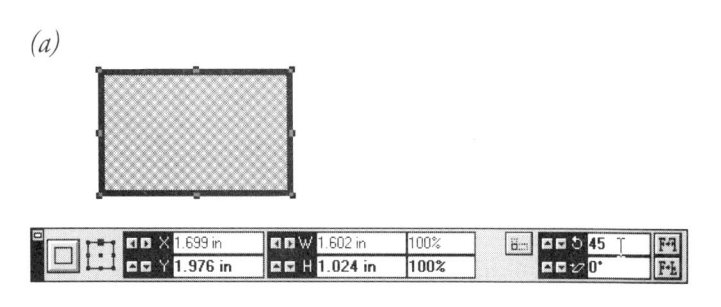

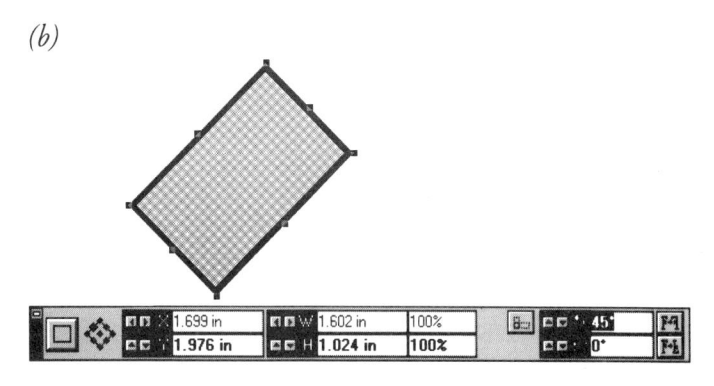

(a)

(b)

109

Chapter 6: Creating Graphics

(a)

(b)

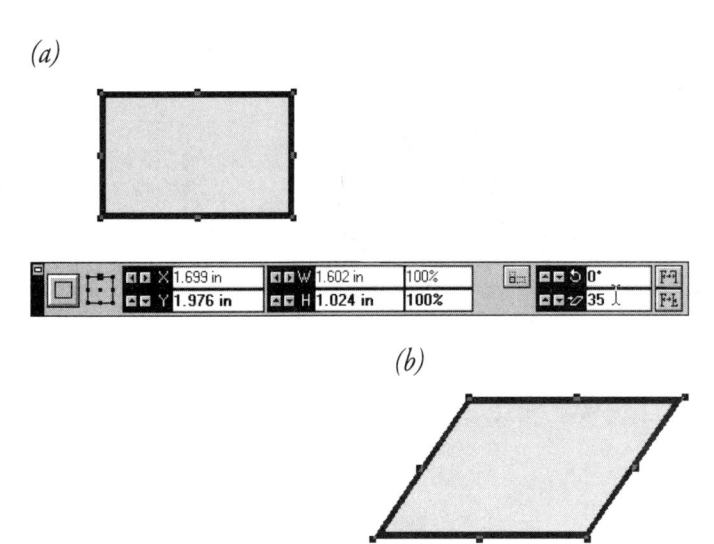

SKEWING GRAPHICS

Figure 43. You can skew objects horizontally by + or - 85 degrees at 0.01 degree increments. Select the object with the pointer tool and select a fixed point on the *Proxy*. Specify a skewing angle in the *Skewing option* edit box (a), and press the Enter key or click on the *Apply* button to apply the skew (b).

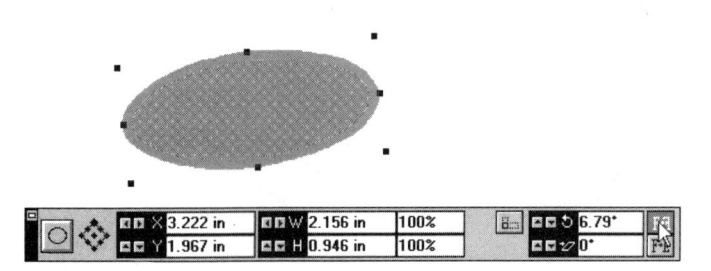

REFLECTING GRAPHICS

Figure 44. Select the object with the pointer tool and select a point on the *Proxy*. PageMaker reflects the object around this point. Click on the *Horizontal* or *Vertical* reflection button (a) and you will see the change immediately (b).

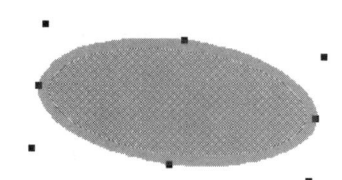

110

REMOVING TRANSFORMATIONS

Figure 45. To remove the transformations you have applied to an object (rotated, reflected or skewed), select the object and select *Remove transformation* from the **Element** menu.

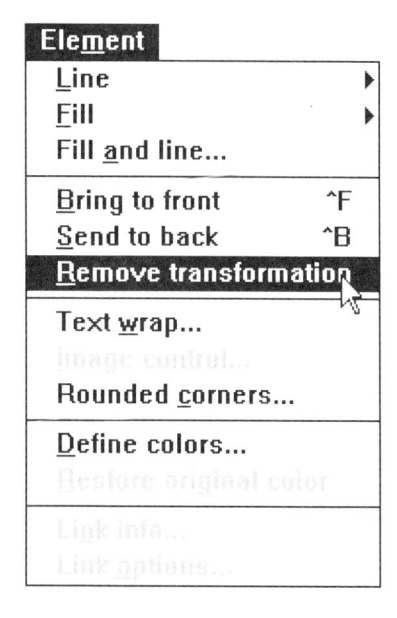

```
Element
 Line                    ▶
 Fill                    ▶
 Fill and line...
 Bring to front       ^F
 Send to back         ^B
 Remove transformation
 Text wrap...
 Image control...
 Rounded corners...
 Define colors...
 Restore original color
 Link info...
 Link options...
```

IMPORTED GRAPHICS   7

THE FORMATS PAGEMAKER SUPPORTS

PageMaker imports a wide variety of graphic files. These include bitmap files and scanned images (these can be paint or TIFF files), object-oriented or vector graphics, EPS files (PostScript-coded files) and WMF files (Windows metafiles).

PageMaker uses a file's extension to determine what sort of file it is and whether PageMaker can accept this format. Figures 1 through 4 provide examples of some of the different types of graphics you can place in PageMaker.

Figure 1. We loaded some of the screen shots taken for this book into PC Paintbrush for editing, and then cut and pasted them into PageMaker. By default these files exist in **bmp** format.

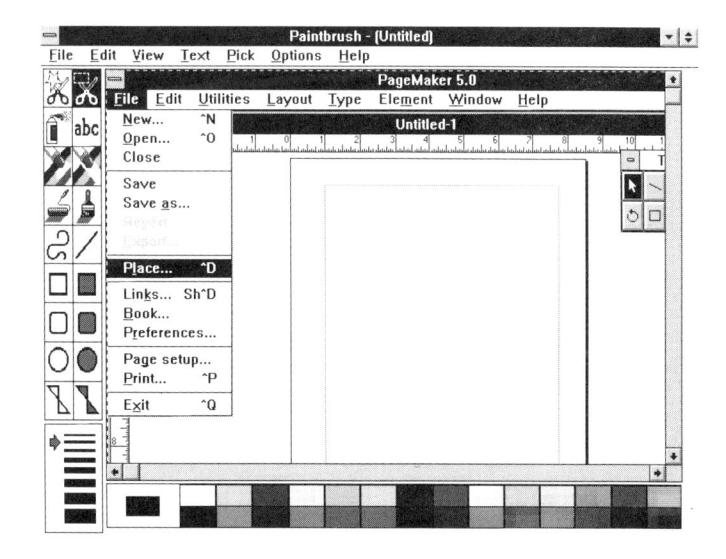

113

Chapter 7: Imported Graphics

Figure 2. EPS graphics are vector based and can be resized without losing resolution and quality. You must have a PostScript printer to print EPS graphics.

Figure 3. The same graphic as Figure 2 but this time TIFF. TIFF graphics are made up of tiny little dots and suffer in resolution when you resize them.

Figure 4. This is a scanned image which can be saved in a number of formats.

Chapter 7: Imported Graphics

LOADING GRAPHICS

Figure 5. Use the *Place* command within the **File** menu to import all types of graphics into PageMaker. This activates the *Place document* dialog box as shown in Figure 6. You can use this command to:

- place a new graphic, or
- replace an existing graphic.

Graphics you place in your document can be part of your text—an inline graphic—or totally independent of the text—an independent graphic.

Figure 6. To add a new graphic to your document, choose the name of the file from the list of files to the left.

Select *As independent graphic* if you wish to place a graphic independent of any text (as opposed to an inline graphic—see Figure 27).

Figure 7. Depending upon the type of graphic you are importing, the mouse cursor takes on one of the following four shapes:

(a) paint graphic;
(b) scanned or TIFF graphic;
(c) draw graphic; and
(d) encapsulated PostScript graphic.

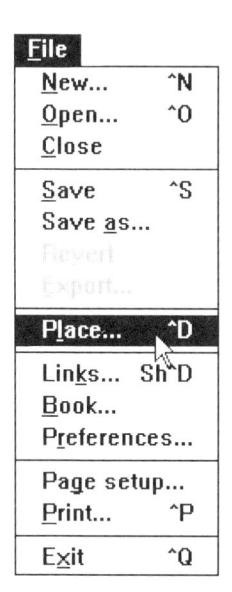

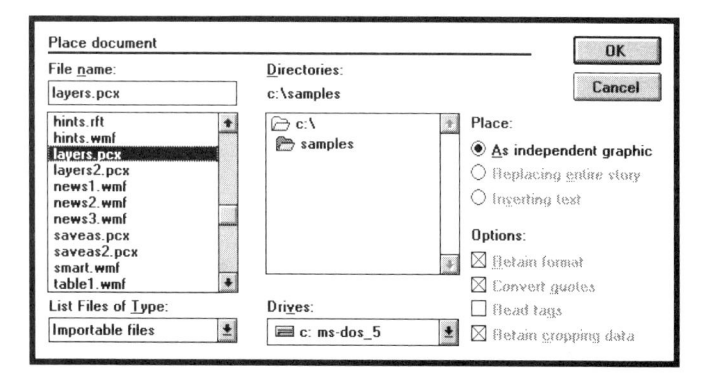

115

Chapter 7: Imported Graphics

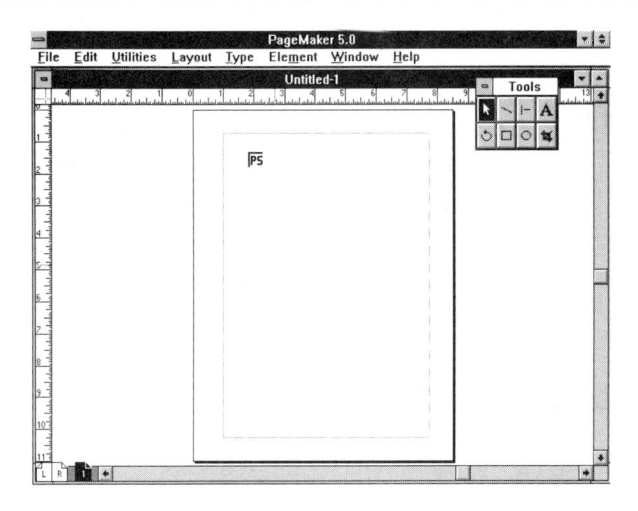

Figure 8. You can place a graphic onto the page in two ways. One way is to position the mouse cursor anywhere on screen and click once. By using this method, you load the graphic onto the page at its original size, which is often very difficult for you to pre-determine.

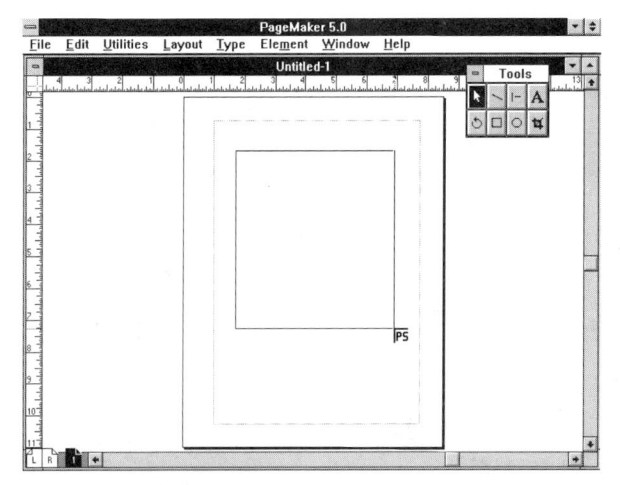

Figure 9. Another way to place a graphic is to drag the mouse until the selection rectangle is the size you would like the graphic to be. This is known as *drag-placing*.

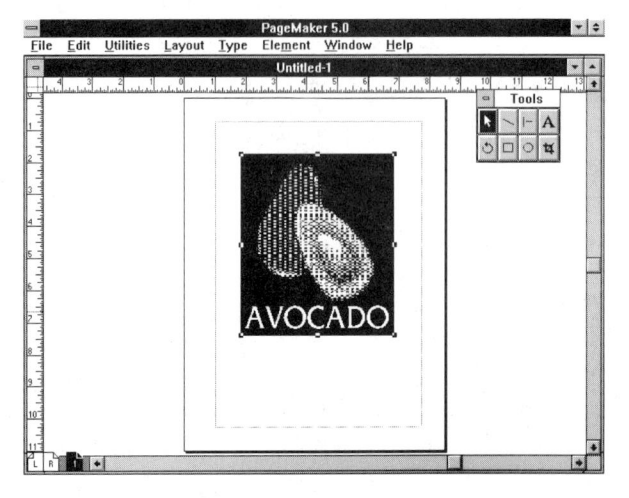

Figure 10. Once you release the mouse button, the graphic will fill the area of the box. To resize the graphic proportionally, hold down the Shift key and select one of the corner handles to resize. The graphic will snap to its true proportions.

Chapter 7: Imported Graphics

REPLACING EXISTING GRAPHICS

Figure 11. To replace an existing graphic, including any resizing and cropping that you have applied, select the graphic on the page, select the graphic file in the *Place document* dialog box and choose *Replacing entire graphic*.

Figure 12. If you place the insertion point in any text before you select the *Place* command, you have the option of placing the graphic as an inline graphic. Figures 27 through 32 explain this procedure.

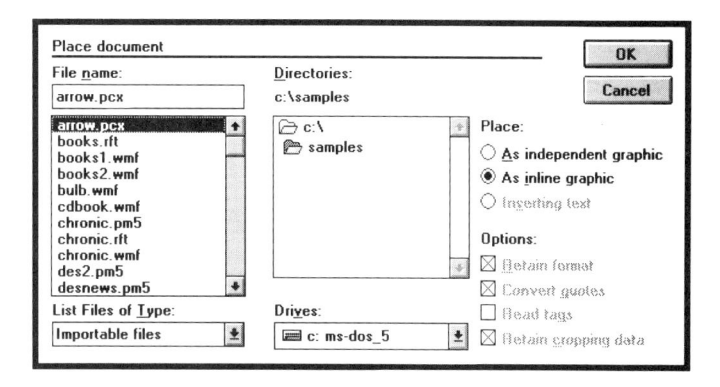

Figure 13. Turn the *Retain cropping data* option on if you have cropped an imported graphic and you wish to update (replace) the link with the original graphic (see the **Cropping graphics** section in this chapter). You can also access this option in the *Link info* dialog box.

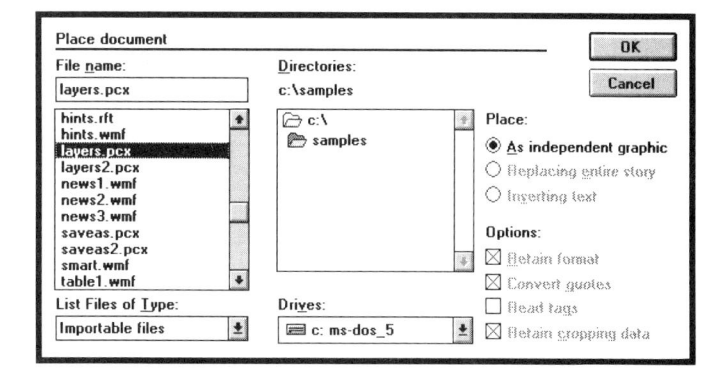

You need apply this option only if you wish to replace or relink graphics using PageMaker's linking options—PageMaker automatically retains cropping information for hot-linked files, OLE-linked or embedded files (see Chapter 3 for more information on links).

117

Chapter 7: Imported Graphics

Cropping tool

Cropping tool cursor

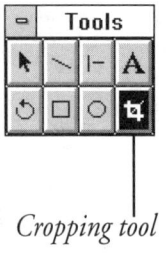

CROPPING GRAPHICS

Figure 14. Use the cropping tool to crop imported graphics. Note that when you select the cropping tool, the cursor changes to the same icon as the cropping tool.

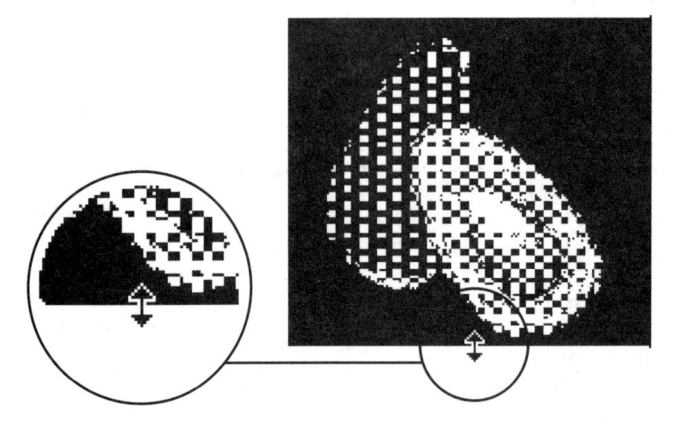

Figure 15. Select the graphic with the cropping tool and position this tool over one of the selection handles. Once the cursor changes to a two-headed arrow, move the mouse pointer towards the center of the graphic. You will find this is similar to resizing a graphic, but in this case you hide part of the graphic. You can crop graphics both horizontally and vertically.

Figure 16. When you have cropped a graphic, you still have access to any part of the graphic you want to bring into view. To move the graphic inside the window, hold the cropping tool down inside the graphic and drag it.

Chapter 7: Imported Graphics

WRAPPING TEXT AROUND GRAPHICS

Figure 17. You can flow text around imported graphics in a variety of ways, using the *Text wrap* command and its associated dialog box. Select a graphic before choosing this command, unless you wish the choices you make in the *Text wrap* dialog box to become the default settings.

Figure 18. Select Wrap off if you wish text to flow through the graphic.

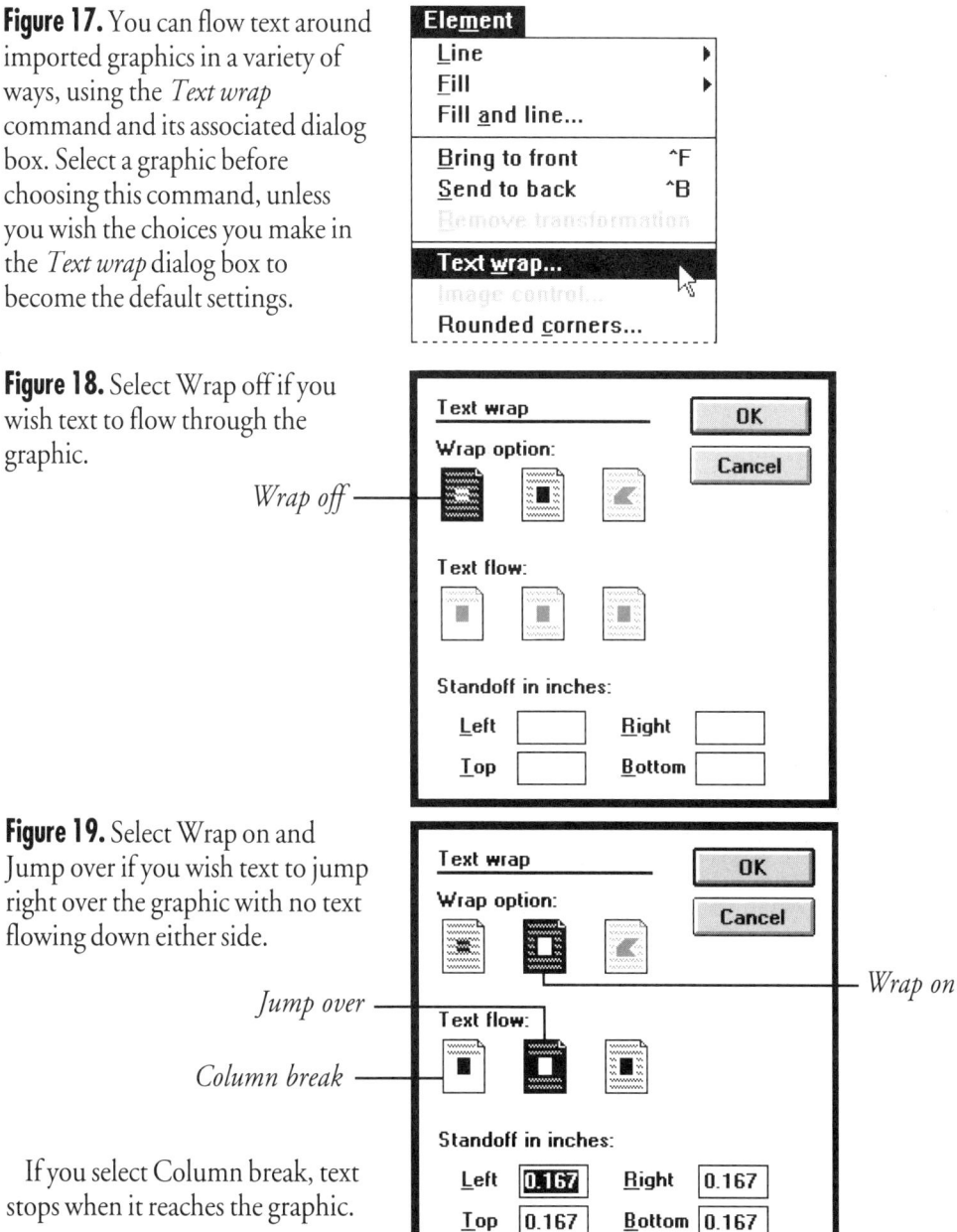

Wrap off

Figure 19. Select Wrap on and Jump over if you wish text to jump right over the graphic with no text flowing down either side.

Jump over

Column break

Wrap on

If you select Column break, text stops when it reaches the graphic.

119

Chapter 7: Imported Graphics

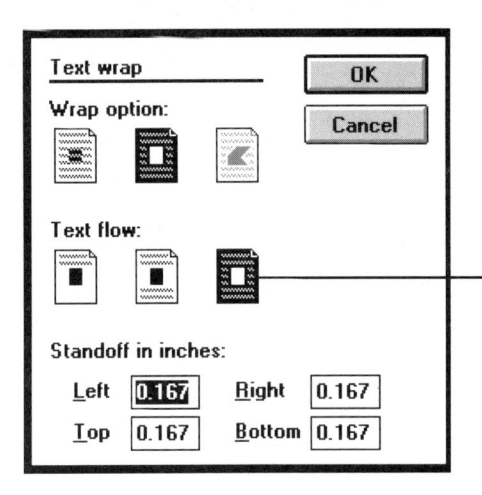

Figure 20. Select Wrap on and Wrap all sides if you wish text to flow regularly around a graphic, including down both sides. See the example shown in Figure 21.

—*Wrap all sides*

Figure 21. This is an example of text flowing regularly around a graphic using the *Text wrap* settings in Figure 20.

120

Chapter 7: Imported Graphics

IRREGULAR WRAP-AROUNDS

Figure 22. Set up the *Text wrap* dialog box with Wrap on and Wrap all sides to get an irregular wrap-around.

As soon as you begin to manipulate the irregular text wrap border around the graphic, PageMaker automatically selects Custom wrap in the *Text wrap* dialog box.

— Custom wrap
— Wrap on
— Wrap all sides

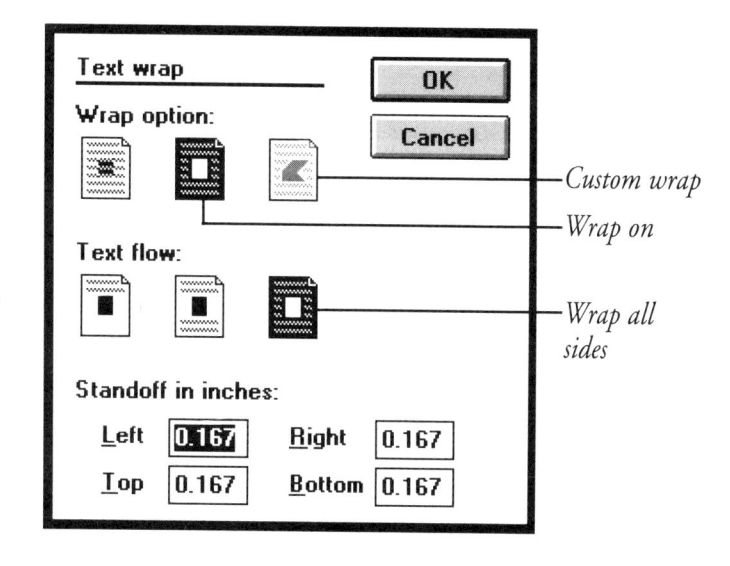

Figure 23. These settings give you two sets of handles around the graphic. The inside handles resize the picture. The outside handles adjust the text wrap to any shape.

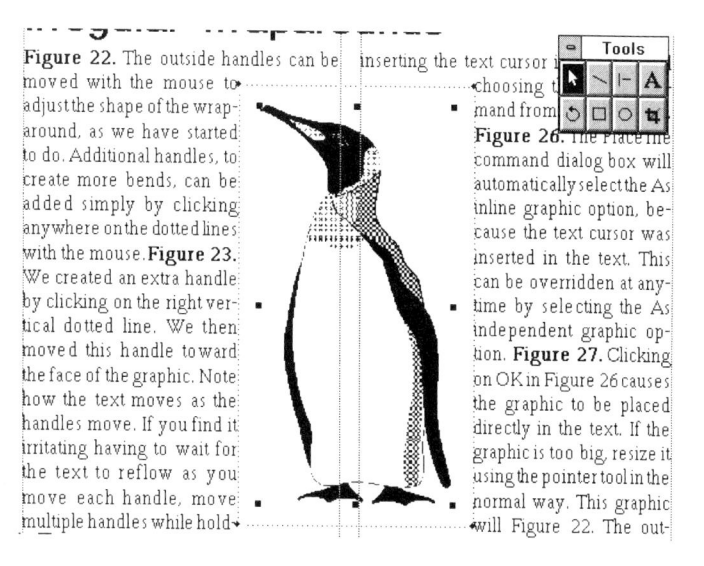

Figure 22. The outside handles can be moved with the mouse to adjust the shape of the wrap-around, as we have started to do. Additional handles, to create more bends, can be added simply by clicking anywhere on the dotted lines with the mouse. **Figure 23.** We created an extra handle by clicking on the right vertical dotted line. We then moved this handle toward the face of the graphic. Note how the text moves as the handles move. If you find it irritating having to wait for the text to reflow as you move each handle, move multiple handles while hold-

inserting the text cursor choosing mand from **Figure 26**. The Place command dialog box will automatically select the As inline graphic option, because the text cursor was inserted in the text. This can be overridden at any-time by selecting the As independent graphic option. **Figure 27.** Clicking on OK in Figure 26 causes the graphic to be placed directly in the text. If the graphic is too big, resize it using the pointer tool in the normal way. This graphic will Figure 22. The out-

121

Chapter 7: Imported Graphics

Figure 22. The outside handles can be moved with the mouse to adjust the shape of the wraparound, as we have started to do. Additional handles, to create more bends, can be added simply by clicking anywhere on the dotted lines with the mouse. **Figure 23.** We created an extra handle by clicking on the right vertical dotted line. We then moved this handle toward the face of the graphic. Note how the text moves as the handles move. If you find it irritating having to wait for the text to reflow as you move each handle, move multiple handles while hold- inserting the text cursor choosing mand from Figure 26. The Place line command dialog box will automatically select the As inline graphic option, because the text cursor was inserted in the text. This can be overridden at anytime by selecting the As independent graphic option. **Figure 27.** Clicking on OK in Figure 26 causes the graphic to be placed directly in the text. If the graphic is too big, resize it using the pointer tool in the normal way. This graphic will Figure 22. The out-

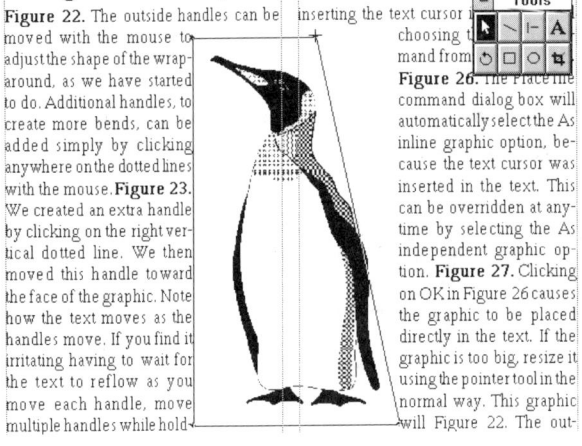

Figure 24. You can move the outside handles with the mouse to adjust the shape of the wrap-around, as we have started to do. You can add extra handles to create more bends simply by clicking anywhere on the dotted lines with the mouse.

Figure 22. The outside handles can be moved with the mouse to adjust the shape of the wraparound, as we have started to do. Additional handles, to create more bends, can be added simply by clicking anywhere on the dotted lines with the mouse. **Figure 23.** We created an extra handle by clicking on the right vertical dotted line. We then moved this handle toward the face of the graphic. Note how the text moves as the handles move. If you find it irritating having to wait for the text to reflow as you move each handle, move multiple handles while holding down choosing the Place com File menu. **Figure 26.** The mand dialog box will au lect the As inline graphic cause the text cursor was inserted in the text. This can be overridden at anytime by selecting the As independent graphic option. **Figure 27.** Clicking on OK in Figure 26 causes the graphic to be placed directly in the text. If the graphic is too big, resize it using the pointer tool in the normal way. This graphic will Figure 22. The outside handles can be moved with the mouse to adjust the shape of the wraparound, as we have started to do. Additional handles, to create more bends,

Figure 25. We created extra handles by clicking on the vertical dotted line and moved these handles individually toward the graphic. See how the text moves as you move the handles. If you find it irritating having to wait for the text to reflow as you move each handle, move multiple handles while holding down the Spacebar. The text will not reflow until you release the Spacebar.

Figure 22. The outside handles can be moved with the mouse to ad- just the shape of the wraparound, as we have started to do. Additional handles, to create more bends, can be added simply by clicking anywhere on the dotted lines with the mouse. **Figure 23.** We created an extra handle by clicking on the right vertical dotted line. We then moved this handle toward the face of the graphic. Note how the text moves as the handles move. If you find it irritating having to wait for the text to reflow as you move each handle, move multiple handles while holding down the Spacebar. The text will not reflow until you release the Spacebar. **Figure 24.** A finished irregu- mand dialog box will se lect the As inline graphi se the text cursor was ins xt. This can be overridden at anytime by selecting the As independent graphic option. **Figure 27.** Clicking on OK in Figure 26 causes the graphic to be placed directly in the text. If the graphic is too big, resize it using the pointer tool in the normal way. This graphic will Figure 22. The outside handles can be moved with the mouse to adjust the shape of the wrap-around, as we have started to do. Additional handles, to create more bends, can be added simply by clicking anywhere on the dotted lines with the mouse. Figure 23. We created

Figure 26. A finished irregular wrap-around.

Chapter 7: Imported Graphics

INLINE GRAPHICS

Inline graphics are graphics that become part of the text. As you move the text, inline graphics move with it.

Figure 27. You create inline graphics by placing the insertion point in the text where you want to put the graphic and choosing *Place* from the **File** menu.

Figure 28. The *Place document* dialog box automatically selects the *As inline graphic* option, because you placed the insertion point in the text. You can override this at any time by selecting the *As independent graphic* option. But for this example we are not going to change this option.

Figure 29. Clicking on *OK* in the *Place document* dialog box causes PageMaker to place the graphic in the text. If the graphic is too big, resize it with the pointer tool. This graphic will now move if you edit the text, or move or resize the text block.

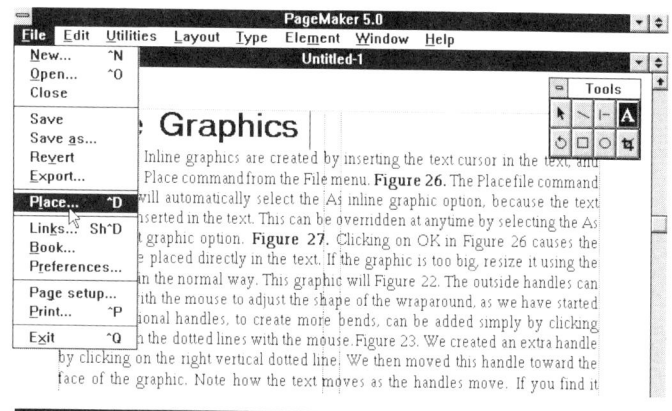

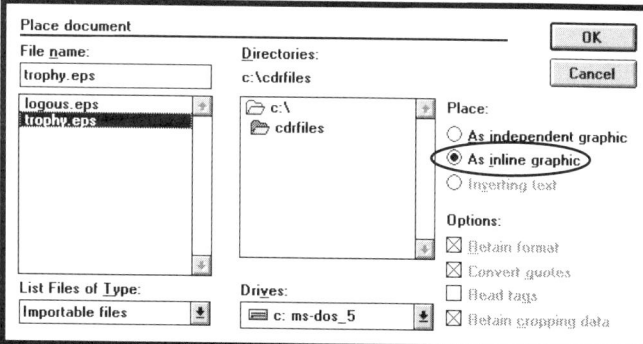

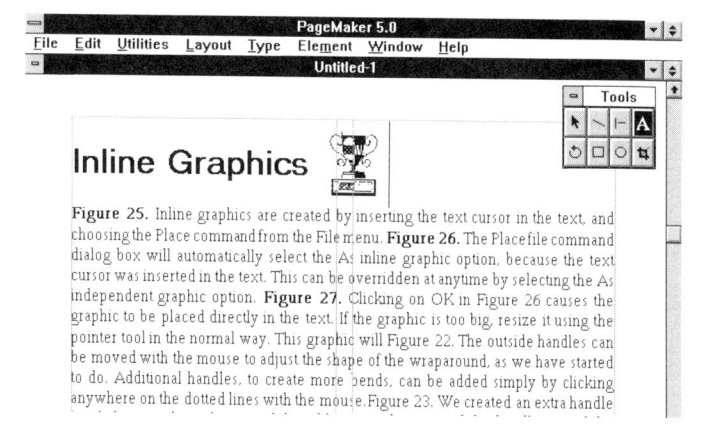

123

Chapter 7: Imported Graphics

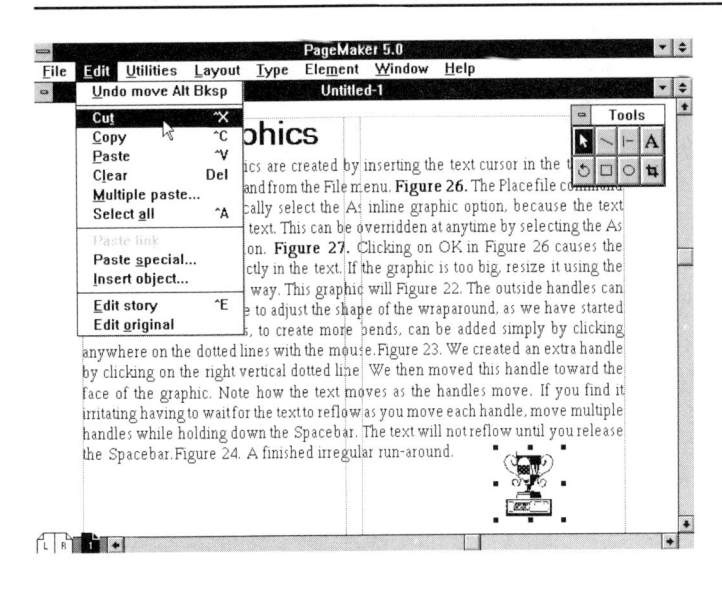

Figure 30. You can turn an independent graphic on the page into an inline graphic in your text as follows:

Select the graphic with the pointer tool and choose *Cut* from the **Edit** menu.

Place the insertion point where you want the graphic in the text and choose *Paste* from the **Edit** menu.

Figure 31. We inserted the cursor into the text and pasted the removed graphic at the insertion point. It now becomes an inline graphic.

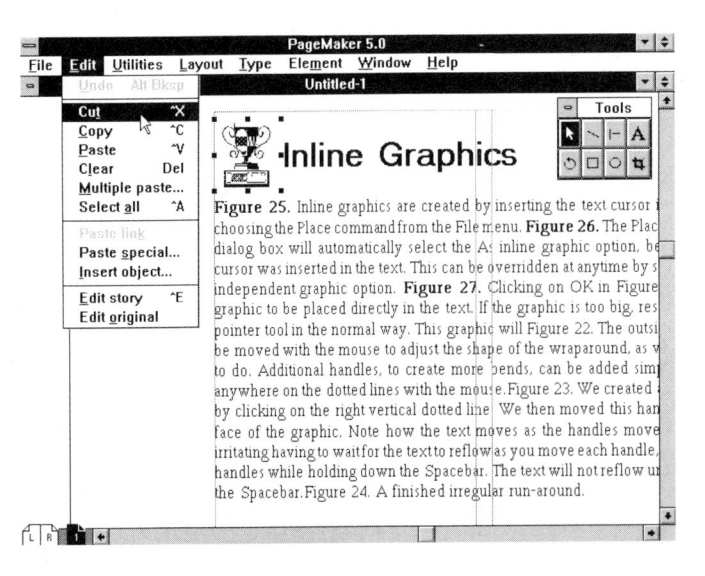

Figure 32. You can turn an inline graphic on your page into an independent graphic as follows:

Select the graphic with the pointer tool, choose *Cut* from the **Edit** menu and then choose *Paste*.

The graphic reappears in the text in the same place. However, you can now select it with the pointer tool and move it independently of the text.

124

Chapter 7: Imported Graphics

IMAGE CONTROL

Figure 33. You can alter the appearance of paint graphics and scanned images using the *Image control* command from the **Element** menu. The *Image control* command is available for black-and-white graphics only.

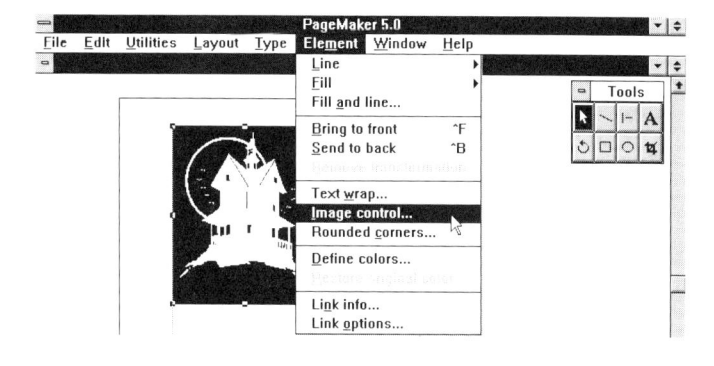

Figure 34. This is the *Image control* dialog box. You can change the lightness, contrast, screen patterns, angle and frequency of a selected graphic. If you change a setting here, press the Tab key to move to the next option and you can then click on the *Apply* button. Using the *Apply* button allows you to keep the *Image control* dialog box on screen while you experiment.

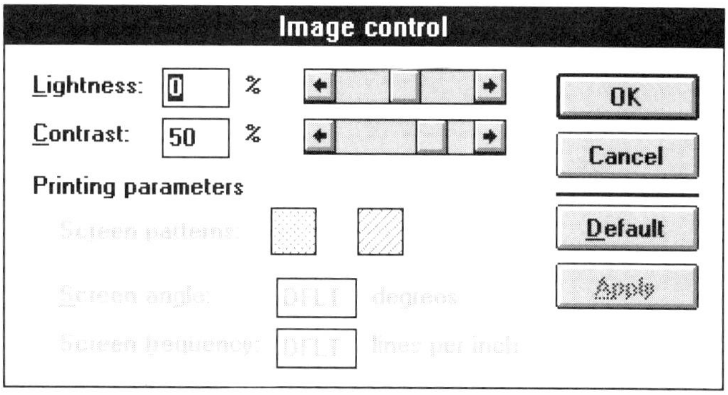

Figure 35. Here we have inverted the image by changing the figure in the *Contrast* box, either directly or using the scroll bar, from 50 to -50.

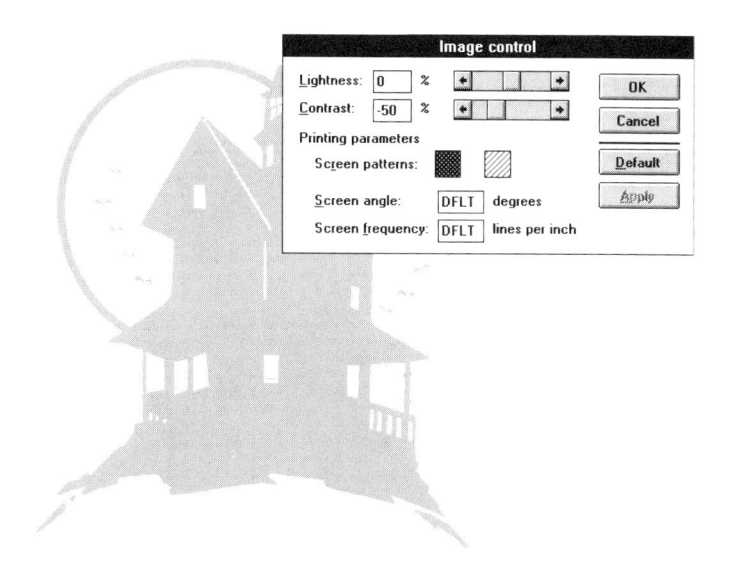

125

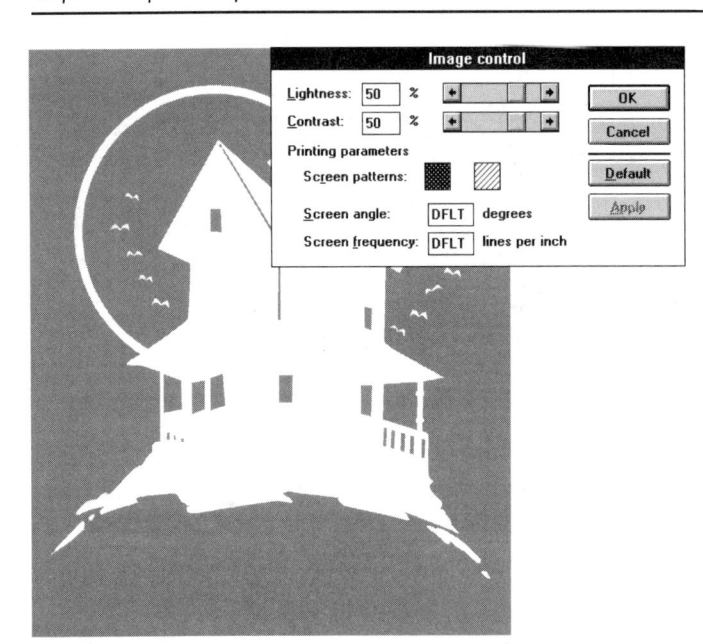

Figure 36. By altering the figures in both *Lightness* and *Contrast*, the image adjusts accordingly after you click on the *Apply* button.

Once you have adjusted the *Lightness* and *Contrast* of the image, you can alter the *Printing parameters* options. Here you have the option of changing the default line or dot angle and frequency settings for special effects.

MULTIPLE PASTE COMMAND

You can use the *Multiple paste* command if you wish to paste multiple copies of an object from the clipboard onto your page. See Chapter 6, Figure 23 for more information.

IMPORTED GRAPHICS AND THE CONTROL PALETTE

You use the Control palette with imported graphics in the same way as you do with internal graphics—for moving, resizing, scaling, rotating, skewing and reflecting of graphics (see **The Control Palette and Graphics** in Chapter 6). However, you can also use the Control palette to crop imported graphics. This is discussed below.

CROPPING

Figure 37. To crop a graphic using the Control palette, select the graphic, click on the *Cropping* option, and select a reference point on the *Proxy*.

Cropping option

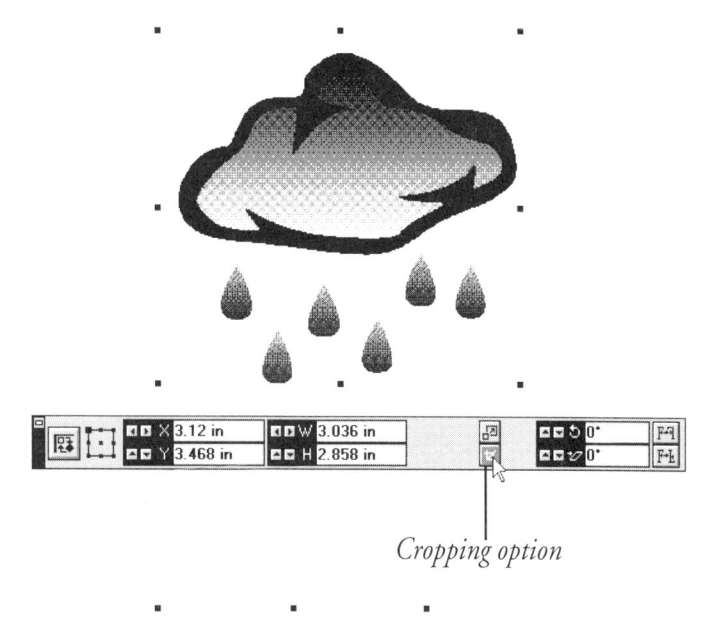

Figure 38. Change the values for *X* and *Y* or *H* and *W* and press the Enter key or click on the *Apply* button to see the results. Here, we have cropped the right side of the graphic by selecting a reference point on the left side of the *Proxy* and decreasing the *W* value.

Figure 39. The other options available when you turn the *Cropping* option off are *Proportional scaling*, and the *Printer-resolution scaling*. Use the latter option to resize monochrome bitmap images to an optimal size for your target printer.

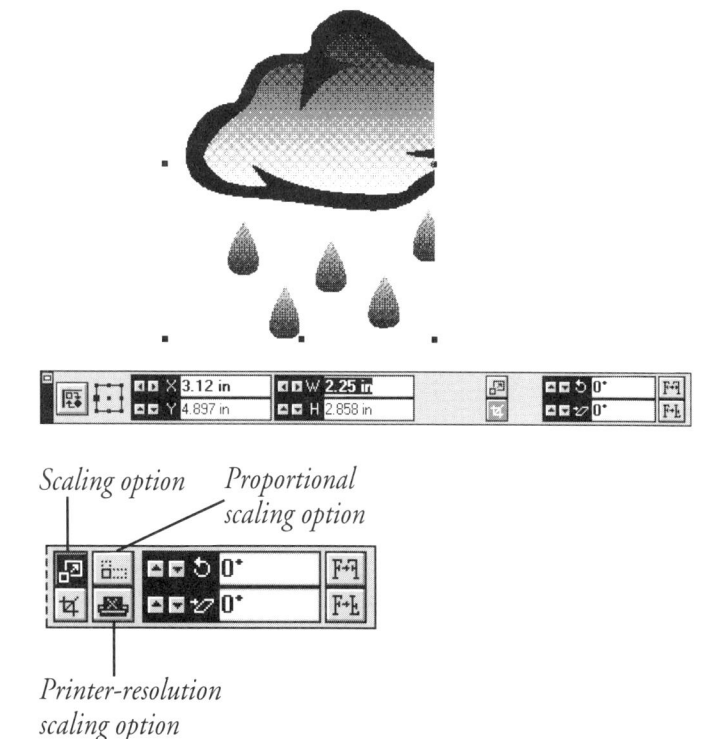

Scaling option *Proportional scaling option*

Printer-resolution scaling option

WORKING WITH TEMPLATES 8

CREATING TEMPLATES

A PageMaker template is like any other normal publication, except that it has a specific application as a "dummy" document. A dummy document can contain formatting information for a standard publication, such as a monthly newsletter. When you open a template, you automatically open an untitled copy of the original document. This allows you to add new information to a document without affecting the original template.

As you will see below, you can include text and graphics in a template, and PageMaker provides a number of features for simple and easy replacement of these objects with updated information.

Note: You can use the text and graphic replacement methods discussed in this chapter in any PageMaker publication.

Figure 1. You create a template in the same way as any other PageMaker publication. Add text and graphics as required, adjust the layout as needed, and use master page items, imported graphics and other elements as you would for any document. The difference is when you save the file — the *Save* command from the **File** menu produces the *Save publication* dialog box. In the right half of this box, click on the *Template* radio button. Name the publication and select *OK* to create a template publication.

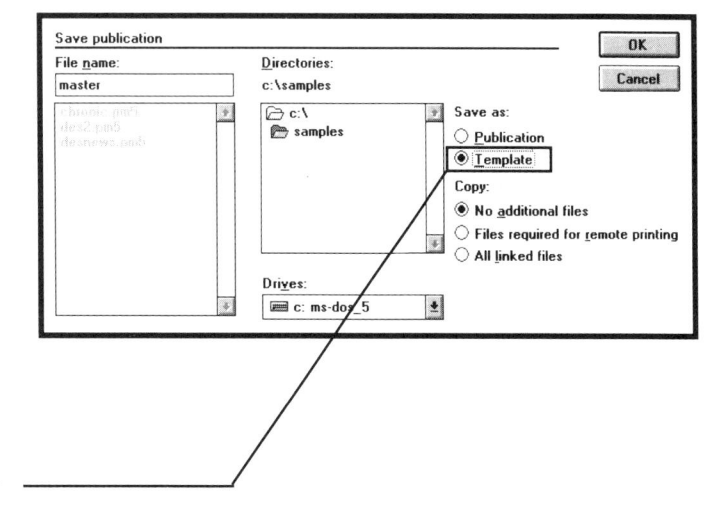

129

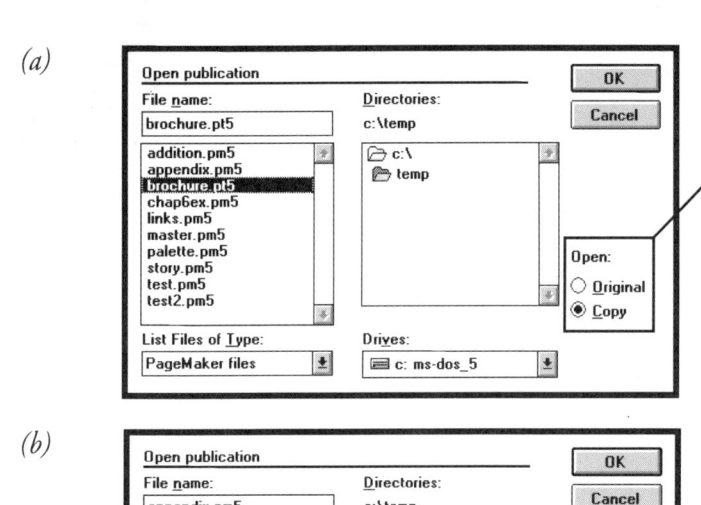

Opening Templates

(a)

(b)

Figure 2. To open a template, use the *Open* command, as for any PageMaker publication. The dialog box automatically defaults to *Copy* when you select a template as shown in (a). You can select *Original* if you wish to alter your original template. (See also the *Open template* addition in Chapter 9.)

Conversely, opening a normal publication automatically defaults to *Original* as shown in (b). You can also override this to open a copy of a publication.

The difference between opening a publication and a template is that a template automatically defaults to *Copy* when you are opening it. A template will also have an extension of **.pt5**.

Using Templates

Figure 3. When you open a copy of a template to change it, you often need to replace the text with a file of your choice. Do this by selecting any part of the text file with the pointer tool (or placing the insertion point anywhere within a story), and choosing *Place* from the **File** menu.

If you wish to replace only part of a text file, select that part with the text tool. In this figure, we have selected a block of text in column one with the pointer tool.

Chapter 8: Working with Templates

TEXT PLACEHOLDERS

Figure 4. The *Replacing entire story* in the *Place document* dialog box lets you replace the story selected in the template. If you have inserted the text cursor in the text, then you can select the *Inserting text* option. If you have selected a portion of text with the text tool, a new option—*Replacing selected text*—appears.

With these methods, you can quickly and easily replace earlier outdated stories with new stories. The old and new text stories do not need to be of the same length.

The text contained within the original template is called a text placeholder.

GRAPHIC PLACEHOLDERS

Figure 5. Replacing old graphics with new imported graphics is even simpler than replacing text. Select the graphic you wish to replace with the pointer tool and choose *Place* from the **File** menu.

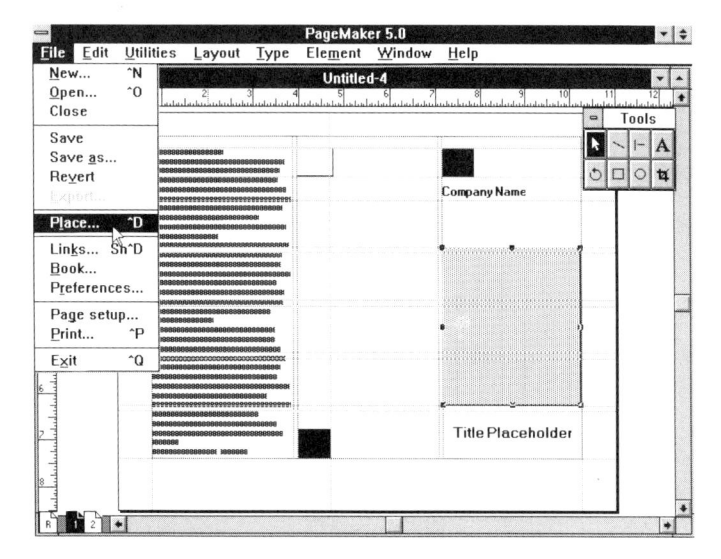

131

Chapter 8: Working with Templates

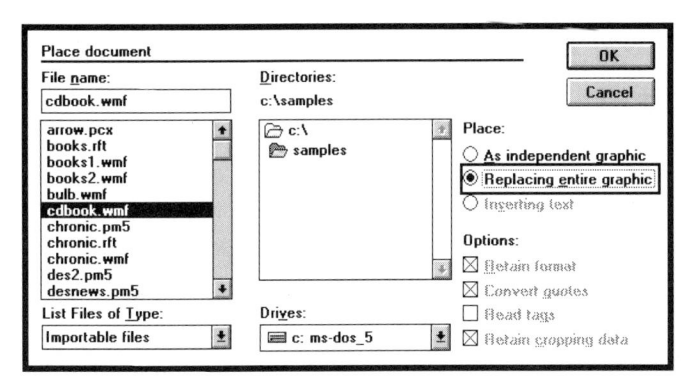

Figure 6. In the *Place document* dialog box you can choose either *Replacing entire graphic* selection or *As independent graphic.* Use the latter option to load graphics in the normal way. Use the former option to replace a selected graphic. Click on *OK* and PageMaker immediately loads the graphic into the selected graphic area on your page.

The graphic contained within the original template is referred to as a graphic placeholder.

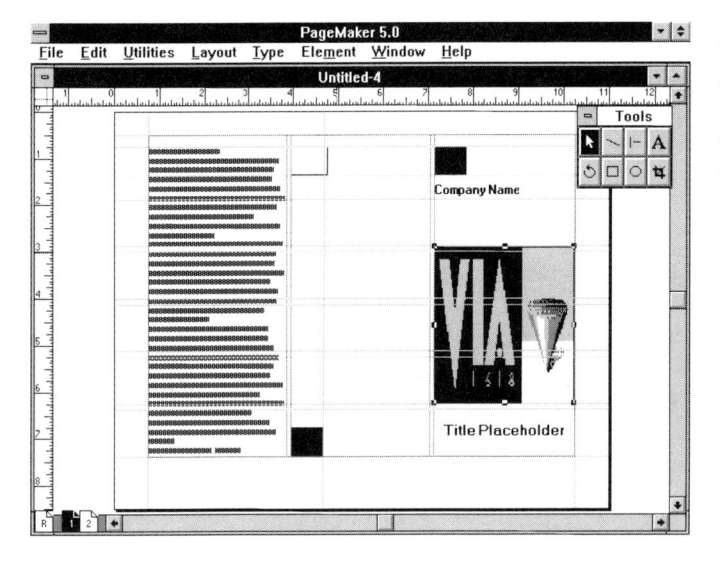

Figure 7. PageMaker keeps the same graphic size and parameters, including cropping and text wrap-around attributes. You can change these if necessary.

132

ALDUS ADDITIONS 9

WHAT ARE ALDUS ADDITIONS?

PageMaker 5 comes with a number of additions which you can find in the *Aldus Additions* submenu in the **Utilities** menu. You can also get additions offered by independent developers as these become available. The additions give you extra features you can use to enhance and compile your publications.

Such features include balancing columns, adding bullets, adding drop capitals, displaying publication information and text continuation notices, and more.

Figure 1. The *Aldus Additions* submenu is in the **Utilities** menu. The additions in the submenu you see here are the ones that you install by default with PageMaker 5.0. Any extra additions you must install separately.

The following pages describe each of the additions in the submenu listed in this figure.

Utilities		
Aldus Additions	More	Run script...
Find... ^8	Acquire image...	Running headers/footers...
Find next Sh^9	Add cont'd line...	Sort pages...
Change... ^9	Balance columns...	Traverse textblocks...
Spelling... ^L	Build booklet...	
Index entry... ^;	Bullets and numbering...	
Show index...	Create color library...	
Create index...	Create keyline..	
Create TOC...	Display pub info...	
	Display story info...	
	Display textblock info...	
	Drop cap...	
	Edit tracks...	
	Expert kerning...	
	Find overset text	
	List styles used	
	Open stories	
	Open template...	
	PS Group it	
	PS Ungroup it	
	Printer styles...	

ACQUIRE IMAGE

The *Acquire image* addition lets you use your scanner from within PageMaker to scan images. This is useful, as you can integrate the process of scanning and placing graphics. To use this addition, you need a scanner that uses the TWAIN standard installed.

133

ADD CONT'D LINE

Figure 2. Use the *Add cont'd line* addition if you want a continuation notice at the top or the bottom of a text file that joins another one on another page.

Figure 3. Select the text block with the pointer tool and select *Add cont'd line* from the *Aldus Additions* submenu.

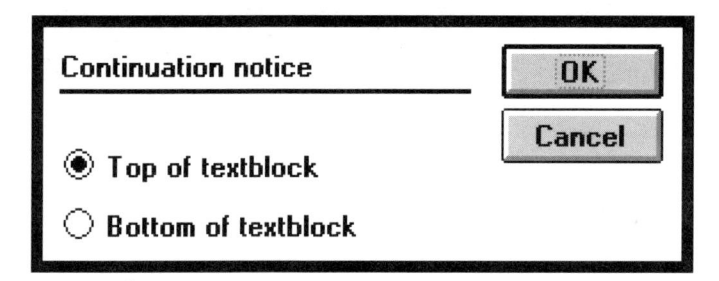

Figure 4. If the text appears on a page in front of the currently selected text block, choose the *Top of textblock* option from the *Continuation notice* dialog box. Choose the *Bottom of textblock* option if the text appears after the page you are on.

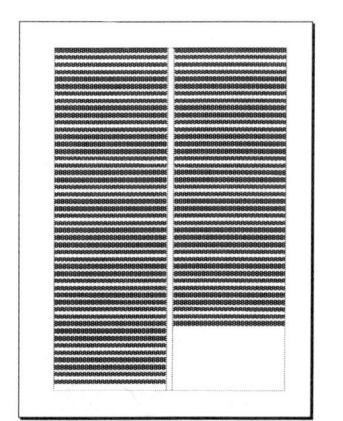

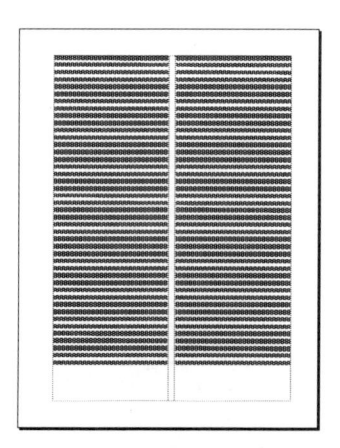

BALANCE COLUMNS

Figure 5. Use the *Balance columns* addition to align multiple columns of a single threaded story. The page to the left is not balanced and the page to the right is.

Figure 6. To use this command, first select the columns you wish to balance and select *Balance columns* from the *Aldus Additions* submenu. This activates the *Balance columns* dialog box shown in Figure 7.

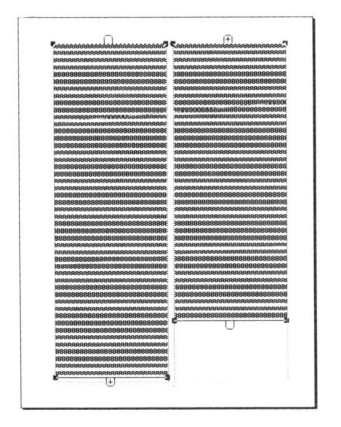

Figure 7. The left *Alignment* option aligns columns from the top of the page downwards and the right *Alignment* option aligns columns from the bottom upwards.

The *Add leftover lines* options allow you to add any remaining uneven lines to the left column or to the right column.

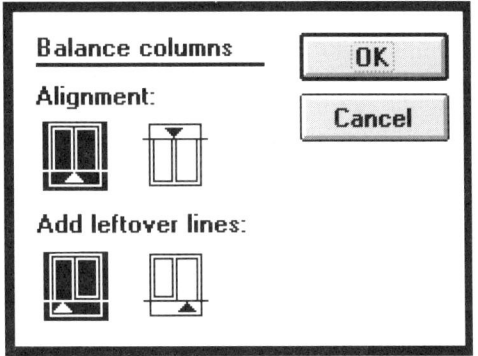

BUILD BOOKLET

Figure 8. With the *Build booklet* addition, you can create a copy of your current publication in booklet form. PageMaker rearranges the pages so that multiple pages print on a single sheet and if you then fold them, the pages assume the correct order.

If you were to print an eight-page, letter-sized brochure for example, you could print to a tabloid paper size and fold the pages in half. The correct page number grouping required for this procedure is displayed here.

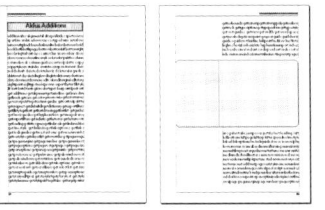

Pages 1 and 8

Pages 2 and 7

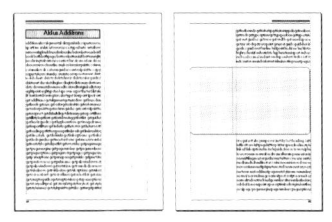

Pages 3 and 6

Pages 4 and 5

With the *Build booklet* addition you can do this automatically without having to think about the correct page imposition.

PREPARING YOUR PUBLICATION

To prepare your publication for building a booklet, you should have completed the following tasks:

- Check that you have at least two and a half times the size of the publication left on your hard disk.

- Check that you have completed the layout.

- Check that you have included your index and table of contents, if required.

- Check that the publication starts on an odd page.

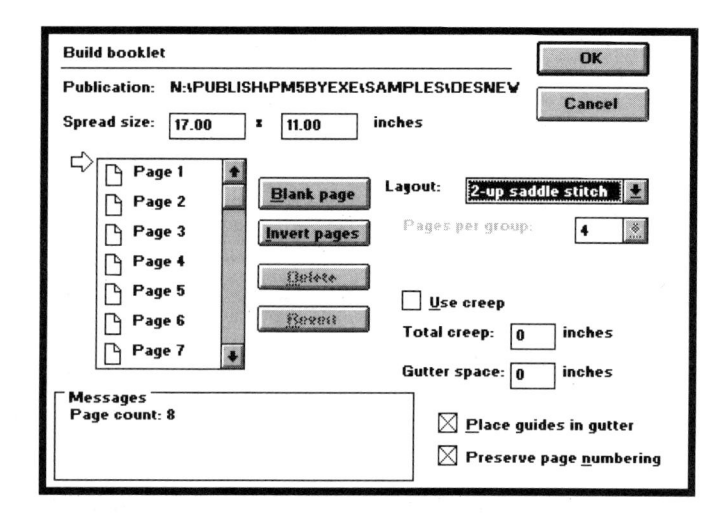

Figure 9. Once you have prepared your publication, you are ready to build a booklet. In the open publication, select *Build booklet* from the *Aldus Additions* sub-menu in the **Utilities** menu. This activates the *Build Booklet* dialog box.

Figure 10. The *Spread size* boxes display the calculated size of the selected *Layout* option. You can adjust the size to provide room for crop marks or bleeds. A warning appears in the *Messages* section if the current spread size is not large enough to accommodate these options.

PageMaker displays any messages or warnings in the *Messages* section.

Figure 11. In the section we have labeled here, you can rearrange, add, and delete pages. To insert a blank page, move the arrow to the left of the list box between the relevant pages by clicking the mouse, then click on *Blank page*. To rearrange the order of the pages from first to last to last to first, click on *Invert pages*. Select a page and click on *Delete* to remove it. Click on *Revert* to undo any unwanted changes you have made.

Figure 12. The *Layout* drop-down list box gives you six options to choose from:

- *None*: this option creates a new publication but does not automatically rearrange the pages or change the spread size.

- *2-up saddle stitch*: the default setting. Double-sided pages are printed, folded and fastened along the fold (see Figure 8 for an example).

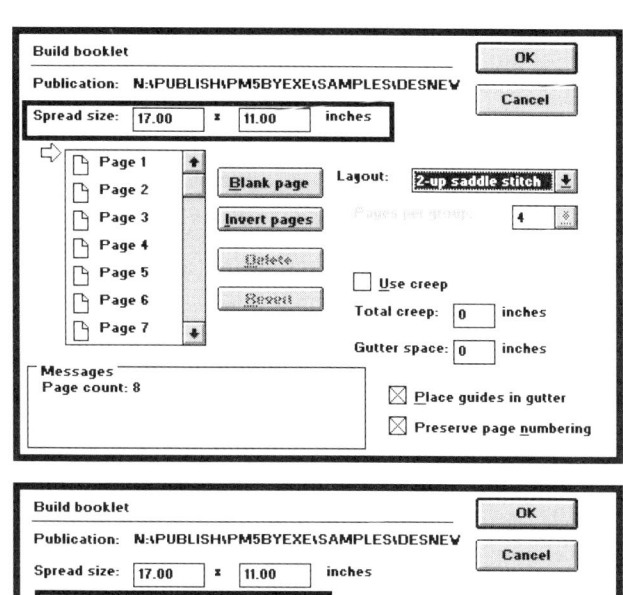

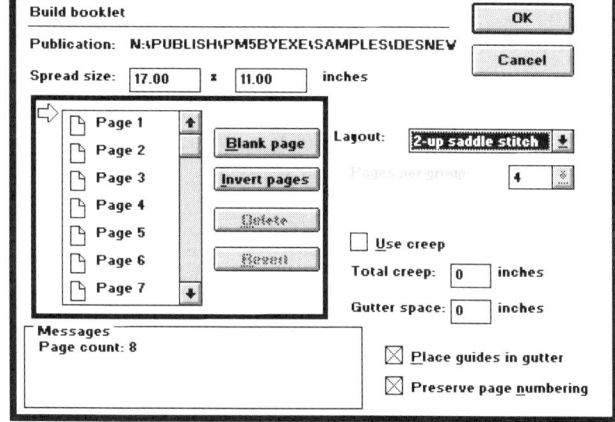

- *2-up perfect bound*: this creates a series of folded booklets that are joined together to create a spine-bound book. You must specify the number of pages per group, PageMaker calculates the number of spreads needed to produce the publication, as well as the correct page imposition.

- *2-3-4-up consecutive*: use these options to create multi-page spreads. Each set of pages is combined side-by-side onto a single page. This allows you to create, for example two-, three-, or four-panel brochures with ease.

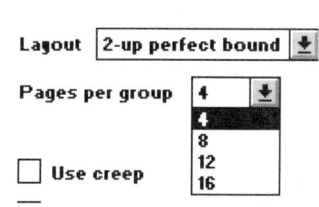

Figure 13. You can change the *Pages per group* option only when you have selected the *2-up perfect bound* option (see above). Select how many pages per group or booklet there will be for your perfect-bound book.

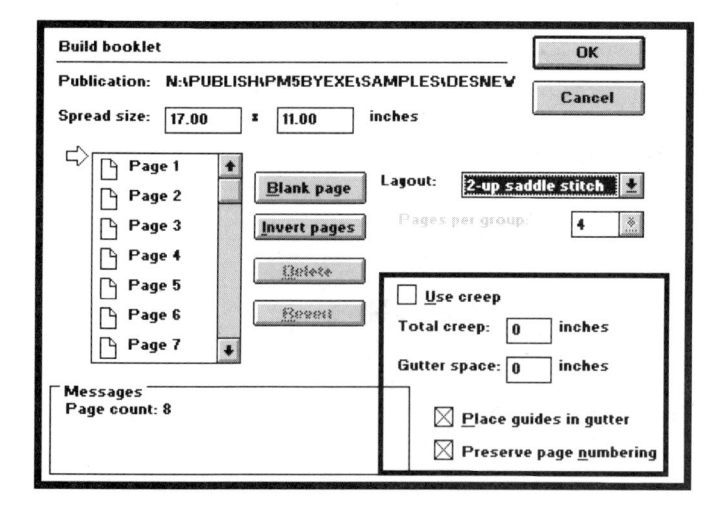

Figure 14. The *Use creep* option counteracts the problems you sometimes encounter when the folded sheets in a large booklet become offset due to the paper thickness. Turn the *Use creep* option on and in the *Total creep* text box insert a value that you estimate to offset the creep affecting your publication. PageMaker then adjusts the placement of the page elements to counter this problem.

Use the *Place guides in gutter* option to position non-printing ruler guides in the gutters of the publication.

Figure 15. Turn the *Preserve page numbering* option on or off to turn the page numbering on or off, respectively. You must have page numbering in the master pages of your document for the numbering to work. PageMaker renumbers and places a number on any blank pages if you turn this option on.

Type a value into the *Gutter space* text box to add space between pages. PageMaker automatically increases the *Spread size* values.

Once you have made all your changes in this dialog box, select *OK*.

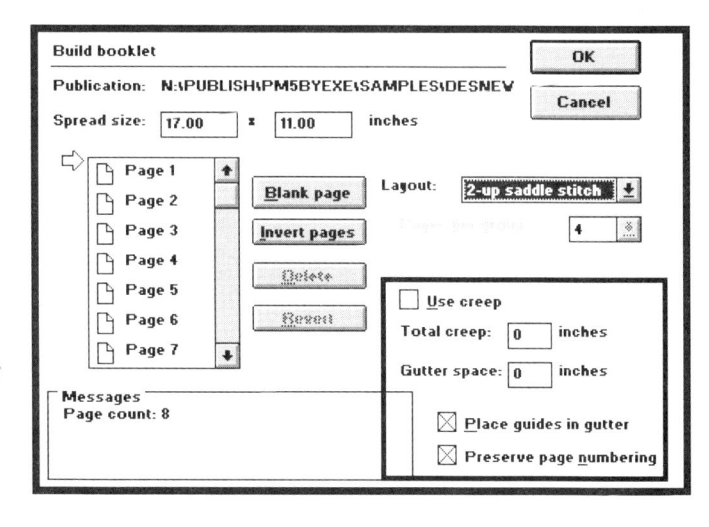

Figure 16. PageMaker creates a new untitled publication and closes the original file. The page size is equal to the dimensions displayed in the *Spread size* edit boxes in the *Build Booklet* dialog box. The page numbering sequence changes according to the type of *Layout* you chose. After PageMaker has created the new publication, you can still manually edit the publication. The master pages are blank as PageMaker has copied all these elements onto the individual pages.

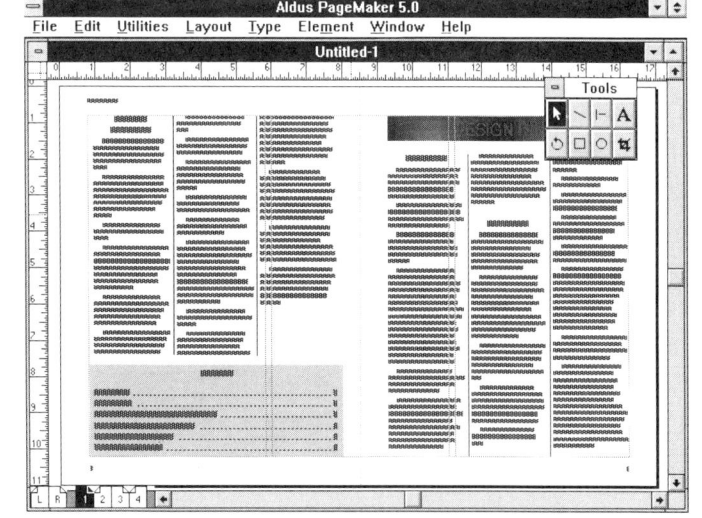

Chapter 9: Aldus Additions

BULLETS AND NUMBERING

Figure 17. With the *Bullets and numbering* addition you can number paragraphs and add bullets or a specified character to any number of paragraphs in your publication.

Figure 12. The Layout submenu gives you six options to choose from, which we describe below:

- *None:* This option creates a new publication, but does not automatically rearrange the pages or change the spread size.

- *2-up saddle stitch:* The default, standard setting. Double-sided pages are printed, folded and fastened along the fold (see Figure 2 for an example).

Figure 18. Before you select the *Bullets and numbering* addition, decide how many paragraphs you will be numbering and place the insertion point at the beginning of the first paragraph you want to mark.

Insertion point

Figure 12. The Layout submenu gives you six options to choose from, which we describe below:

None: This option creates a new publication, but does not automatically rearrange the pages or change the spread size.

2-up saddle stitch: The default, standard setting. Double-sided pages are printed, folded and fastened along the fold (see Figure 2 for an example).

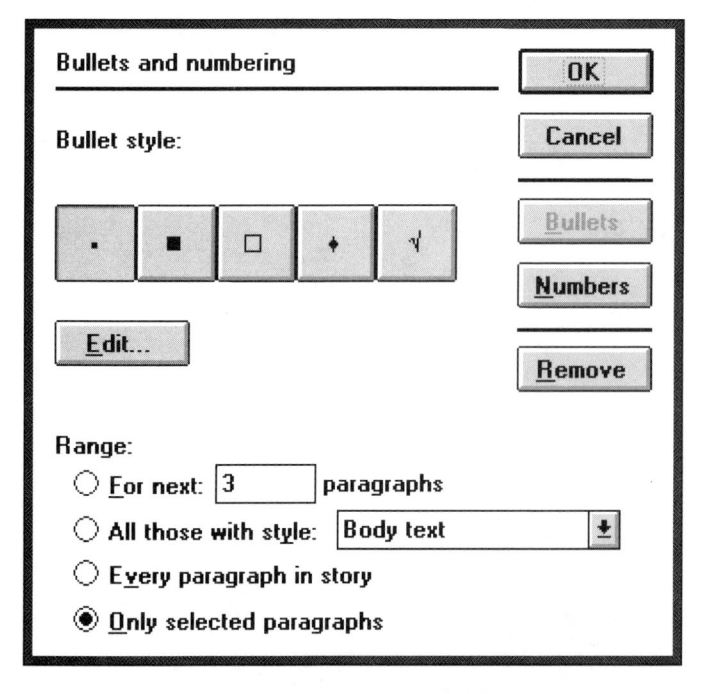

Figure 19. Select *Bullets and numbering* from the *Aldus Additions* submenu in the **Utilities** menu. The options in this dialog box are explained below:

- Choose the *Bullet style* you wish to use.
- Enter the number of paragraphs to be marked in the *For next: x paragraphs* option;

or

- select the *All those with style* to number or mark only paragraphs to which you have applied a specific style;

or

140

- select *Every paragraph in story* to mark every paragraph in the story;

or

- select *Only selected paragraphs* if you only wish to mark the paragraphs you have selected.

Figure 20. Click on the *Edit* button to change the bullet character you wish to use. In the *Edit bullet* dialog box that appears you can change the *Bullet character code* to a different ASCII character number, as well as the *Font* and the *Size* of the character. PageMaker displays your changed character in the *Example* box.

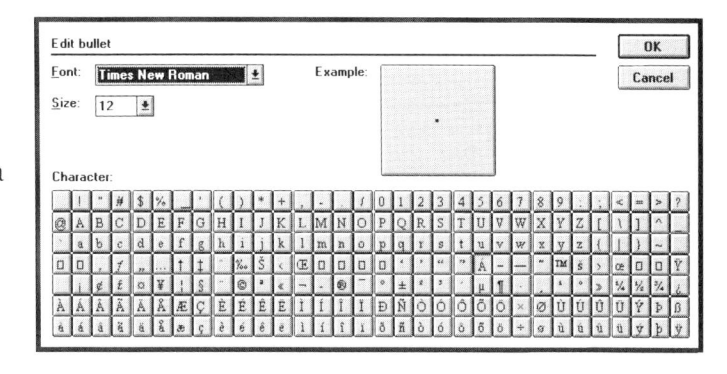

Figure 21. To number paragraphs in your story, click on the *Numbers* button to activate the options shown here. Choose a *Numbering style*, a *Separator* character, and the number you want to start at. The *Range* options are the same as they are for the *Bullets* options.

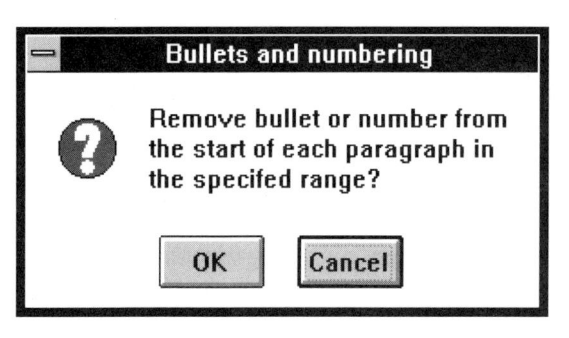

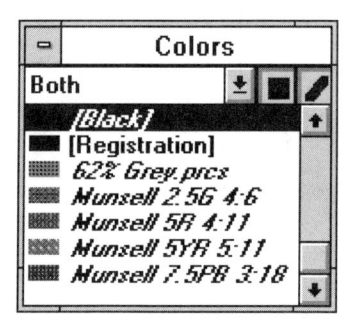

REMOVING BULLETS AND NUMBERING

Figure 22. Click on the *Remove* button if you want to remove any numbering and bullets you have applied. You must have the insertion point in the text and specify a *Range* before doing this.

CREATE COLOR LIBRARY

Figure 23. The *Create color library* addition lets you name and save a group of colors in your color palette so that you can open this color library file at any time. To create your own color library, add the colors you need to the color palette using the *Define colors* command (see Chapter 12, **Colors** for more information).

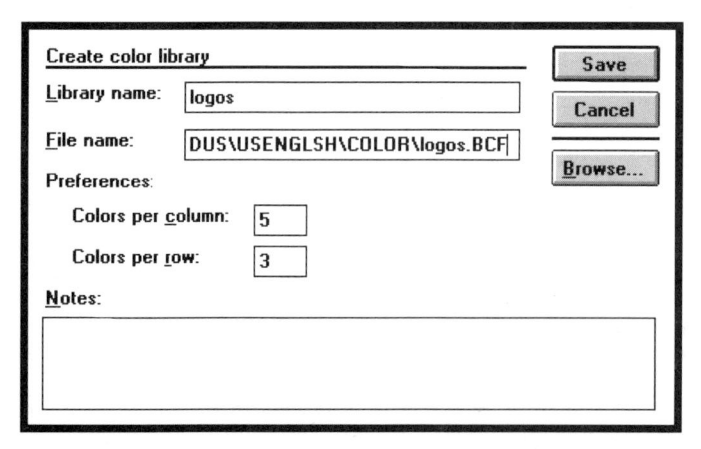

Figure 24. Next choose the *Create color library* addition to activate the *Create color library* dialog box. Type in a name for the library, the number of colors per column and per row (maximum of 10 each way) and optionally any comments about the library. Click on *Save* to save the library as a **bcf** file, or browse to change its location.

Chapter 9: Aldus Additions

Figure 25. You must save all color files inside the language directory. Once you click on *OK* or *Save* in either dialog box, PageMaker saves the color library.

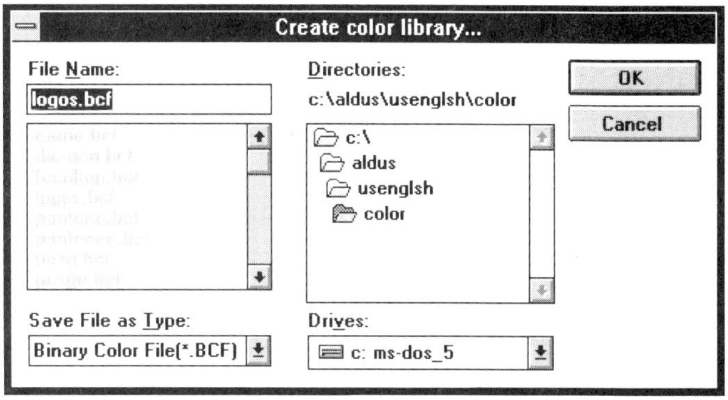

Figure 26. To access a color library in a different publication, click on the *New* button in the *Define colors* dialog box, select the library name from the list of libraries and click on *OK*.

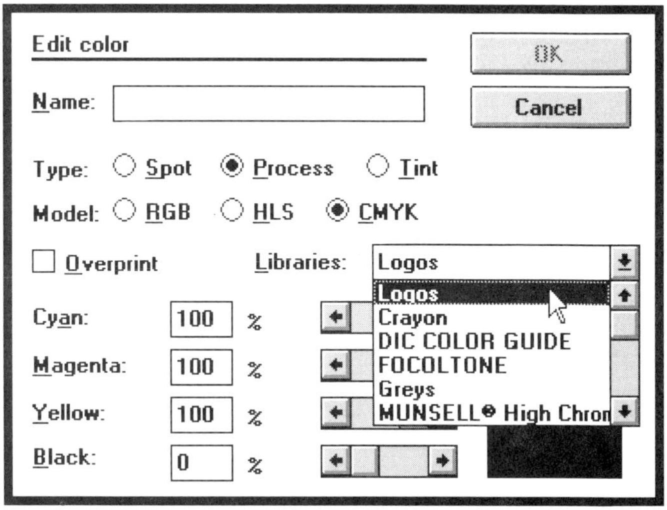

Figure 27. In the *Library* dialog box, drag-select the colors you want to add to the library palette and click on *OK* until you return to your document. When you activate the Color palette, PageMaker adds the selected colors to the list.

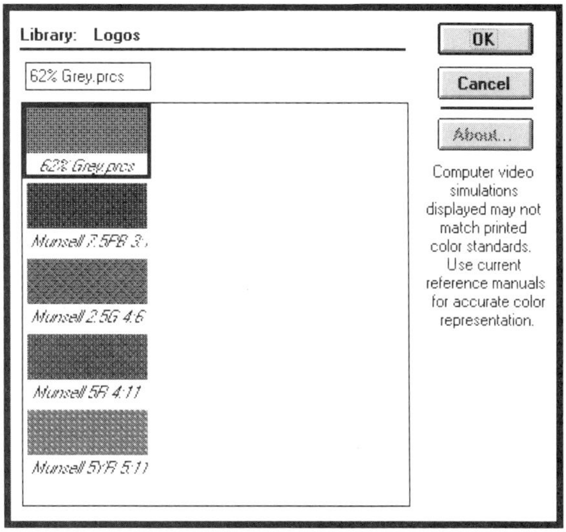

143

CREATE KEYLINE

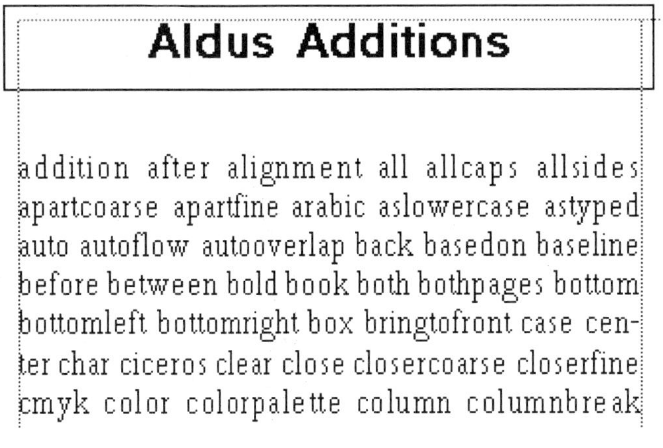

Figure 28. With the *Create keyline* addition, you can insert a box or a keyline around a selected object. A keyline proof is a bare-bones visual guide for the printer indicating with boxes where text and graphics lie on the page and also shows where to print different colors. You can choose to put the box either behind or in front of the selected object. You can define the distance the box is offset from the object and also set the fill and line attributes of the box. You can change the fill and line attributes even after you have inserted the box.

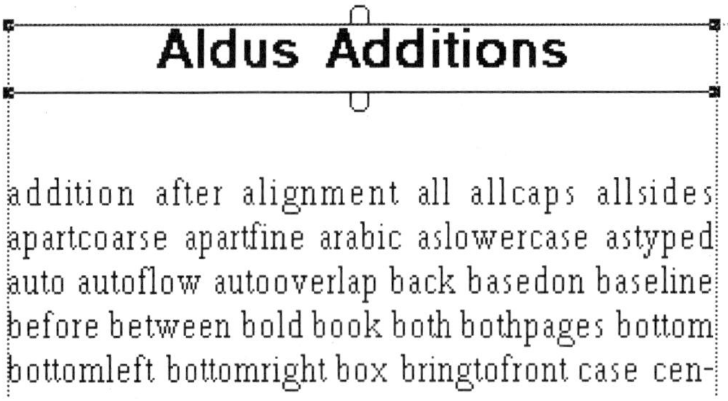

Figure 29. Select the object you wish to box using the pointer tool and then select *Create keyline* from the *Aldus Additions* sub-menu. This activates the *Create keyline* dialog box.

Figure 30. Define the distance between the selected object and the box in points. Choose whether you would like the box to sit in front or behind the selected object. If you click on the *Attributes* button you activate the *Fill and line* dialog box where you can define the box's outline color and thickness, as well as its fill color. Turn the *Knock out under keyline* option on to define an overlap thickness (see Chapter 12, **Color** for more information on knockouts).

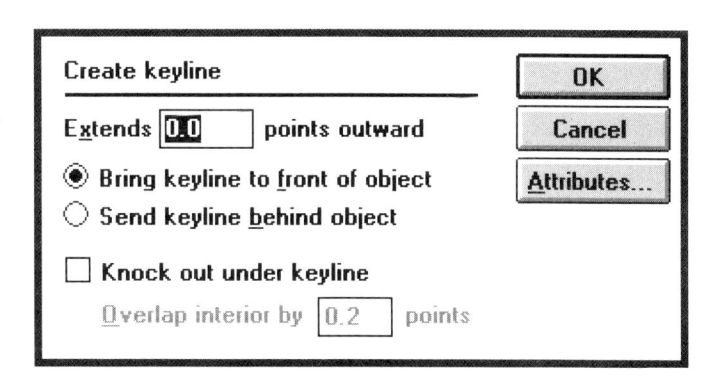

DISPLAY PUB INFO

Figure 31. Use the *Display pub info* addition to display information about the currently opened file. PageMaker lets you save this as a text file.

You can choose to display fonts used and fonts available, links to graphics and text files, and the style names and their definitions. Do this by selecting or de-selecting the check boxes at the bottom of the dialog box.

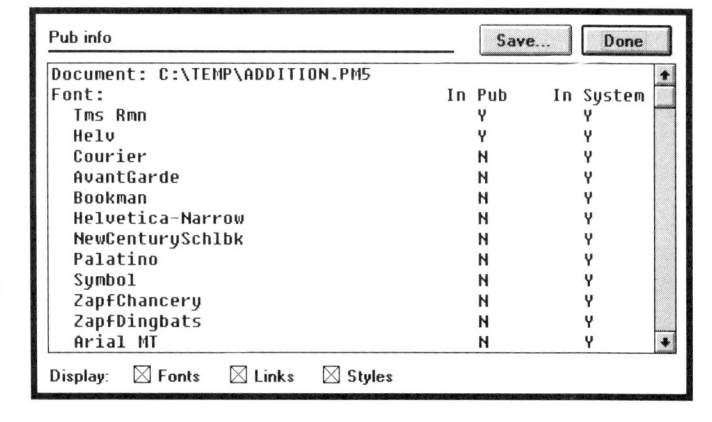

Figure 32. Click on the *Save* button to save the information as a text file. This activates the *Save As* dialog box. Type in a name or use the suggested name and then select *OK*. You can then load this into PageMaker and print it out.

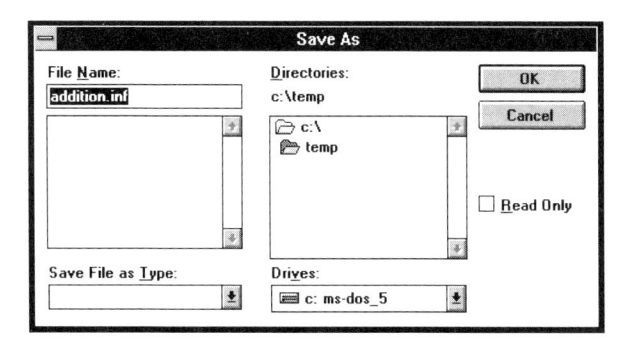

Display Story Info

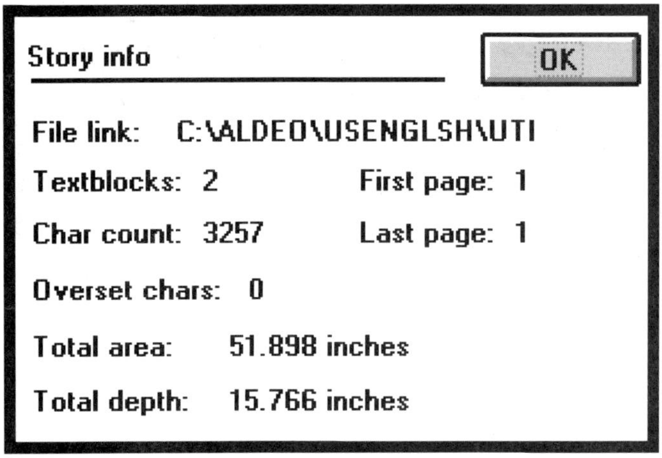

Figure 33. Use the *Display story info* addition to display information about the currently selected story. PageMaker activates the *Display story info* dialog box, showing you the link to the file, the number of text blocks and characters, the page numbers on which you placed the story, any overset characters, and the total area and depth of the selected text file.

Display Textblock Info

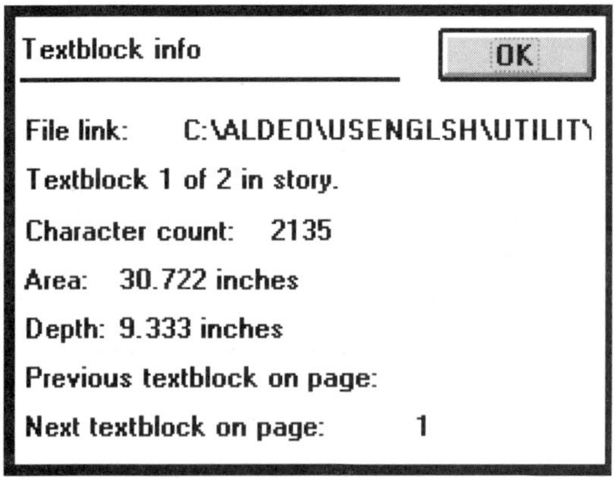

Figure 34. The *Display textblock info* addition gives much the same information as the *Display story info* addition, but only for the selected text block.

Drop Cap

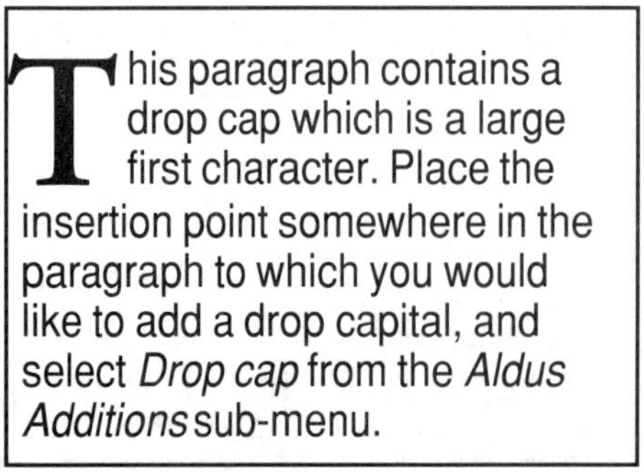

Figure 35. Use the *Drop cap* addition to create a large first letter of a paragraph, as shown here.

> This paragraph contains a drop cap which is a large first character. Place the insertion point somewhere in the paragraph to which you would like to add a drop capital, and select *Drop cap* from the *Aldus Additions* sub-menu.

Figure 36. Place the insertion point somewhere in the paragraph you would like to add a drop capital to, and select *Drop cap* from the *Aldus Additions* submenu.

Insertion point

> Th(is)paragraph contains a drop cap which is a large first character. Place the insertion point somewhere in the paragraph to which you would like to add a drop capital, and select *Drop cap* from the *Aldus Additions* sub-menu.

Figure 37. In the *Drop cap* dialog box, you can change the number of lines for the capital size, and which paragraphs to use by using the *Prev* and *Next* buttons. You can preview the drop capital by clicking on the *Apply* button, and you can remove a drop cap with the *Remove* button.

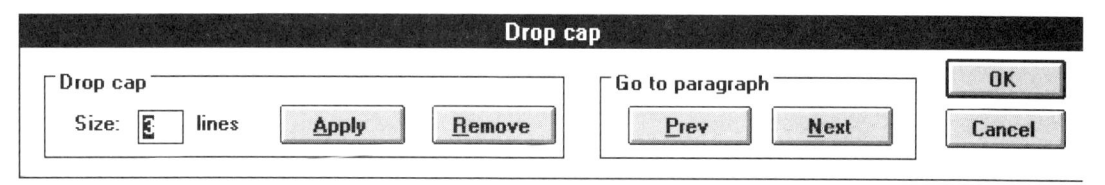

```
┌─ Drop cap ─────────────────────────┐  ┌─ Go to paragraph ──────┐   ┌────────┐
│  Size: [E]  lines   [Apply] [Remove] │  │   [Prev]    [Next]    │   │   OK   │
└────────────────────────────────────┘  └────────────────────────┘   │ Cancel │
                                                                      └────────┘
```

EDIT TRACKS

Figure 38. The *Edit Tracks* addition allows you to customize the tracking options you have in the *Track* command in the **Type** menu. These commands are *Very loose, Loose, Normal, Tight,* and *Very tight.* (See the **Type** menu in Chapter 4 for more information on these commands.)

TRACKING COMMANDS	*No track*
TRACKING COMMANDS	*Very loose*
TRACKING COMMANDS	*Loose*
TRACKING COMMANDS	*Normal*
TRACKING COMMANDS	*Tight*
TRACKING COMMANDS	*Very tight*

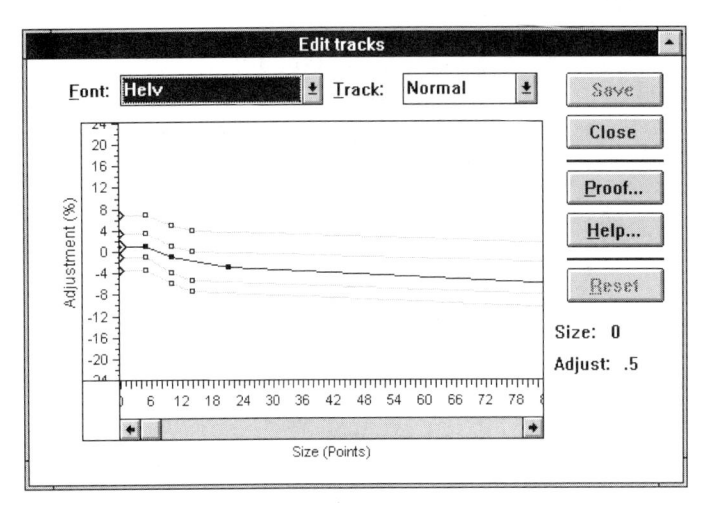

Figure 39. To edit one of these tracks, select the *Edit Tracks* addition and then select the font and track that you wish to edit from their respective drop-down menus. Alternatively, you can click on a track line to select it. In this example, we are editing the font *Helvetica* and the track *Normal*.

Each line represents one track. *Very loose* is the top line and *Very tight* is the bottom one. The steepness of the line determines how much the letter spacing is tightened or loosened. A flat line, for example, keeps the spacing proportionally the same at all sizes.

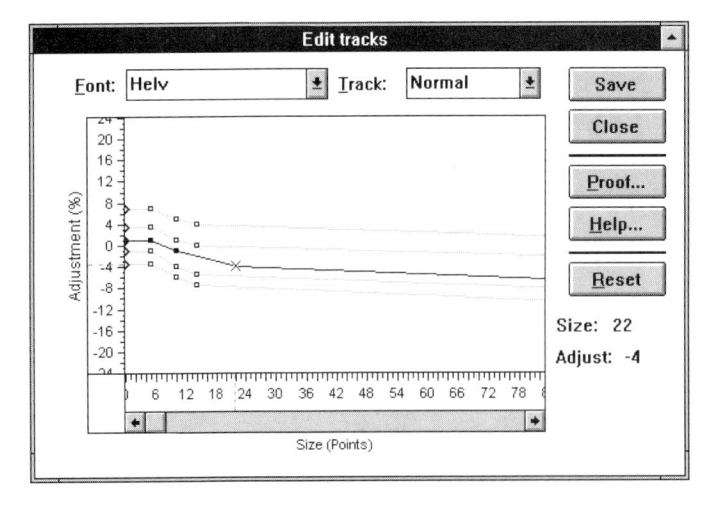

Figure 40. To adjust the tracking values, drag a handle to a new position. The values of the handle you have selected appear in the bottom right of the dialog box as you move it. In this example we are moving a handle of the *Normal* tracking line.

To add a track handle, hold down the Alt key and click on a track line. To delete one, hold down the Alt key and click on a handle you want to delete.

Chapter 9: Aldus Additions

Figure 41. If you want to view a sample of the new tracking values you have created, click on the *Proof* button in the *Edit Tracks* dialog box. Select the tracks and the point sizes to include and whether you want the short or long text sample. You can change the display text in the edit box by selecting it and typing in the text you want.

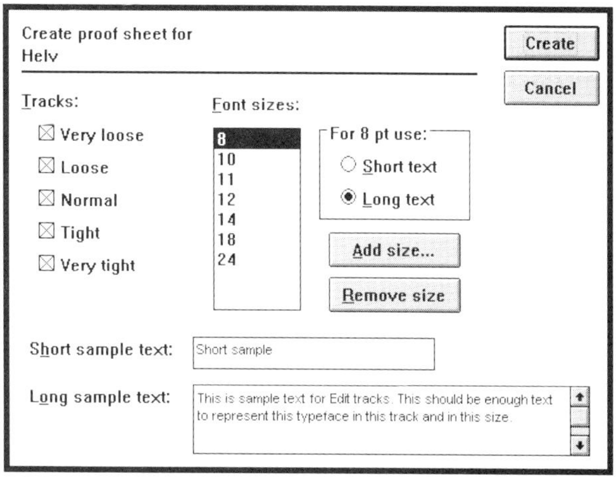

Figure 42. After you select *Create* in the *Create proof sheet* dialog box, PageMaker creates an untitled publication with the sample text showing you the changed tracking values for your evaluation.

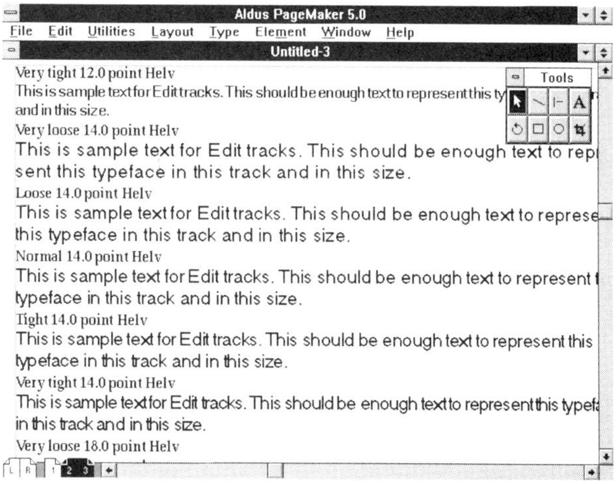

EXPERT KERNING

Figure 43. The *Expert kerning* addition lets you finely adjust the letter-spacing between character pairs.

Note: You can use *Expert kerning* only on PostScript Type 1 fonts and only then if they are installed on your computer. We recommend that you use this addition only on small blocks of text, as it can be time consuming.

Kerning

Kerning   *Kerning strength of 2 applied*

Kerning   *Kerning strength of 0 applied*

149

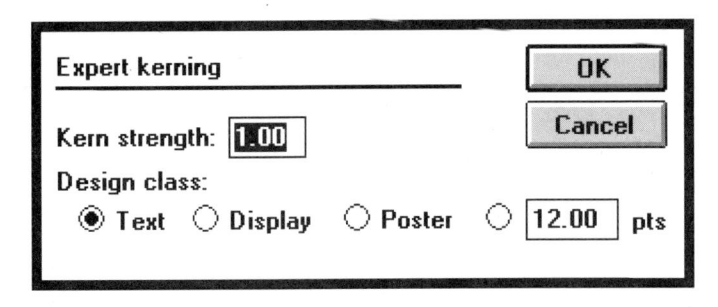

Figure 44. To kern your highlighted text, in the *Expert kerning* dialog box, choose a kerning strength between 0.0 and 2.0. The higher the value, the tighter the kerning. If you don't know the source of the master design of the font, click on the *Text* option below the *Design class* section.

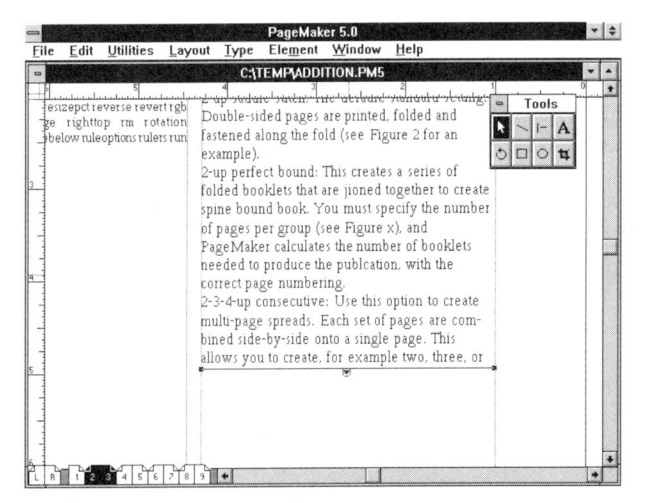

FIND OVERSET TEXT

Figure 45. Use the *Find overset text* addition to find any stories which still have unplaced text. When you select this addition, PageMaker finds and selects any text blocks that contain unplaced text. You can then manually flow the text into the next available space.

If there is more than one story with unplaced text, select the command again until PageMaker has found all unplaced stories.

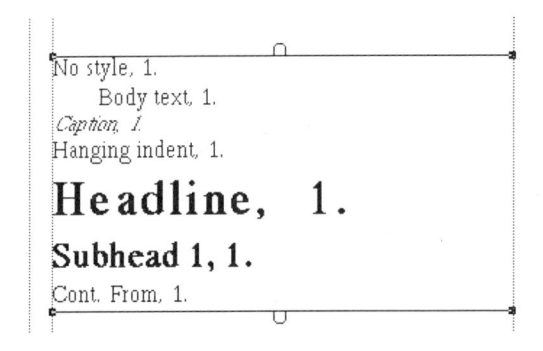

LIST STYLES USED

Figure 46. Use the *List styles used* addition to list all the styles you have used in selected story. You must select a text block of the story whose styles you want to view. PageMaker displays the styles you have used, followed by the number of paragraphs in that style.

Chapter 9: Aldus Additions

OPEN STORIES

Figure 47. Use the *Open stories* addition to open all the stories in the current publication in cascaded story windows. This allows you to view and edit all stories at once.

OPEN TEMPLATE

Figure 48. The *Open template* addition lets you choose a document type from a number of predesigned templates for common publishing tasks. It opens up as an untitled publication containing preformatted components. All you have to do is add your own text and graphics.

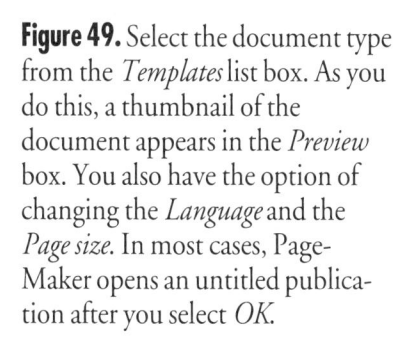

Figure 49. Select the document type from the *Templates* list box. As you do this, a thumbnail of the document appears in the *Preview* box. You also have the option of changing the *Language* and the *Page size*. In most cases, Page-Maker opens an untitled publication after you select *OK*.

In some cases, PageMaker prompts you for more information before it opens the publication.

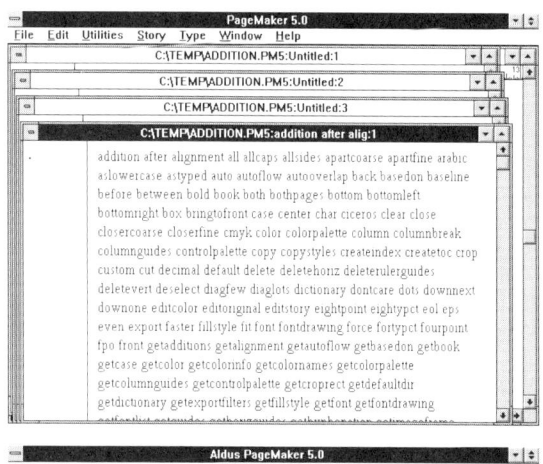

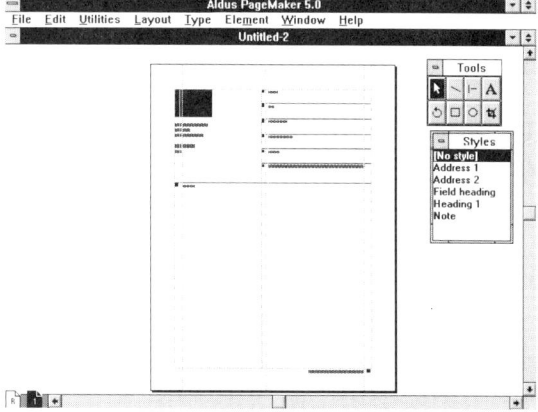

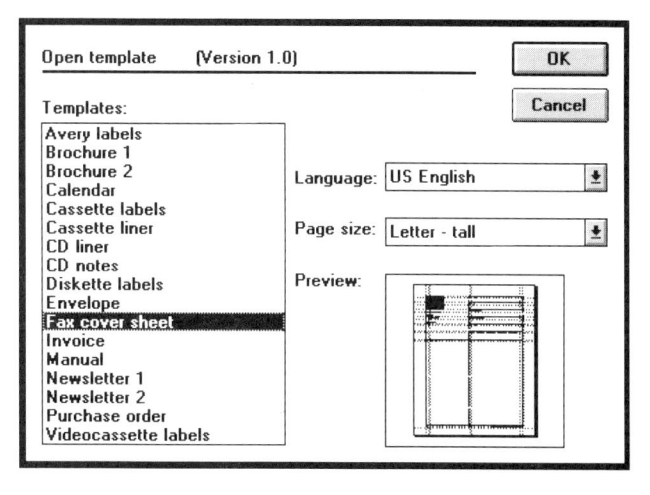

151

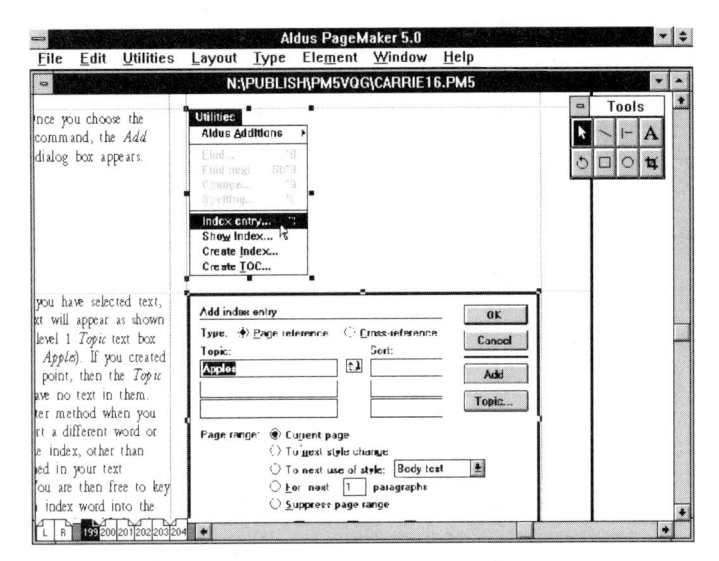

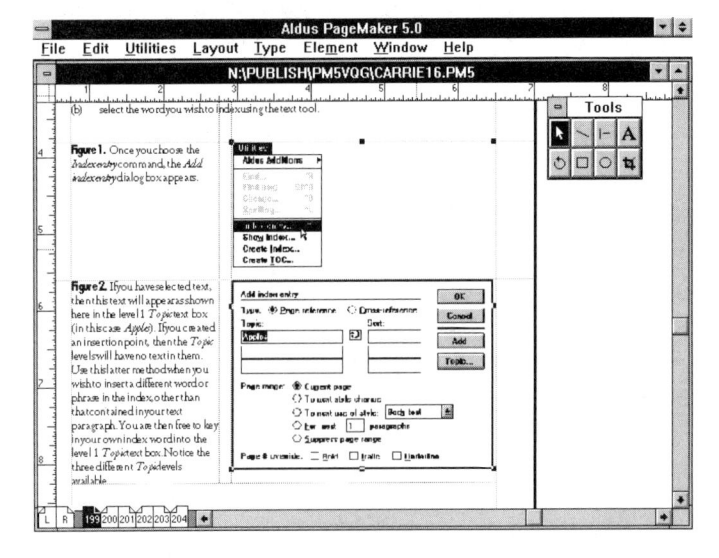

PS Group It

Figure 50. The *PS Group it* addition allows you to combine separate objects so you can manipulate them as one object. When you group the objects, PageMaker converts them to an Encapsulated Postscript (EPS) graphic which replaces the grouped objects.

You can resize, stretch, rotate, and crop grouped objects as well as adding grouped objects to other grouped objects.

Figure 51. To group objects, select the objects to be grouped with the pointer tool and select the *PS Group it* addition.

PS Ungroup It

Figure 52. If you want to ungroup any object you have grouped together, select the grouped object and then the *PS Ungroup it* addition. PageMaker then asks you whether you want to delete the group file, so if you have several copies of the group in your publication, they are all deleted. If you don't want to have to make this decision each time you ungroup objects, you can specify what you want to do in the options below. Once you have done this, PageMaker converts the EPS graphic file back to its original components.

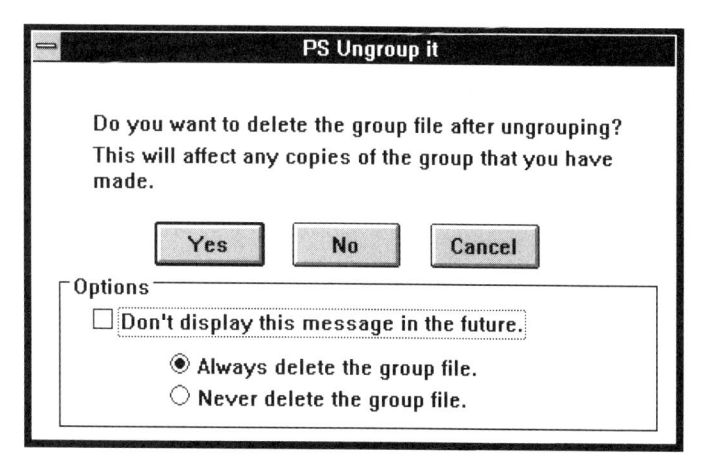

Printer Styles

The *Printer styles* addition lets you print a number of Page-Maker publications at once with different printer specifications. For example, you can print publications with different page sizes, orientations and page ranges without having to open each publication individually.

Figure 53. When you activate the *Printer style* dialog box, you can select the files you wish to print from the *File name* box, changing the directory if required. You can then create new printer styles or edit existing ones to apply to the selected publications you wish to print. The *Printer styles* contain the information used to print each document. This process is explained below.

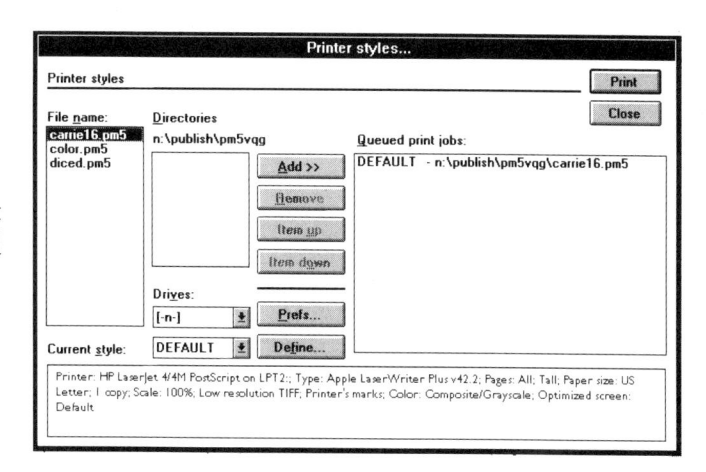

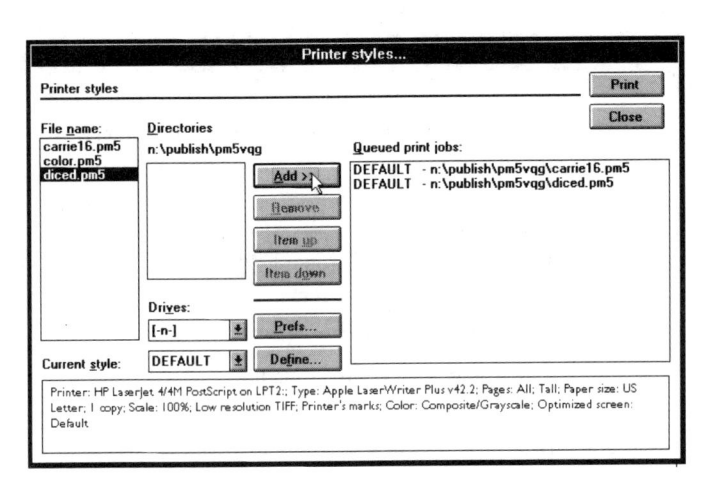

PRINTING MULTIPLE FILES

Figure 54. Select the file you want to add to the *Queued print jobs* list from the *File name* box and click on the *Add* button. Repeat this to add more files to the list. Use the *Remove* button to remove a selected file from the *Queued print jobs* list, and the *Item up* and *Item down* buttons to rearrange the order of the selected file in the list on the right. This is the order that the files print in.

You can click on the *Print* button to print the selected files in the queue, or you may want to modify the printer styles and preferences before printing. To temporarily override print settings of a publication in the queue (the range—for example), double-click on the file name, modify the setting in the *Print document* dialog box and select *OK*.

INCLUDING PRINT JOB INFORMATION

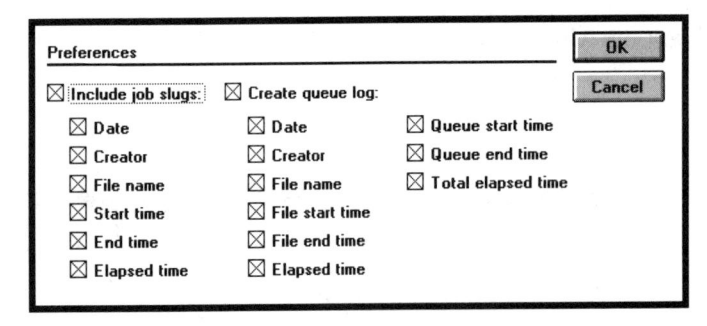

Figure 55. Click on the *Prefs* button to activate this *Preferences* dialog box. To include print file information, select *Include job slugs* (if you want to include any of the selected options in the dialog box) and *Create queue log* (if you want to include information on the number of files printed and printing time). Next, check the boxes here that correspond to the information you require. When you select *OK* and then *Print* in the *Printer styles* dialog box, PageMaker prints the selected files with the print file information.

Chapter 9: Aldus Additions

CREATING AND MODIFYING A PRINTER STYLE

Figure 56. To create or modify a printer style, click on the *Define* button to activate the *Define styles* dialog box.

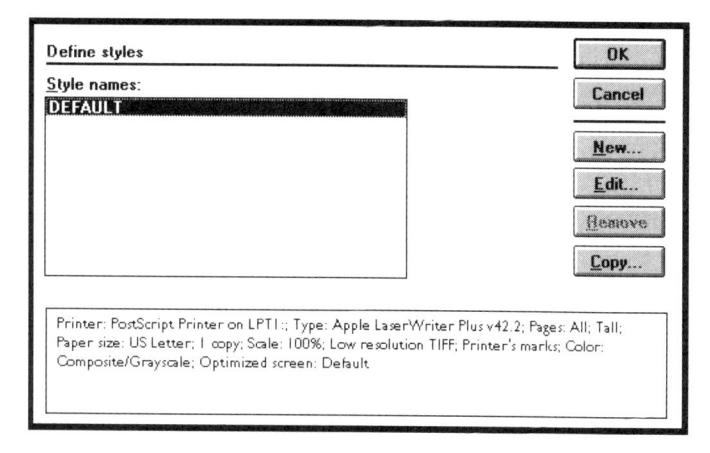

Figure 57. To create a new printer style, click on the *New* button to activate the *New style* dialog box, type in a name and click on *OK*. To modify a selected style, click on the *Edit* button.

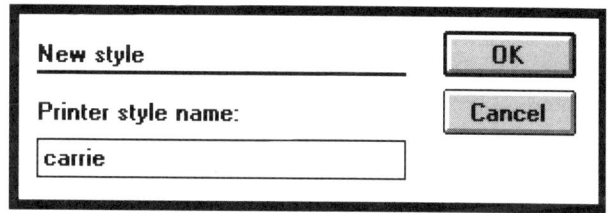

Figure 58. In the *Printer style* dialog box that appears, you can change any of the options available here to become part of the printer style you are creating or editing. (See Chapter 13, **Printing** for more information on the options in this dialog box.)

When you have made the required changes, select *OK* until you return to the *Printer styles* dialog box. Your new style appears in the *Style names* list in the *Define styles* dialog box. If you were editing a style, the changes are reflected at the bottom of the *Define styles* dialog box when you select the style name from the list.

155

Chapter 9: Aldus Additions

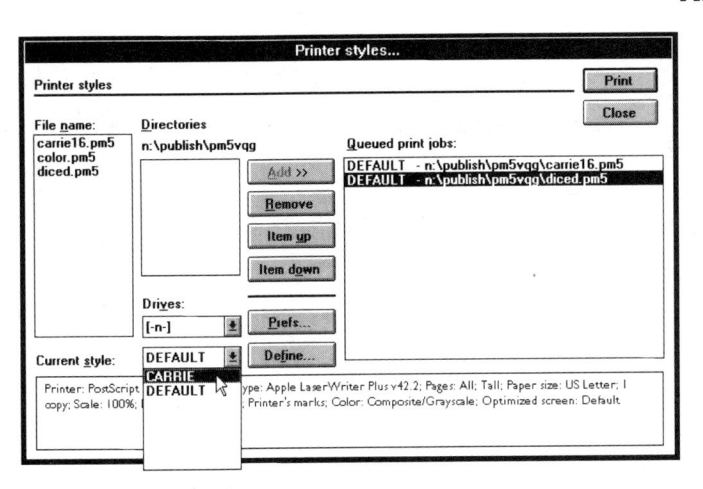

APPLYING PRINTER STYLES

Figure 59. To apply a different printer style to a selected publication in the *Queued print jobs* list, activate the *Current style* drop-down list and click on a new style name.

When you apply printer styles to publications in the list, it only affects the current print job and does not modify the print settings within the publication.

To print the publications in the *Queued print job* list, select the ones you want to print and click on the *Print* button.

RUNNING HEADERS/FOOTERS

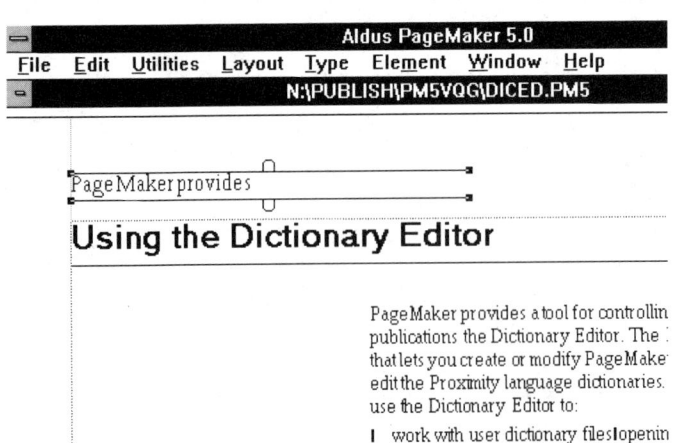

Figure 60. The *Running headers/footers* addition allows you to create headers and footers based on the content of the text on the page. For example, if you are working on a glossary of terms, you can use this addition to add headers and footers that match the first or last term on the page.

Figure 61. Select the text block on the page and then select the *Running headers/footers* addition. The *First instance* and *Last instance* options let you choose whether PageMaker includes specified text from the beginning or the end of the first or last paragraph (of the selected style).

You can have PageMaker search for a specific style from the *Styles* submenu or you can select *None* so that PageMaker searches only for specific text. Next choose an option from the *Insert* drop-down list box (or click on *Edit* to customize a search pattern—see Figure 62).

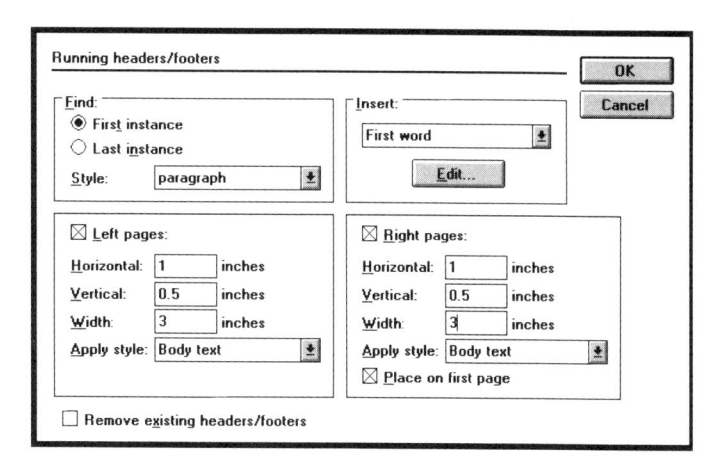

Note: To define both headers and footers, you must use this addition twice and specify different *Horizontal* and *Vertical* positions.

Figure 62. Turn the *Left pages* or the *Right pages* option on (or both). Enter the *Horizontal* or *Vertical* value where you want the headers or footers to be. This is measured from the zero point on the rulers. Also enter a *Width* value for the width of the header or footer text block and choose a style. You can also choose a style from the *Apply style* drop-down list that PageMaker can apply to the headers and footers.

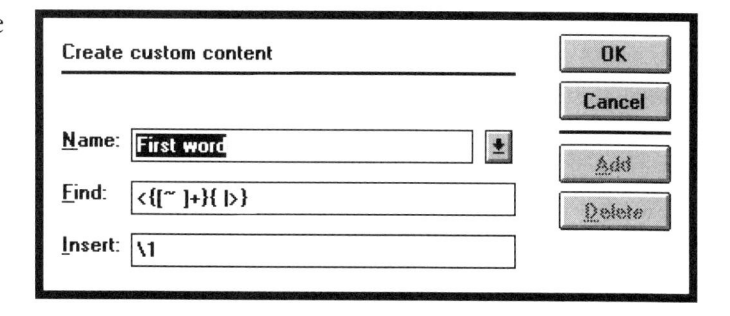

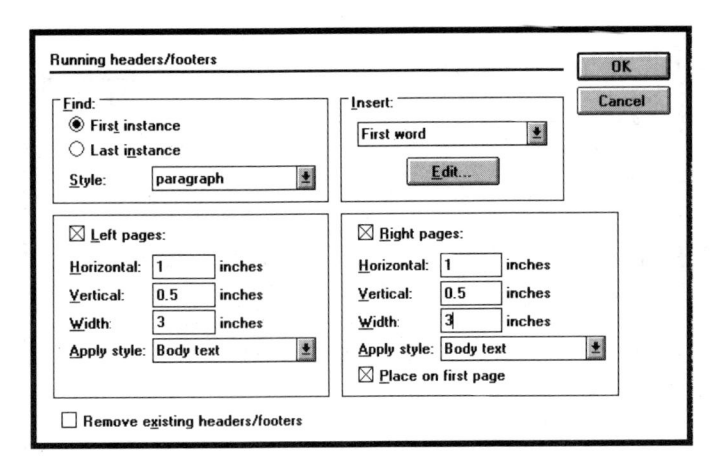

Figure 63. If you click on the *Edit* button, the *Create custom content* dialog box appears. You can type in specific text in the *Name* text box.

You can edit an existing search pattern or add a new pattern by clicking on the *Edit* button in the *Running headers/footers* dialog box.

DELETING HEADERS AND FOOTERS

Figure 64. Select the first text block from where you started the headers or footers and choose the *Running headers/footers* addition. Click on the *Remove existing headers/footers* command and select *OK*. PageMaker removes all headers and footers.

RUN SCRIPT

The *Run script* addition allows you to select a script for Page-Maker to execute. A script is a set of instructions, written in PageMaker's script language, that performs steps for which you would normally use the mouse or the keyboard.

Scripts are similar to macros you often use in word processors—they allow you to automate time-consuming and often-performed tasks. There are two ways you can run a script. You can run a script created in PageMaker or you can run a script created in another program and saved as a text-only file.

Figure 65. To run a script you have created in PageMaker (use the *PageMaker 5.0 Script Language Guide* for information on how to write your own script), select the script text in the publication with the pointer tool and then select the *Run script* addition. You can also run a part of the script that you have selected with the text tool. In the *Run script* dialog box click on the *Run selection* button.

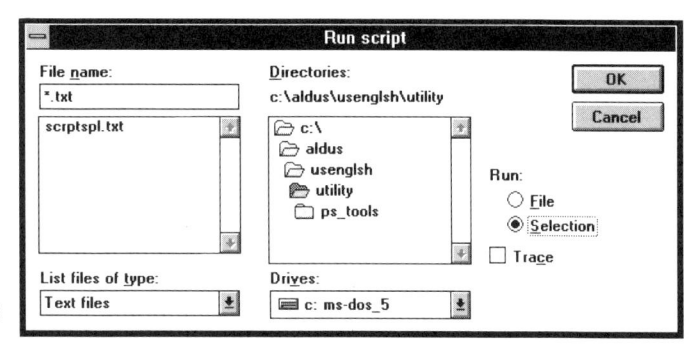

If you select the *Trace* option before you run a script, a window opens and you can scroll through the selected text to review each step or you can stop PageMaker carrying out the script as it is running.

Figure 66. To run a script that has been saved as a text-only file, you can place the text in your publication and use the first method described. You could also find the text file within the *Run script* dialog box and click on *OK*.

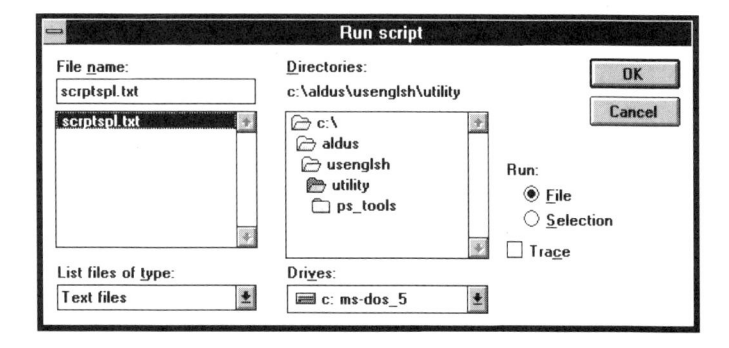

SORT PAGES

Figure 67. The *Sort pages* addition lets you arrange pages in your current publication by moving thumbnail representations of your pages into the order you would like. If you are re-arranging a double-sided document, you may need to manually adjust text and graphics to accommodate for a left page becoming a right page.

PageMaker doesn't change the threads of text in a number of text blocks if you sort pages in this way.

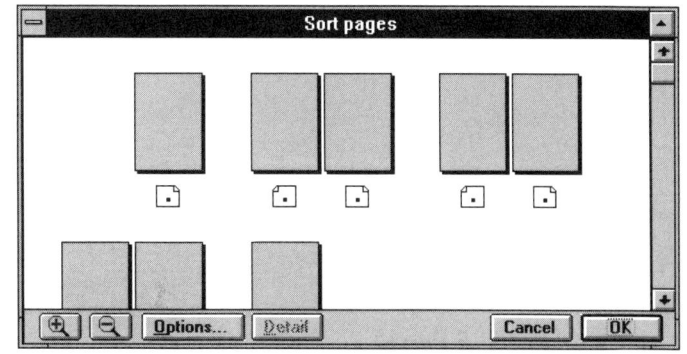

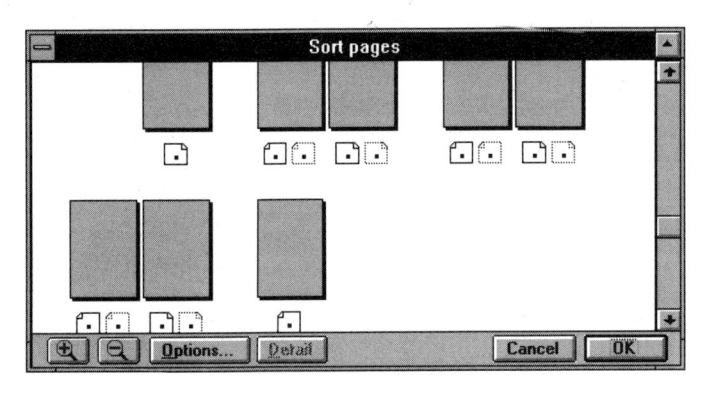

Figure 68. Select the page or pages you want to move (use the Shift key to select multiple pages, use the Ctrl key to select one page of two facing pages), drag the pages to the left or the right of the page where you want to move them and release the mouse. Here we have moved pages 2 and 3 to where 6 and 7 were. When you release the mouse, PageMaker dims the icons below the original page and places new icons to the left of them, indicating that you have put a new page there.

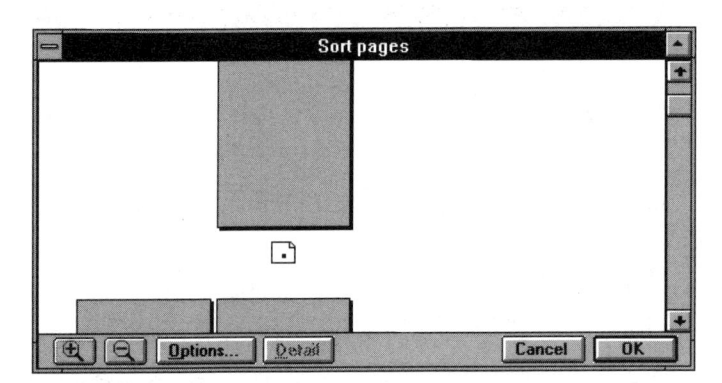

Figure 69. Click on the *magnifying* icon to enlarge the thumbnails. You can enlarge them to three levels. Click on the *reduction* icon the same number of times you clicked on the magnifying icon to bring the thumbnails back to the original size.

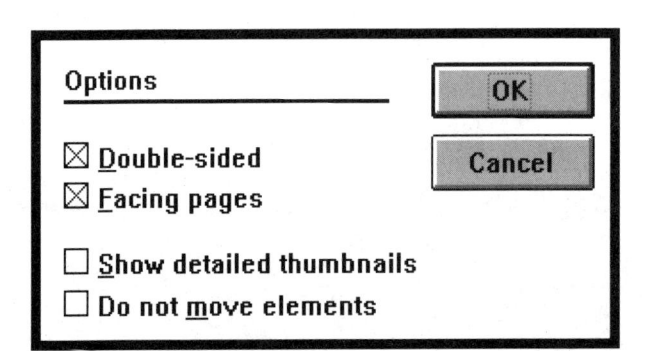

Figure 70. Click on the *Options* button in the *Sort pages* dialog box to activate the *Options* dialog box. Here you can change a double-sided document to a single-sided document and vice versa.

Chapter 9: Aldus Additions

Figure 71. Select the *Show detailed thumbnails* option to view the elements of the pages more clearly. Select the *Do not move elements* option if you do not want PageMaker to adjust elements relative to the inside and outside margins of a double-sided publication.

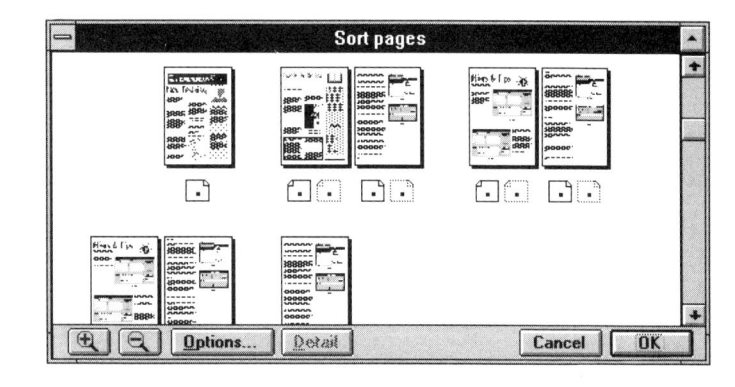

Once you have made all the necessary changes, select the *OK* button in the relevant dialog boxes and PageMaker automatically sorts the pages of your publication into the new order.

TRAVERSE TEXTBLOCKS

Figure 72. Select the *Traverse textblocks* addition to locate the first, previous, next, or last text block of the selected text block in a story. This addition is handy if you are working with a large publication with a number of different stories, and you need to locate a specific part of a threaded text file.

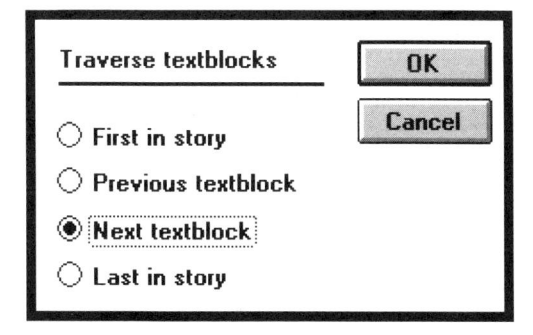

161

Chapter 9: Aldus Additions

VP CONVERTER

Note: You can get this addition from your computer dealer.

Figure 73. The *VP Converter* addition lets you convert a Ventura Publisher file into PageMaker format so that you can open it as a PageMaker publication.

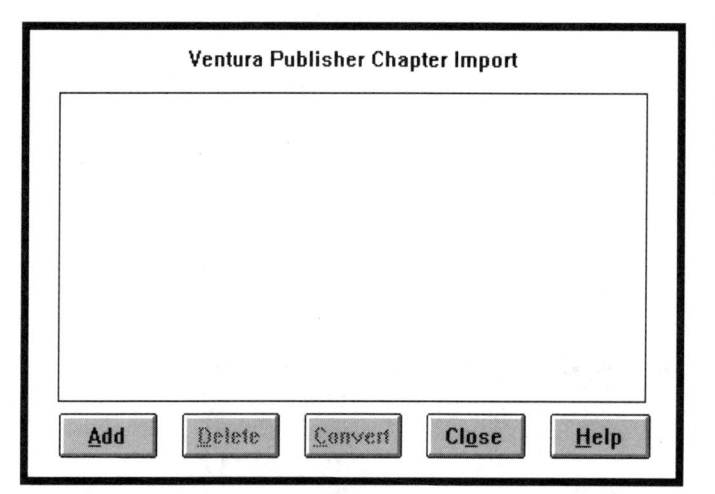

Figure 74. In the *Ventura Publisher Chapter Import* dialog box, you must click on the *Add* button to find and select the Ventura files you want to convert.

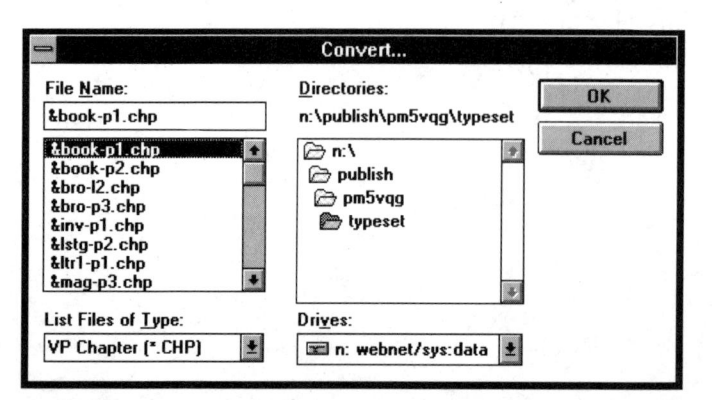

Figure 75. You can only add one Ventura file at a time so after you have selected the file and clicked on *OK*, you must click on the *Add* button again to add more files.

Chapter 9: Aldus Additions

Figure 76. When you have added the required files, click on the *Convert* button. PageMaker converts all the files in the list and opens them as new PageMaker files.

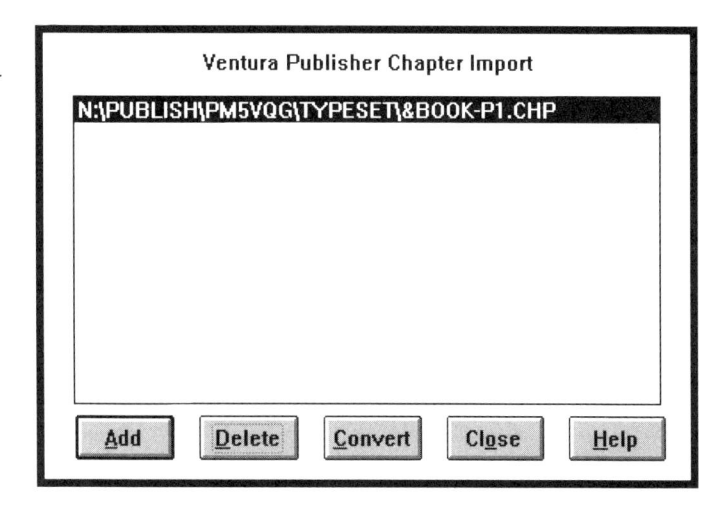

Figure 77. PageMaker converts the Ventura files in the list into open PageMaker files. You can see in the publication title bar that PageMaker has kept the name and path of the original Ventura file but changes the extension to PM5. PageMaker copies the styles, page formatting and graphics across from Ventura.

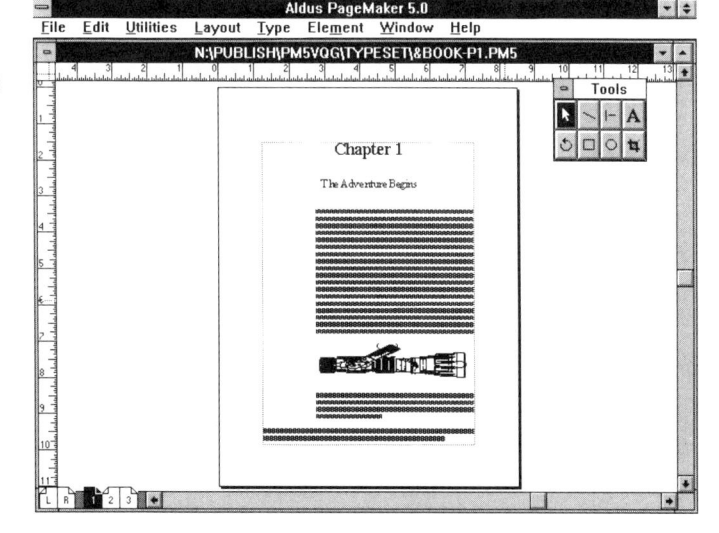

PageMaker Defaults   10

Application and Publication Defaults

PageMaker is shipped with preset options for many of its settings. These may differ between US, International English and other foreign language settings. PageMaker includes two kinds of defaults: *application* and *publication*. *Application* defaults are wide-ranging and apply to every new publication that you open. You can set them up before you enter a new or existing publication. *Publication* defaults apply to the currently open publication only.

APPLICATION DEFAULTS

If you wish to have the same settings for every new PageMaker file, then using *application* defaults is the best choice. For example, the number of columns by default is one. If you wish to change this to three columns, you would alter this before you open a new PageMaker file. You can select all menus in PageMaker before you open or start a new document (see Figure 1).

Figure 1. To change any *application* defaults, open PageMaker by double-clicking on the PageMaker icon (or choose *Close* from the **File** menu if you have a PageMaker publication open). You will then be at the Page-Maker 5 desktop level. Normally, at this level, you select *New* for a new publication or *Open* to select a previously saved publication.

165

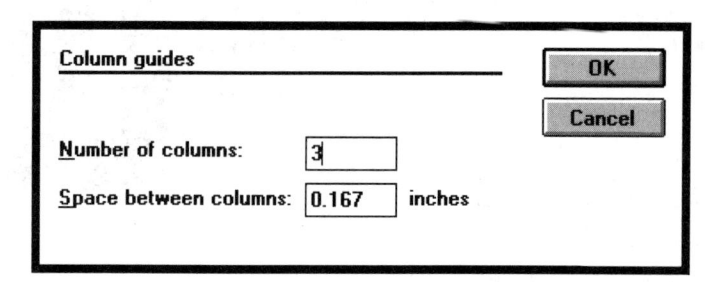

Figure 2. Before selecting *New* or *Open*, you can change any default setting, which then applies to all new publications until you change it again at the desktop. Here we have changed the *Column guides* option to 3.

Figure 3. We have set the page size to *Custom*, the orientation to *Tall* and the number of pages at 3 through the *Page setup* command in the **File** menu. All new documents you create will now open with these parameters as standard.

To determine which options you can set and change at the PageMaker desktop, check each menu in turn. You can select and alter all commands in black (except of course *New*, *Open* and *Exit*).

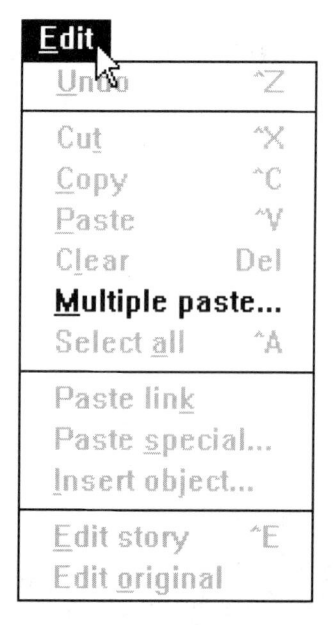

Figure 4. You cannot select the commands that appear in gray at the desktop. All but one command in the **Edit** menu is grayed out. Such commands are not associated with default settings, as you apply them when you are manipulating a publication.

PUBLICATION DEFAULTS

Publication defaults are different to *application* defaults in that you set them up inside an already open publication, and they apply to that publication only. (You can use publication defaults to override application defaults.) For example, you may wish to change the default text option for typing text within a single publication. Normally this is set by default at Times 12 point.

Figure 5. In this example, the next time we draw a graphic, it will have a line thickness of 4 points.

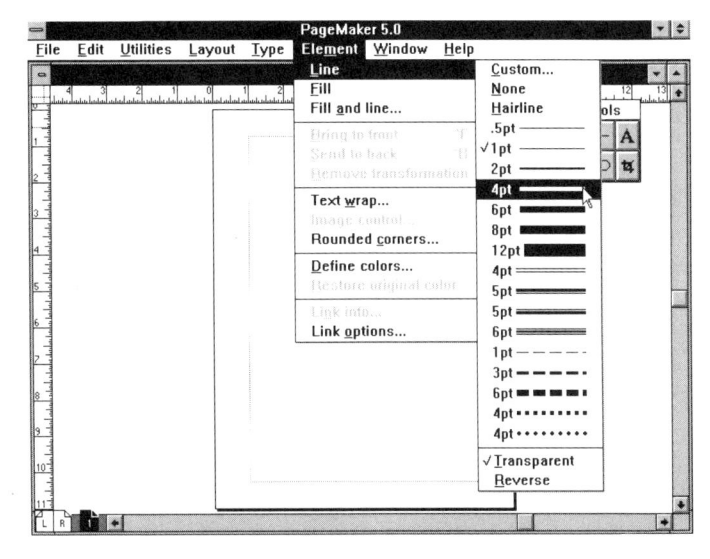

Figure 6. From inside a publication, we are adjusting the default text type to 12 point Palatino. Again, you can adjust any default setting in this way. When you do this, ensure that you have selected the pointer tool and you have no text or graphics selected on the page.

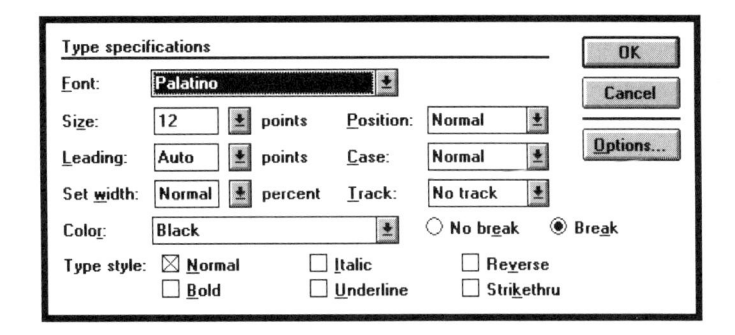

USING STYLES 11

WHAT IS A STYLE?

A style is a set of formatting attributes that you apply to text. When you use styles, you save time by simultaneously applying many formatting changes to indicated text. You name the style and then specify its attributes. The style name then appears both in the *Style* sub-menu in the **Type** menu and the Style palette. This creates consistency within the publication and between publications, as you can copy styles from one publication to another.

Figure 1. PageMaker's provides a number of default styles, containing text and paragraph attribute descriptions that you can apply to text. To access these styles choose *Style palette* from the **Window** menu.

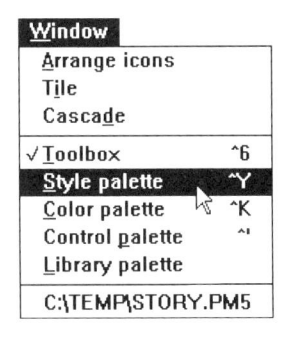

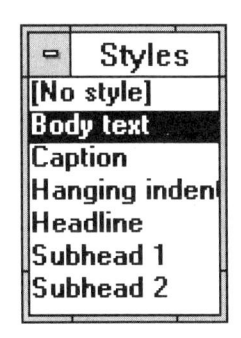

APPLYING STYLES

Figure 2. The result of applying a style to text means that you apply all the text and paragraph attribute descriptions contained in the style to the text. In this figure we have placed the insertion point in the top paragraph (the heading). If we click on the *Headline* style in the Style palette, we apply this style to the whole paragraph. Figure 3 shows the immediate result.

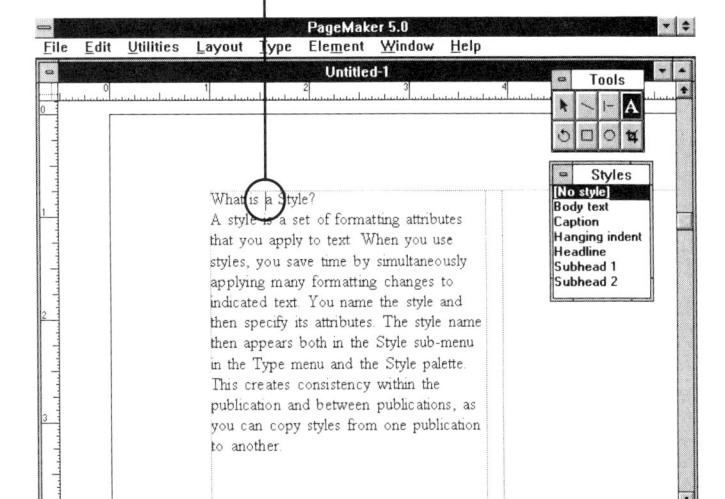

Insertion point

169

Chapter 11: Using Styles

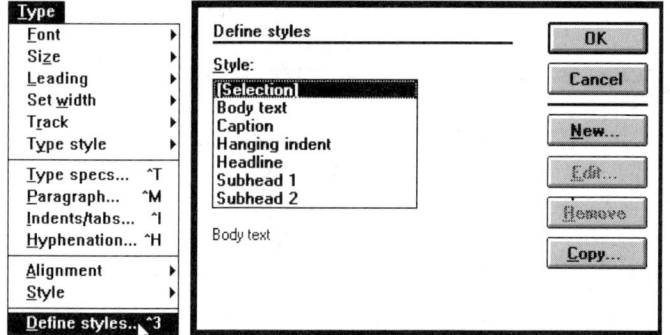

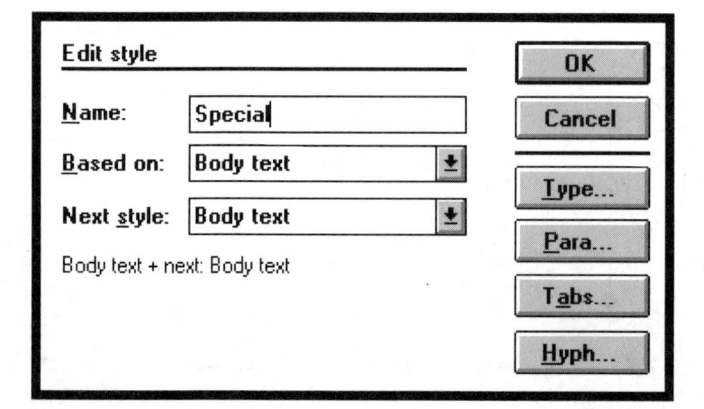

Figure 3. The paragraph now takes on the text attributes defined under the *Headline* style.

Note: You need only place the insertion point in the paragraph you want to apply the style to—you do not have to highlight it.

CREATING STYLES

Figure 4. You create new styles by selecting *Define styles* from the **Type** menu or by pressing the Ctrl key and clicking on a style name in the Style palette. This activates the *Define styles* dialog box. The *Style* list contains all the current style names.

If you click on a style name in the list, its specifications appear at the bottom of the dialog box. Click on the *New* button to create a new style. The *Edit style* dialog box (Figure 5) appears.

Figure 5. Type the name of the new style in the *Name* edit box. We have typed in the word *Special*. The four buttons to the right, *Type, Para, Tabs,* and *Hyph,* allow you to set a variety of text and paragraph specifications for any new style. Click on the button you require. See Figures 6 through 9 for more details.

170

Chapter 11: Using Styles

Figure 6. You get the *Type specifications* dialog box by clicking on the *Type* button in the *Edit style* dialog box. Choose the attributes you need and click on *OK*. You are then returned to the *Edit Style* dialog box. See Chapter 4, **Text** for more information on the *Type specifications* dialog box.

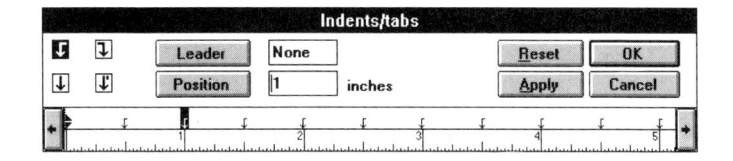

Figure 7. You get the *Paragraph specifications* dialog box by clicking on the *Para* button in the *Edit style* dialog box. Clicking on *OK* after you make any changes returns you to the *Edit style* dialog box. The options available in the *Paragraph specifications* dialog box are explained in Chapter 4, **Text**.

Figure 8. You can change tabs and indents in the *Indents/tabs* dialog box, which you get by clicking on the *Tabs* button in the *Edit style* dialog box. Clicking on *OK* once you have made changes returns you to the *Edit style* dialog box. The *Indents/tabs* dialog box is explained in Chapter 4, **Text**.

171

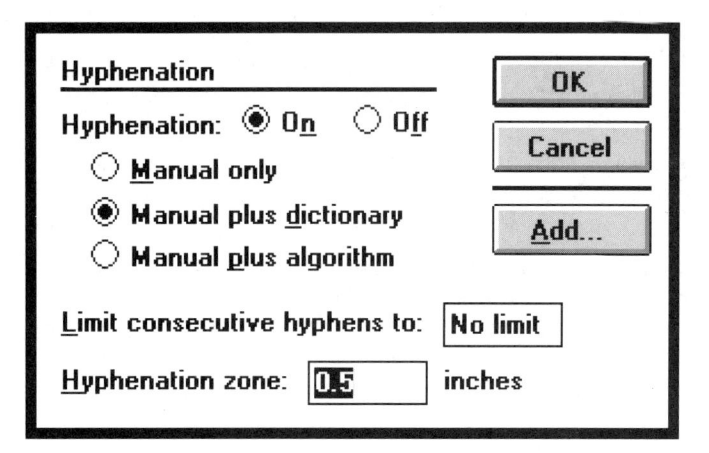

Figure 9. You activate the *Hyphenation* dialog box by clicking on the *Hyph* button in the *Edit style* dialog box. Clicking on *OK*, once you have made changes returns you to *Edit style* dialog box. The *Hyphenation* dialog box is discussed in Chapter 4, **Text**.

Figure 10. This is the *Define styles* dialog box after the changes shown in Figures 6 through 9. Page-Maker includes and highlights the style *Special* in the list. PageMaker displays the attributes we gave to the *Special* style below the list box.

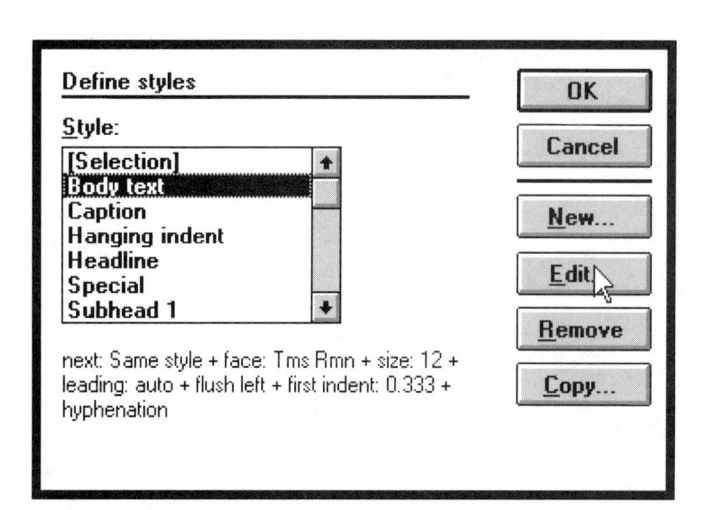

EDITING STYLES

Figure 11. To edit a style, start with the *Define styles* dialog box shown in Figure 10, then highlight the style you need to edit and click on the *Edit* button as shown in the figure.

Figure 12. This activates the *Edit style* dialog box. As we selected *Body text* in Figure 11, the dialog box automatically displays this style. You can now edit it using the options described in Figures 6 through 9.

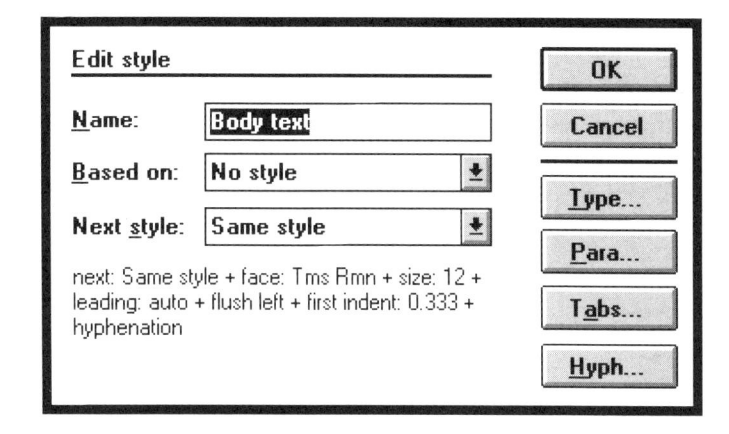

Figure 13. If you change the attributes of selected text (without using the *Define styles* command) to which you have applied a style, PageMaker adds a "+" next to the style name in the Style palette.

> This text has the Caption style applied to it, and we have *changed the attributes of a selected part of the paragraph.*

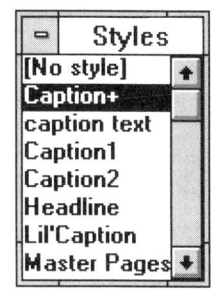

REMOVING A STYLE

Figure 14. To remove a style, select the style name in the *Define styles* dialog box (in our case *Special*) and click on *Remove*.

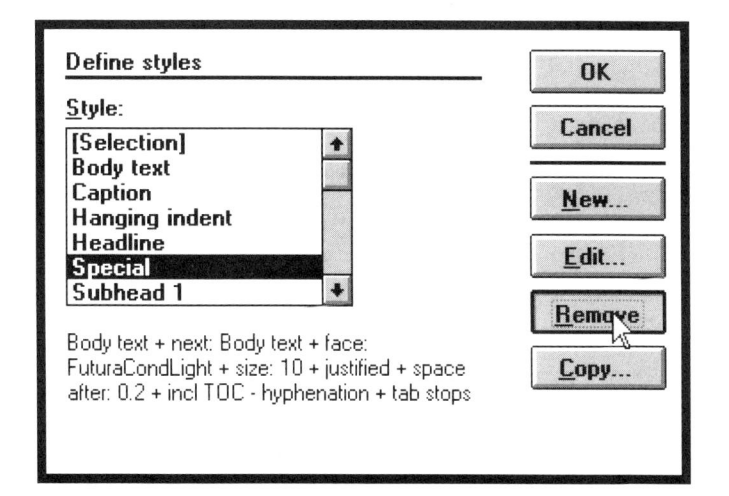

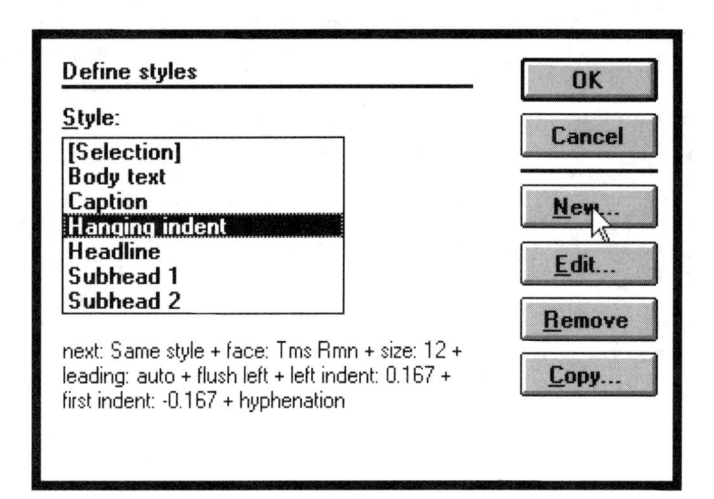

BASED ON

Figure 15. To add a new style which is based upon an existing style, select the style name on which you want to base the new style (in our case *Hanging indent*) and then click on *New* in the *Define styles* dialog box.

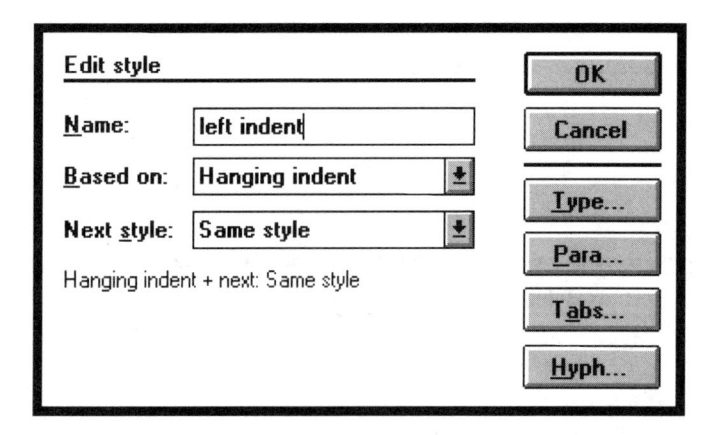

Figure 16. The *Edit style* dialog box appears with the name *Hanging indent* in the *Based on* box. The new style name you are defining (say *left indent*) will start off with the same attributes as *Hanging indent*. Make any necessary changes to *left indent* using the same approach outlined in Figures 6 through 9. You could also select a different style from the *Based on* drop-down list once you are in this dialog box.

NEXT STYLE

Figure 17. The *Next style* drop-down list in the *Edit styles* dialog box contains the list of current styles available in the publication. Selecting a style from this list activates this style when you press the Enter key (start a new paragraph) after using the style you are creating or editing.

COPYING STYLES

Figure 18. You can copy styles from other PageMaker publications. This feature imports a list of styles and adds them onto the current styles list from another publication.

Click on the *Copy* button from the *Define styles* dialog box to activate the *Copy styles* dialog box.

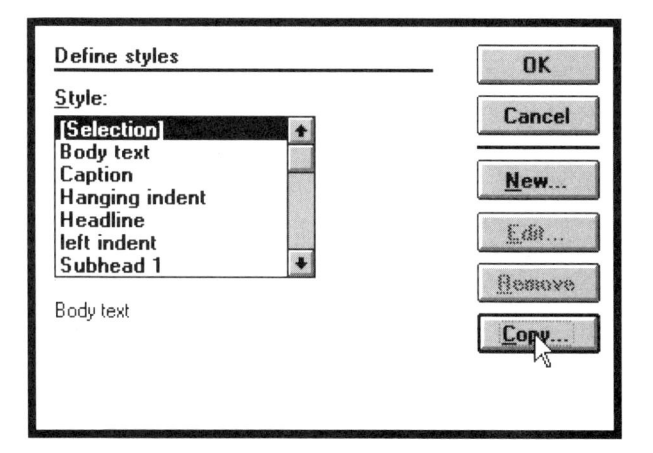

Figure 19. Find and select the required publication from this dialog box and select *OK*. Any styles with matching names will be replaced with the new style if you select *Yes* in the Prompt box that appears.

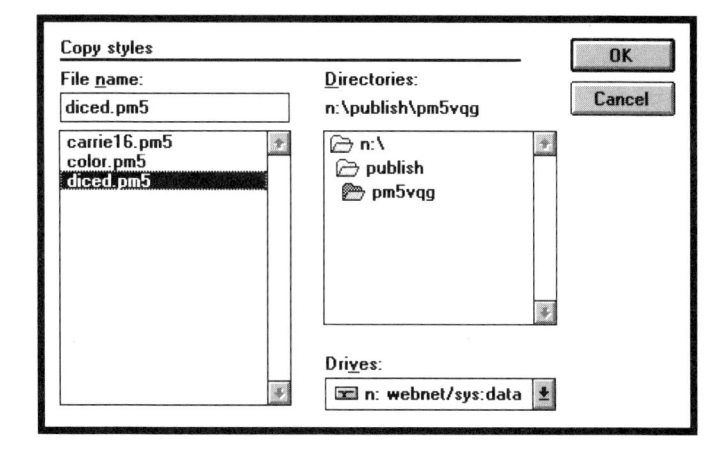

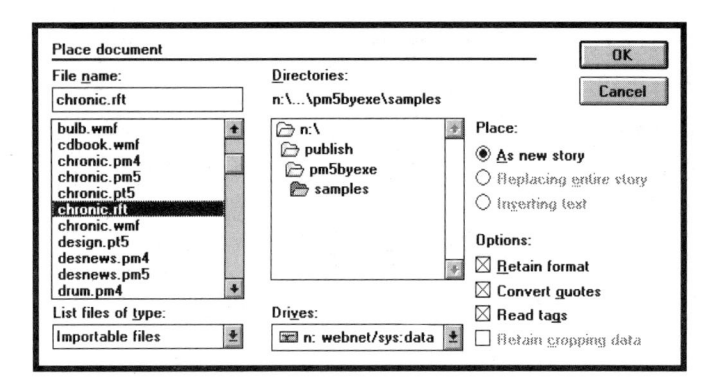

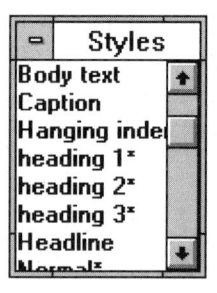

IMPORTING STYLES

Figure 20. You can import style names from word processing documents by including style names in angle brackets (<>) at the beginning of each paragraph in your word processor file. These can then come across into your PageMaker document with the named style automatically applied to that paragraph if you choose the *Read tags* option when you place the document. Some word processing packages such as Word Perfect, Word and Word for Windows automatically bring their own styles into PageMaker when you import them.

Figure 21. You will see a "*" next to any style names that you have imported with word processing text files.

THE CONTROL PALETTE AND STYLES

You can use the Control palette both to apply existing styles to a selected paragraphs, and to create new styles based on the formatting of selected text.

Figure 22. Activate the *Control palette* and click on the *Paragraph view* button.

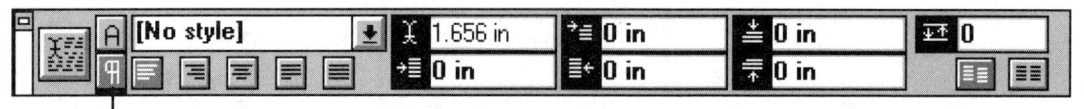

Paragraph view button

Chapter 11: Using Styles

APPLYING STYLES USING THE CONTROL PALETTE

Figure 23. It is easy to apply styles using the Control palette. Insert the text cursor into a paragraph (as we have done here) or select a number of paragraphs. The current style (if any) is displayed in the *Paragraph style* window in the Control palette—in this case *Headline*.

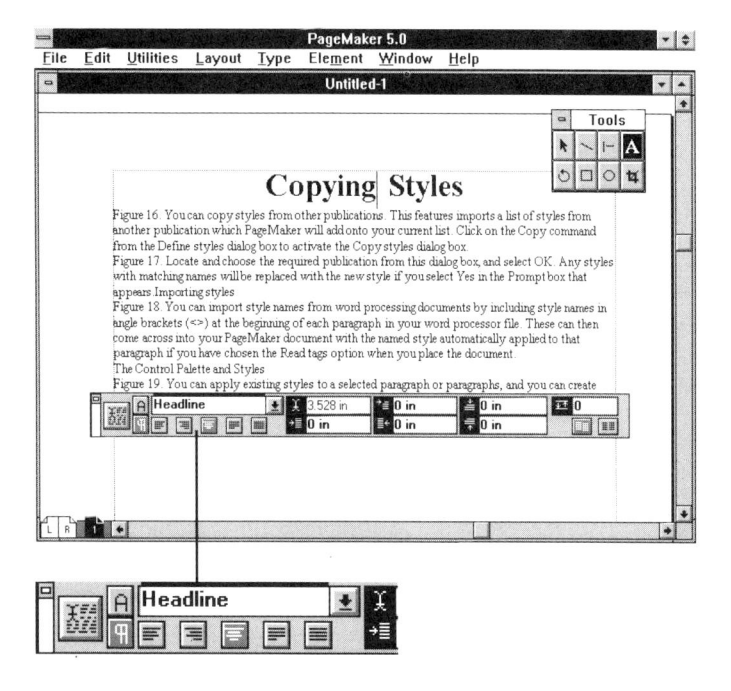

Figure 24. Hold the mouse down on the down arrow to activate the drop-down list of styles. Select the style you want and release the mouse.

Alternatively, you can type the first few letters of the style name into the edit box and press Enter.

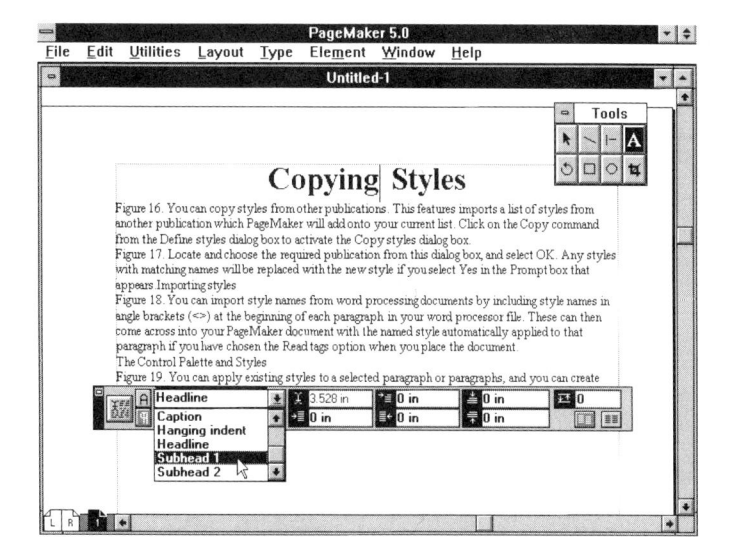

Chapter 11: Using Styles

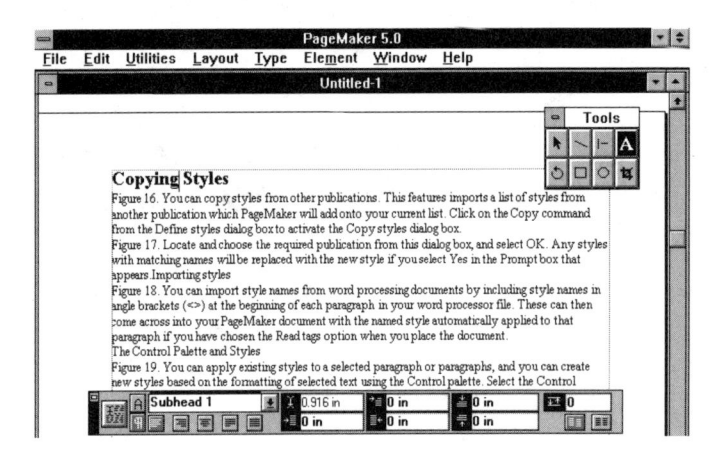

Figure 25. The results display immediately.

CREATING STYLES USING THE CONTROL PALETTE

Figure 26. Format a paragraph of text with the attributes you want to include in the new style. Select the paragraph with the text tool and select the current style name in the *Paragraph style* window.

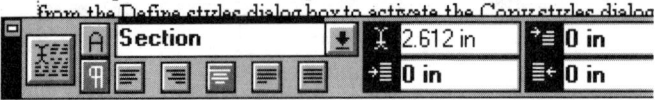

Figure 27. Type a new, unused name over the top of the old one and press the Enter key.

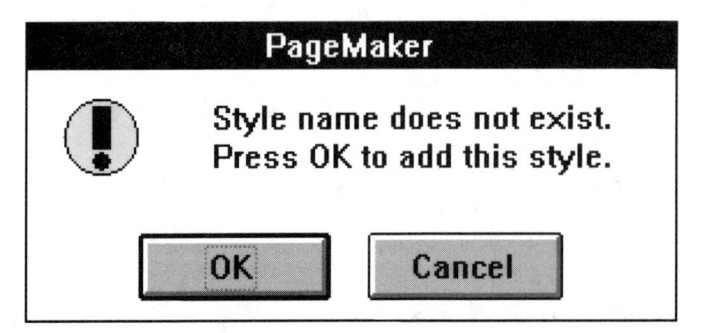

Figure 28. PageMaker responds with this alert box; select *OK*. When you return to the screen, the new style name, in this case *Section*, appears in the list of styles.

You can edit any styles you create in the *Define styles* dialog box, as described in Figures 11 and 12.

USING COLOR 12

SPOT AND PROCESS COLORS

If you are working with color it is necessary to understand the difference between spot and process colors. In Page-Maker, you can define both spot and process colors and apply them to objects and text.

SPOT COLORS

Figure 1. Spot colors are printed using premixed inks. There are hundreds of different spot colors from which to choose. When you send a file to a bureau for color separations of spot colors, the printer must make a separation for each color you have used—so 10 colors equals 10 separations.

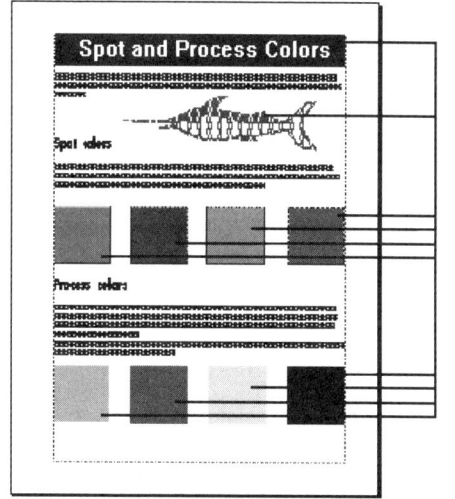

The printer must make a separation for each different spot color used

PROCESS COLORS

Figure 2. Process colors are made up of varying combinations of four basic colors—cyan (C), magenta (M), yellow (Y), and black (K). When you send a file to a bureau for color separations of process colors, a separation for each of the four process colors is made, regardless of how many colors you have used in your publication.

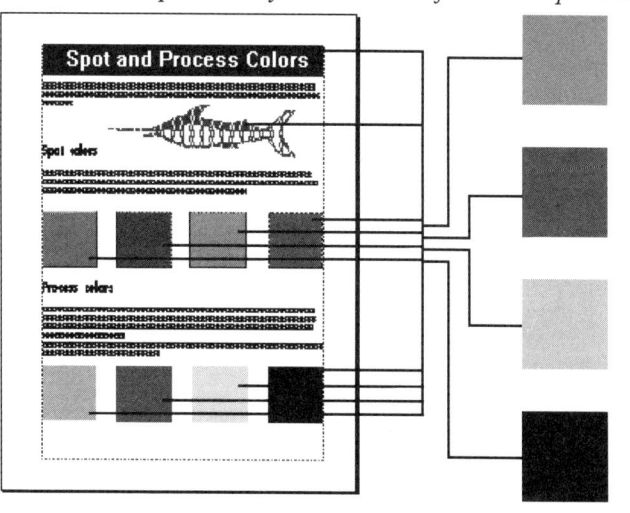

The printer only needs to make four color separations

179

Use spot colors when you are using less than four colors, or when you need precise color matching of inks (for example fluorescent or metallic). Use process colors when you are using four or more colors or you have imported scanned color photographs.

You can use both spot and process colors if you need precise color matching as well as a variety of other colors. This may occur, for example, in a brochure that includes color photographs (four color process) and a corporate logo in a specific spot color.

APPLYING COLOR TO TEXT AND GRAPHICS

Figure 3. You can apply color to text and graphics—including monochrome bitmaps. (You must select text with the text tool before applying color to it.) Activate the Color palette by selecting *Color palette* in the **Window** menu.

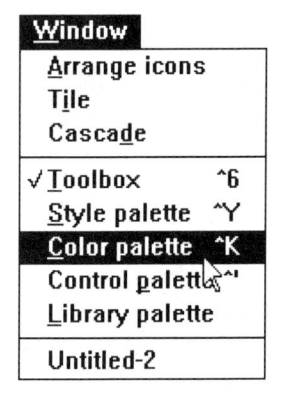

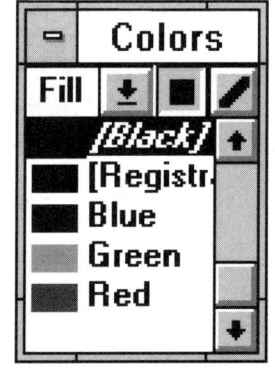

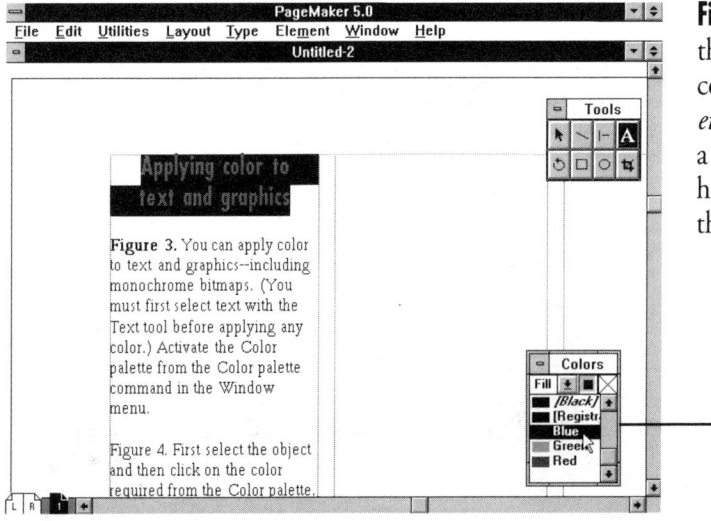

Figure 4. To apply color first select the object and then click on the color required from the *Color palette*. In this figure we have selected a paragraph with the text tool, and have applied the color blue through the *Color palette*.

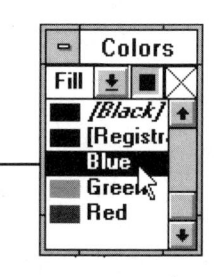

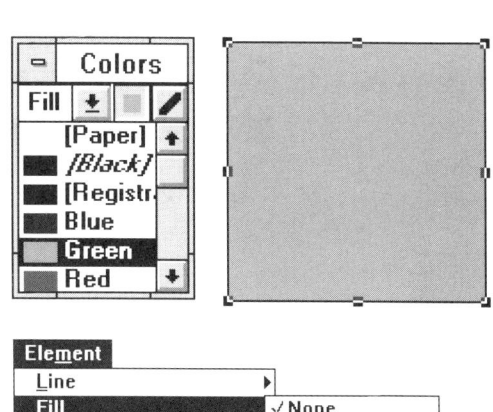

Chapter 12: Using Color

Figure 5. To apply color to an object, select the object and click on a color from the Color palette. PageMaker displays the results immediately.

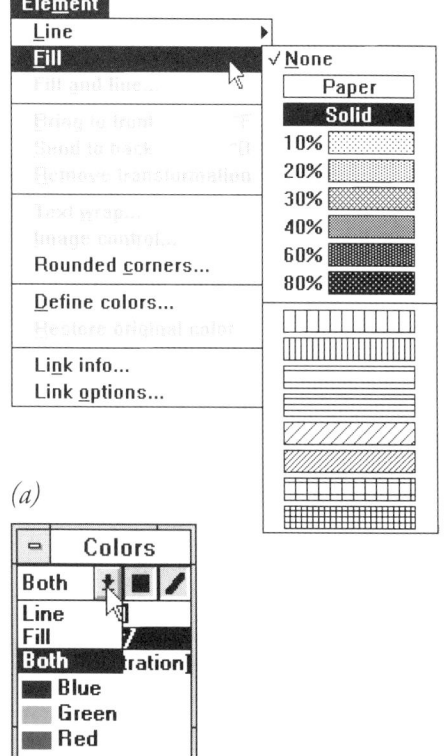

Figure 6. To change the percentage of the fill, you can apply one of the percentage options in the *Fill* submenu from the **Element** command.

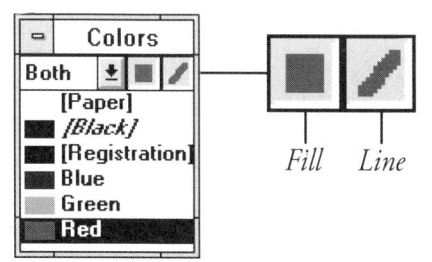

Figure 7. You can apply separate colors for both the line and fill of a selected object from the Color palette.
(a) To apply the color to both the fill and outline, click on the down arrow in the *Color palette* and choose *Both*. To color the *Line* and *Fill* options individually, click on the down arrow and select the *Fill* and Line options alternately.
(b) Alternatively, to switch between the *Line* and *Fill* options, click on the Line or Fill icons in the *Color palette*.

  Note: You cannot change the outline color of text.

(a)

(b)

Fill   Line

181

Chapter 12: Using Color

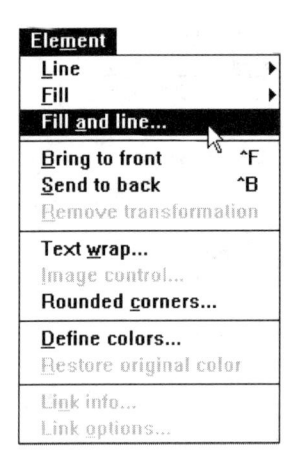

Figure 8. An alternative way to apply color to an object is to select *Fill and line* from the **Element** menu.

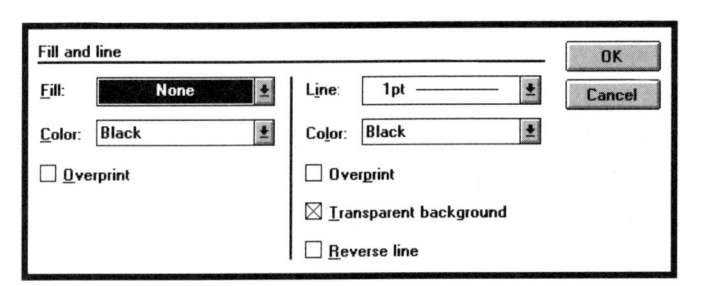

Figure 9. In the *Fill and line* dialog box, you can change both options at the same time.

overprint concept

knockout concept

OVERPRINT OPTION

Figure 10. The default setting for colors in PageMaker is *Knockout*. You can override this with the *Overprint* option in the *Fill and line* dialog box. The *Knockout* option means that when you have two overlapping objects both filled with color, the top object prints but the bottom object does not print where the two objects overlap (this is visible in color separations). When you select the *Overprint* option for a color, this color prints on top of any other color it overlaps, creating a third color that you may not possibly want.

CREATING COLORS

PageMaker supports Pantone and other color libraries as well as giving you the option of defining your own colors. You can also choose pre-defined colors from 14 commercial color libraries. (For more information on commercial color libraries see the *Aldus PageMaker 5 Commercial Printing Guide* or talk to your printer.)

Figure 11. You create new colors by selecting *Define colors* from the **Element** menu. This activates the *Define colors* dialog box. The list shows the various colors that are currently defined; these include the default colors provided with PageMaker. To create a new color, click on the *New* button. This activates the *Edit color* dialog box.

Alternatively, to open this dialog box, use the Ctrl key and click on a color in the Color palette.

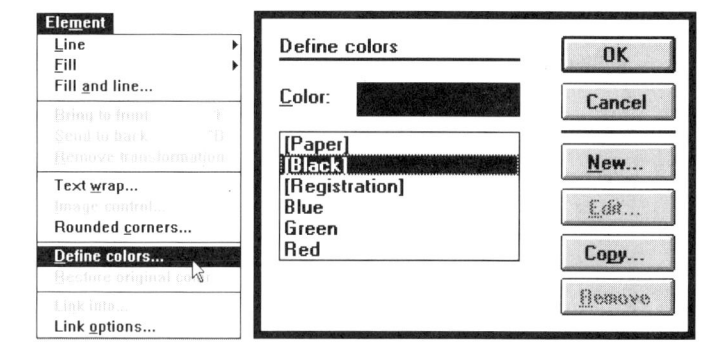

Figure 12. In the *Edit color* dialog box, type the name of the color you are creating in the *Name* edit box. Then choose the *Type* of color you wish to create: *Spot, Process* or *Tint*, and then choose the *Model* type: *RGB, HLS* or *CMYK*. You can adjust the color percentages or degrees using any of the *Model* options; the top half of the color rectangle constantly changes to reflect the new color.

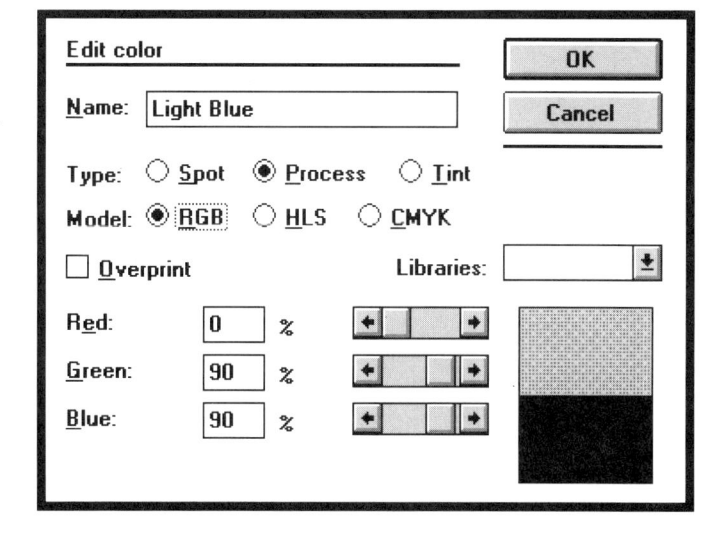

Chapter 12: Using Color

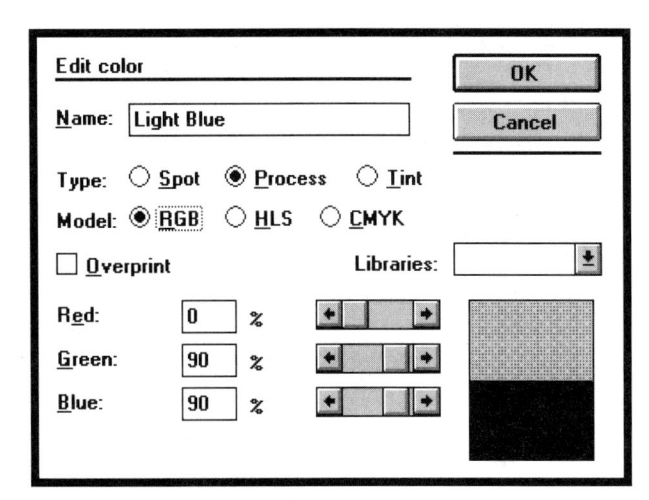

Figure 13. The RGB model allows you to define a color by varying the percentages of red, green, and blue.

Figure 14. The HLS model is similar to RGB but you define the hue in degrees from 0 to 360.

Figure 15. To define a color using the CMYK model, adjust the percentages of cyan, magenta, yellow and black.

The CMYK model for defining colors is the most common method used for printing.

Chapter 12: Using Color

Figure 16. Regardless of which *Type* you select (*Spot*, *Process*, or *Tint*), you can choose any library (spot or process) from the *Libraries* drop-down list. Each library listed is a commercial color-matching system. You may not have all these color libraries installed. It is wise to use the appropriate color reference manuals that you can get from printers if you want accurate results.

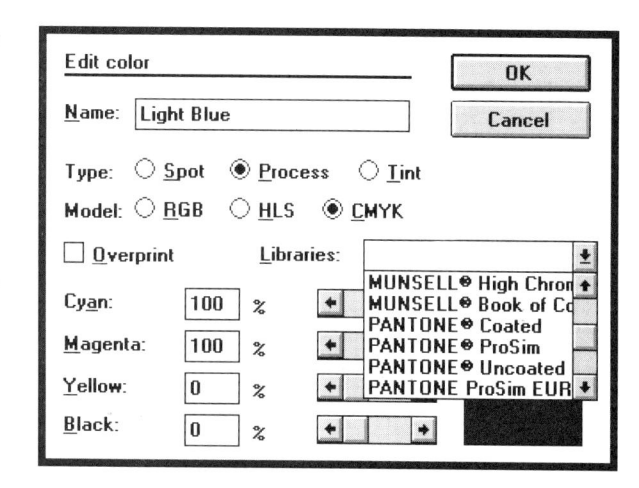

Figure 17. This table shows what *Type* of color each library contains.

Color Matching System	Type of Color	Color Matching System	Type of Color
Crayon	Process	Pantone ProSim	Spot
DIC Color Guide	Spot	Pantone Uncoated	Spot
Focoltone	Process	Pantone ProSim Euro	Spot
Greys	Spot and Process	Pantone Process	Process
Munsell High Chroma Colors	Process	Pantone Process Euro	Process
Munsell Book of Color	Process	TOYOpc	Spot
Pantone Coated	Spot	Trumatch 4-Color Selector	Process

Figure 18. If you choose the *PANTONE* option from the list, for example, this activates the *Library* dialog box shown here. The other libraries appear with a similar dialog box. You choose Pantone colors by scrolling to the one you require, and clicking on it with the mouse. Alternatively, if you know the color, enter the name or its number directly into the *PANTONE* text box at the top of the dialog box, and click on *OK*.

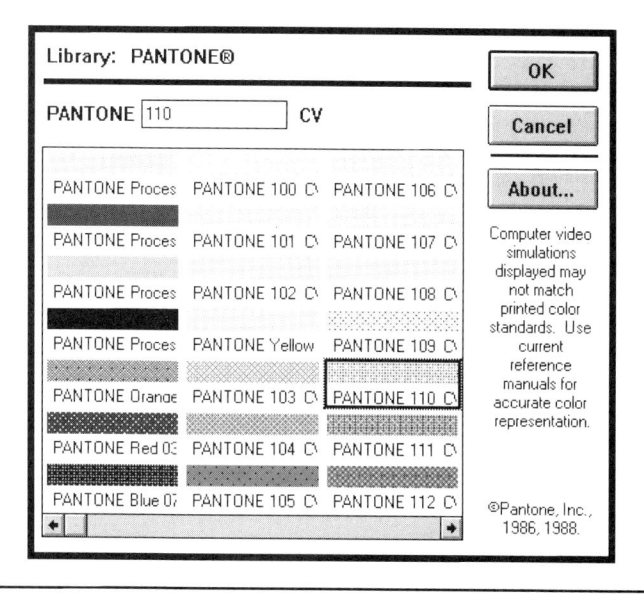

185

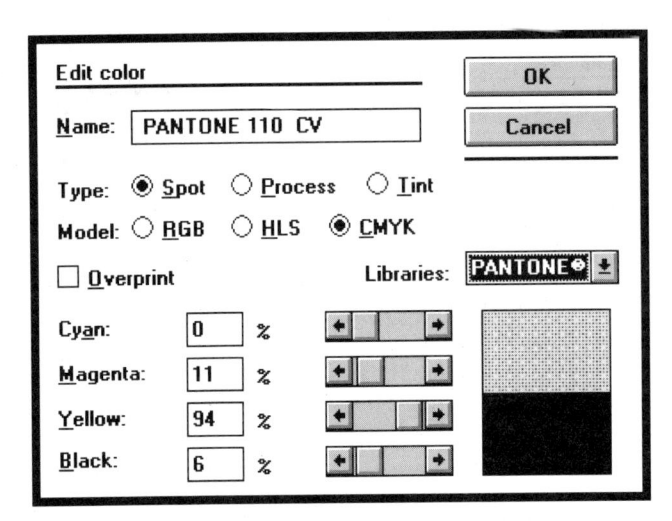

Figure 19. If you leave the *Name* text box blank in the *Edit color* dialog box, then you make a selection from the *Libraries* box, PageMaker automatically inserts the name of the selected color in the *Name* text box. You should keep this name for color identification purposes rather than renaming it.

Figure 20. To create a tint, which is a lighter version of a spot color, click on the *Tint* option and select the spot color that exists from the *Base Color* drop-down list. Choose a percentage of that color from the *Tint* option, and then type in a new name in the *Name* text box.

Tints are a useful way of creating more shades without adding to the separation output. A tint prints on the same separation as the color it is derived from.

Figure 21. After defining a color using any of the above methods, click on *OK* in the *Edit color* dialog box to return to the *Define colors* dialog box again. This figure shows the Pantone spot color we chose in Figure 18 now appearing in the *Color* name list. PageMaker will also display this name in the *Color palette*.

EDITING COLORS

Figure 22. You edit colors the same way you create them. The *Edit color* dialog box allows you to change any color at any time.

To edit a color, select the color you wish to edit from the list in the *Define colors* dialog box and click on the *Edit* button. You cannot edit the default colors of *Black* and *Registration*.

Alternatively, to activate the *Edit color* dialog box, use the Ctrl key and click on the color you wish to edit in the *Color palette*. (See the *Create color library* addition in Chapter 9, **Aldus Additions** for more information on creating your own color library.)

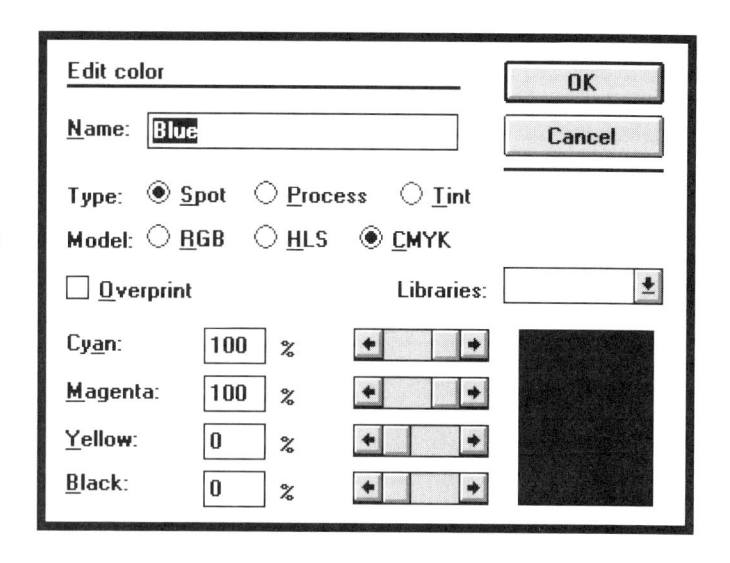

COPYING AND REMOVING COLORS

Figure 23. To copy colors from other PageMaker publications, click on the *Copy* button and then select the relevant publication from the dialog box that appears.

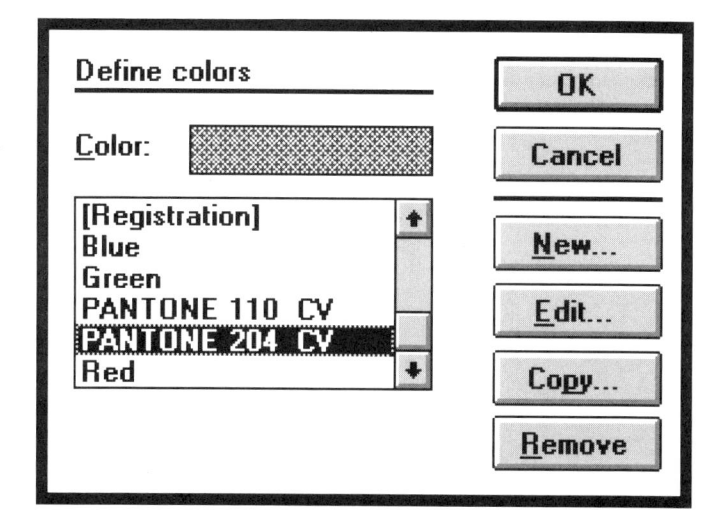

Chapter 12: Using Color

187

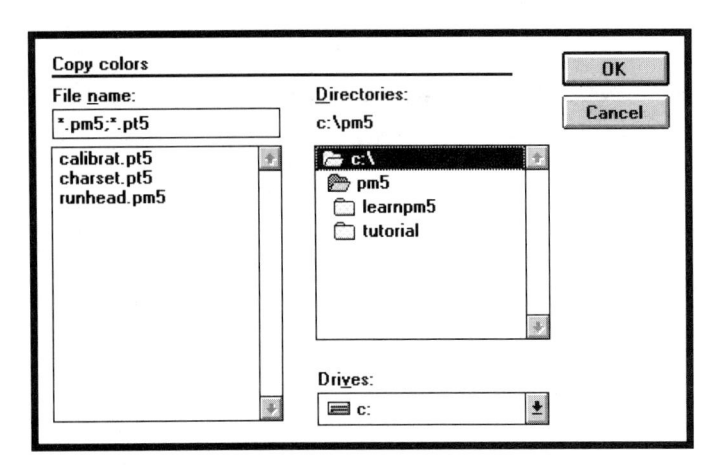

Figure 24. This is the *Copy colors* dialog box that you activate by clicking on the *Copy* button of the *Define colors* dialog box. In the *File list* box, select the file from which you wish to copy the colors and click on *OK*.

To remove a color, select it and click on the *Remove* button in the *Define colors* dialog box (Figure 23).

PRINTING 13

PRINT DIALOG BOX

You can print during any stage of the creation of a publication. You can print the whole document or just a couple of pages, you can scale the size of the pages, add crop marks and print full color separations. The *Print* command in the **File** menu allows you to make a hard copy of the current PageMaker publication.

Figure 1. You should select your target printer when you are setting up your document. To do this, choose the printer you plan to print the final output on from the *Compose to printer* drop-down list in the *Page setup* dialog box. Select the final output printer from this list even if you plan to print interim copies on a different printer.

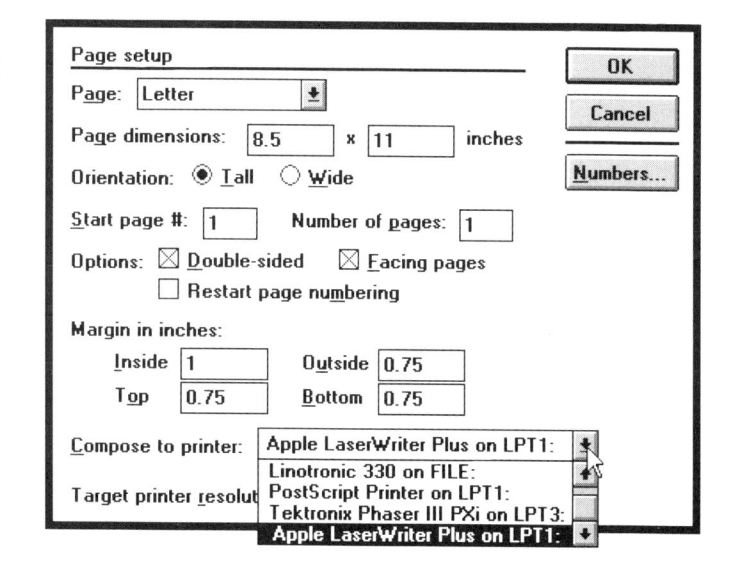

Figure 2. Any time you want to print your publication select *Print* from the **File** menu.

Note: The *Print* dialog box options in this chapter are for a PostScript printer driver only. Non-Postscript printer drivers will have different options.

189

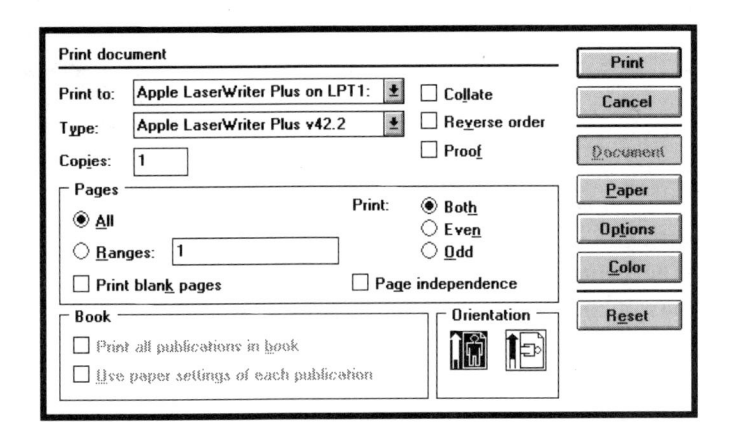

PRINTING OPTIONS

Figure 3. Selecting the *Print* command activates the *Print document* dialog box. This dialog box contains the PostScript options. If you do not have a PostScript printer not all these options will be available to you.

The *Print to* option displays the name of the target printer that you have chosen (see Figure 1). If it does not, use the drop-down list to make your selection.

The *Type* option allows you to select the specific printer model. The drop-down list contains the PPD (PostScript printer description) names for the corresponding printers in the *Print to* drop-down list. Selecting the correct PPD file from this list lets you print more successfully. It is supplied by the printer manufacturer and holds specific information about the printer.

The *Copies* option lets you specify the number of copies of your publication you want printed. You can enter any figure between 1 and 32,000 in this text box which, by default, is set to 1.

Use the *Collate* option to print multiple copies of a publication that contains more than one page. If your document contains many complex graphics, collating automatically can be a very slow process.

When you select the *Reverse order* option, your pages will print in the opposite order to how your printer would print them, either first to last or last to first.

Use the *Proof* option to print all graphics as rectangles only. This speeds up printing considerably.

The *Pages* options let you select all or some of your document to print. To print the whole publication, click on the *All* option. To print part of the publication click on the *Ranges* option (e.g. 1–6) or you can print several ranges (e.g. 2, 5–6, 8–13.) The *Both* option is the default setting to print both odd and even pages, or you can choose to print *Even* or *Odd* pages only—useful for double-sided printing.

To print on both sides of the page using a single-sided printer, print the even pages by selecting the *Even* choice, then, place the even pages back into the printer, and choose to print *Odd* pages.

The *Print blank pages* option allows you to choose to print any pages that are blank. If you check *Page independence,* then PageMaker downloads all the font information with each page rather than once for the whole publication. Unless you specifically need the font information for each page, such as if you use page imposition software that requires it, you should leave this option unchecked.

The *Book* options let you control printing of publications belonging to a book list (see Chapter 14). To print all the publications in the current book list, select *Print all publications in book*. To print each publication in the book list using its own printer settings, select *Use paper settings of each publication*. This allows you to print documents, for example, of different page sizes, or to different printer bins. The options not affected by this setting are the orientation, the number of copies, the *Collate* option and the page range.

Note: If your current book list is empty, you will not be able to access the two options in the *Book* section.

Figure 4. In the *Orientation* section of the *Print document* dialog box, you can select either *Portrait* (vertical) or *Landscape* (horizontal).

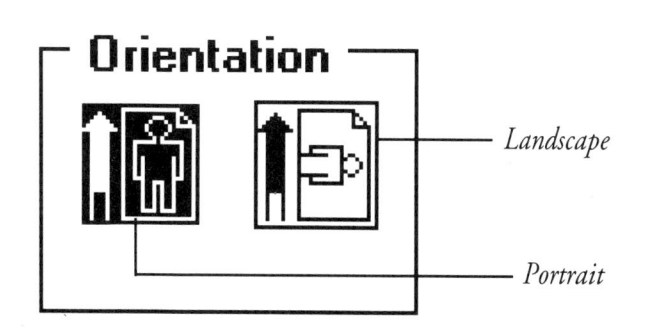

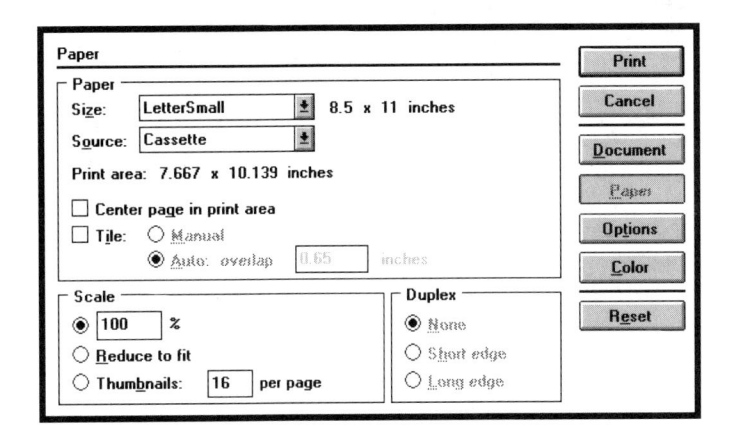

PAPER

Figure 5. Click on the *Paper* button in the *Print document* dialog box to access your printer's settings. Here, you can change the paper size, the paper source and you can center your document on the page.

Note: Because different printers have different capabilities, the options available here may vary depending upon your printer.

The *Tile* option allows you to print page sizes larger than the printer is capable, on separate pages that you can tile together and slightly overlap. You split each page into segments (called tiles) that will fit onto the printer's page. You set the amount of image or page that will overlap in the *Auto overlap* figure box. Selecting *Manual* for this option lets you determine how each tiled page will print.

The % option in the *Scale* section allows you to scale the size of your page between 6 and 1600%, in increments as small as 0.1%. If you need to reduce or enlarge the pages of your document to better fit the paper in your printer, enter a percentage in the % text box. If you are printing an enlarged version of your page, you may need to use the *Tile* option (see Figure 11).

The *Reduce to fit* option automatically scales the size of your page down to fit on your printer's page size.

The *Thumbnails* option allows you to print a miniature version of your publication. You can print up to 100 miniature pages of a publication on the one page. The default setting is 16, which prints 16 thumbnails per page.

If your printer can print on both sides of the page you can use the *Duplex* options to control how it does this. Choose *None* to print your document single-sided. If you are printing portrait, the *Short edge* option allows you to print both sides so that they read correctly when you bind them along the short edge of the paper. The *Long edge* option allows you to print both sides so that they read correctly when you bind them along the long edge of the paper.

OPTIONS

Figure 6. When you click on the *Options* button at the right of the dialog box, these settings become available to you.

In the *Graphics* section, you can choose *Normal* or *Optimized* to print a normal or a higher resolution copy of your document's graphics.

If you have TIFF files in your document, you can print them at a lower resolution by choosing the *Low TIFF resolution* option or you can choose not to print them at all by selecting the *Omit TIFF files* option. You can use these options to speed up printing considerably.

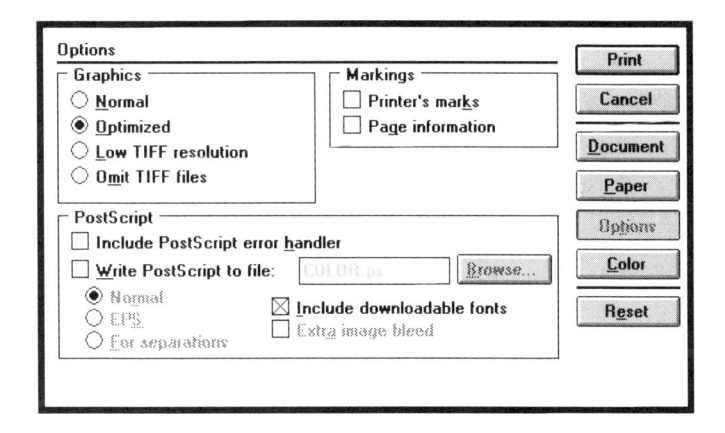

If you select the *Printer's marks* option, PageMaker can place items such as crop marks, registration marks, color-control bars and density bars on the printout. If you are printing, for example, a letter-sized page on letter-size paper, these marks do not appear.

The *Page information* option allows you to print information on the file name, the current date, and the colors used in the lower-left corner of each page. (See Figure 20 for information on creating a print file through this dialog box.)

If you want to print your PageMaker document to a file and not to a printer, use the PostScript options in the *Options* dialog box (Figure 6). You may want to print your document to a file because the printer you are using is in a different location, or you are sending it to a service bureau for printing.

To print the file to disk, first select the *Write PostScript to file* option in the *PostScript* section. Key in the name of the print file in the edit box next to the *Write PostScript to file* option. Click on the *Browse* button to activate a dialog box from where you select a drive and directory to save the print file.

If you choose the *Normal* option, the file is given a *ps* extension by default. Choose the *EPS* option to create an encapsulated PostScript file for any page in your document (you can only print one page at a time when you choose this option). An EPS file created this way is given an *eps* extension by default and you can place it into PageMaker.

Choose the *For separations* option if you plan to have the print file separated by an outside separation program more advanced than PageMaker's separating capabilities. The file in this case will have an *sep* extension.

The *Include downloadable fonts* option includes any fonts in the document that you need to download to your printer before printing.

POSTSCRIPT ERRORS

When you check the *Include PostScript error handler* option, your printer prints a message on a page if an error occurs while printing. This message tells you the PostScript command that caused the error and a brief suggestion on how to fix the problem.

PRINTING COLOR

Figure 7. Clicking on the *Color* button activates the options shown here.

Selecting the *Composite* option allows you to print your color document, as normal, to a color or black and white printer. The *Grayscale* option will print a color version of a document to a color printer, or a grayscale version to a non-color printer. When you print a grayscale version, PageMaker simulates the intensity of the color in shades of gray.

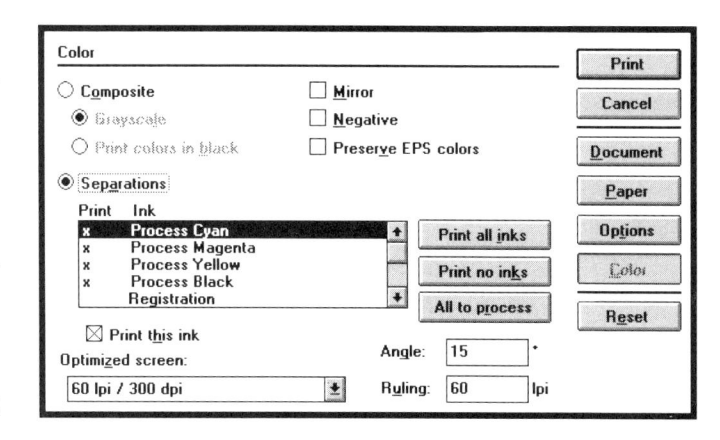

The *Print colors in black* option will print your publication in percentages of black. The *Mirror* option mirrors your document when you print it. The *Negative* option prints your document as a negative, and the *Preserve EPS colors* prints the colors saved with the EPS graphics in your files, rather than any colors you have applied in PageMaker.

Select the *Separations* option to print spot and process color separations. If you wish to print only specific colors as separations, click on the required color in the *Print ink* list box and click on the *Print this ink* option. You can also double-click on the color. The colors that you select or that PageMaker has pre-selected have an "**x**" to the left of the ink name.

Use the *Print all inks* button if you wish to print a color separation for every color in the *Print Ink* list box. After you click on this button, PageMaker places a mark to the left of every color name. Click on the *Print no inks* button to specify that you do not want to print separations. You can then select a specific color and click on *Print this ink*.

Click on the *All to process* button to temporarily convert all spot colors to process for printing. PageMaker converts spot colors to the closest possible process color it can, which may not exactly match the original color.

Use the *Optimized screen* drop-down list to specify the screen ruling that you will print your composite publication or color separations. The list displays the screen ruling and resolution combinations listed in the printer's PPD file. Each printer comes with a PPD file that contains certain information about the printer. The option you select here is reflected in the *Angle* and *Ruling* text boxes.

You can also enter a custom screen angle for your publication, but default angles defined for each specific printer give the best results. You can specify a custom screen ruling, but the rulings defined for each printer give the best results. You will need to get more information from your bureau on the best options to choose here.

Use the *Document* button to return to the *Print document* dialog box.

When you have selected all the required print options, click on the *Print* button.

Multiple Publication Features 14

Book Command

PageMaker's *Book* command allows you to link together multiple PageMaker publications to form one large document. With this command, you compile a list of the names of all publications that form part of a total document. You can link many chapters together to form a complete book.

Figure 1. Through the *Book* command, you can create a list of PageMaker publications that become part of a book list. These may be for example, all the separate chapters of a book.

Once you have created a book list, you can include all the publications when you generate a table of contents and index (see Chapters 15 and 16 for more information on these features). You can also print these multiple publications without having to open each publication individually.

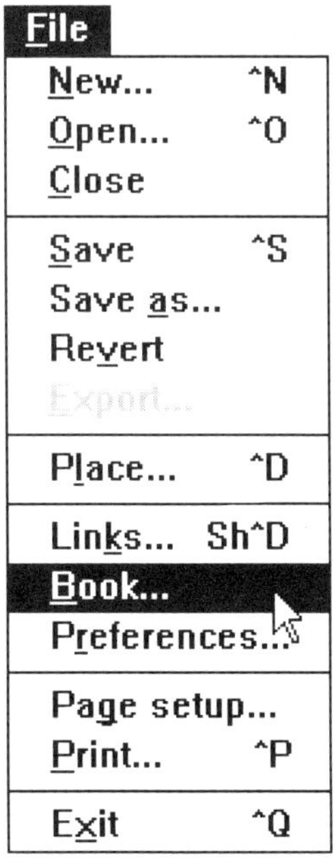

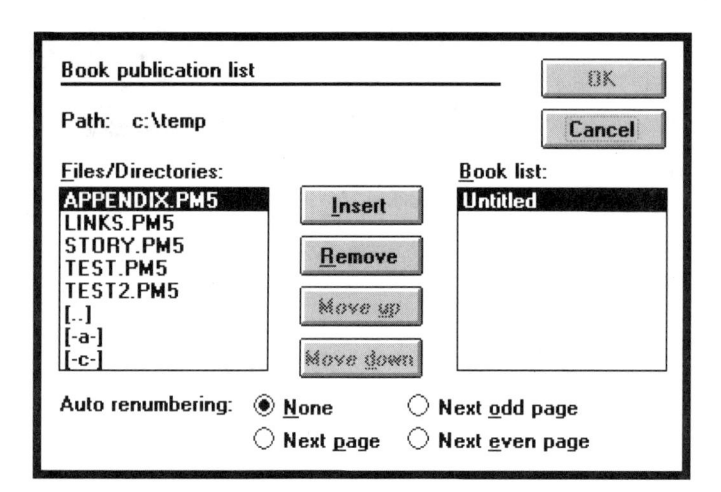

CREATING A BOOK LIST

Figure 2. The *Book publication list* dialog box appears after you select the *Book* command (Figure 1). The *Book list* list box, on the right of this dialog box, is where Page-Maker adds the names of the different publications you specify to create the *Book list*. The *Files/Directories* list box allows you to search through your PageMaker publications on disk to find the documents you wish to add.

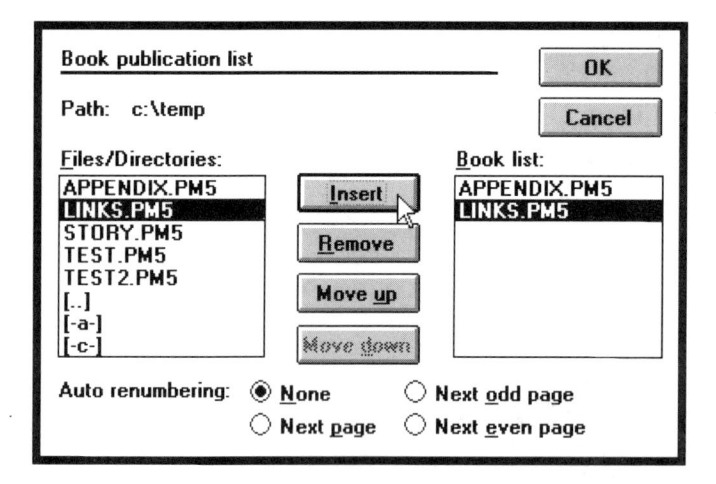

Figure 3. You add to the *Book list* by clicking on a specific publication listed on the left, and then clicking on the *Insert* button. This places the publication in the *Book list*. Repeat this procedure for all required publications. You may also double-click on the name of the publication in the *Files/Directories* list box as an alternative method for adding publications. This will automatically add the selected file name to the *Book list*.

Chapter 14: Multiple Publication Features

Figure 4. You can easily remove documents from the *Book list* by clicking on the name you wish to delete and then clicking on the *Remove* button. This automatically deletes the publication from the list.

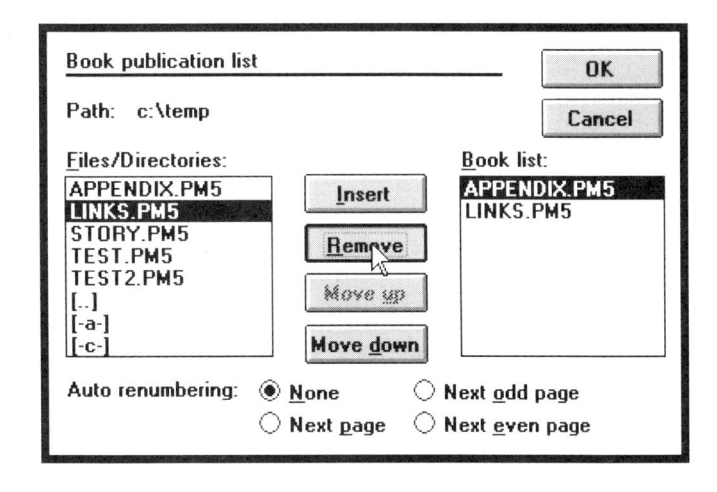

Figure 5. It is important to ensure that the publications in the *Book list* are in the correct order, as this is the order in which the *Book list* prints, and also determines page numbering (only if you are using the *Auto renumbering* feature). You can change this order by using the *Move up* and *Move down* buttons. Highlight the publications you wish to move, and click on the *Move up* or *Move down* buttons as required.

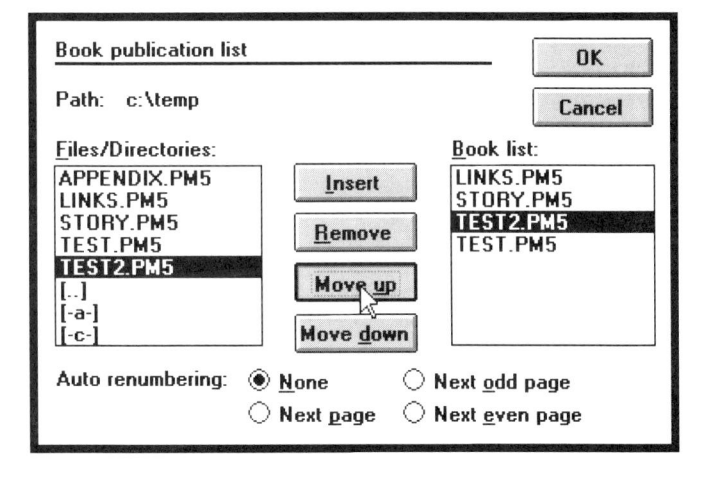

PRINTING A BOOK LIST

Figure 6. The *Print document* dialog box lets you print a single publication or the entire *Book list*. To print the entire list, click in the *Print all publications in book* option in this dialog box.

199

You can copy the book list to every publication in the list by holding down the Ctrl key and choosing *Book* from the **File** menu in the file where you created the book list. If you later modify the list in any one of the publications you must re-copy them by following this same procedure.

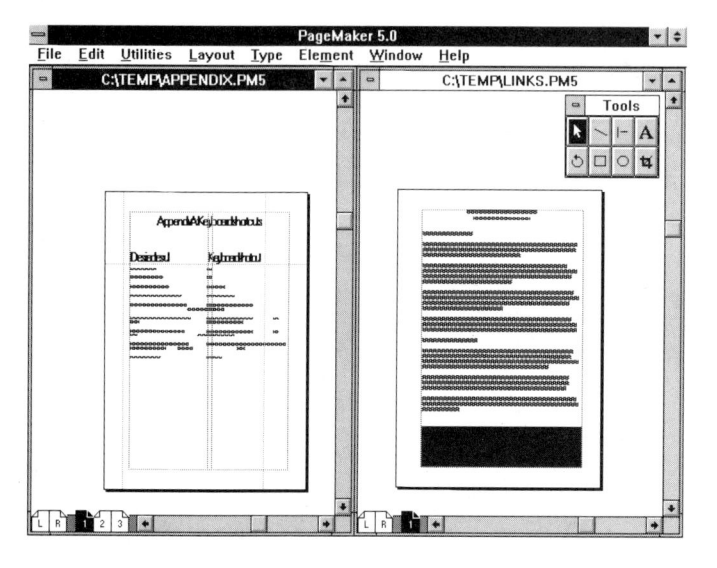

COPYING AND PASTING BETWEEN PUBLICATIONS

Figure 7. You can copy information between multiple opened documents by dragging selected text and graphics from one open window to another. In this figure we have opened two publications.

We are now going to copy the graphic from the publication window on the right to the one on the left.

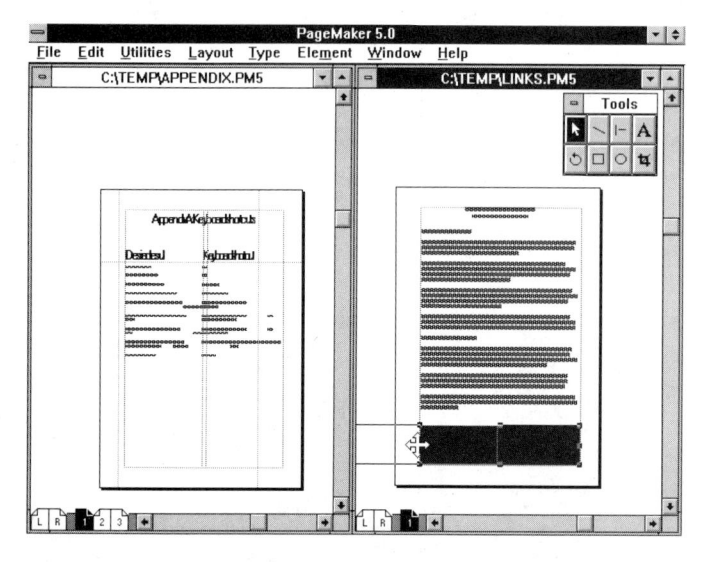

Figure 8. Select the item you want to copy to the other publication (it can include both text and graphics), and drag it with the mouse from one publication window into another.

Figure 9. You can see the result here. When you drag an object from one publication to another, PageMaker makes a copy of the object in the other open publication.

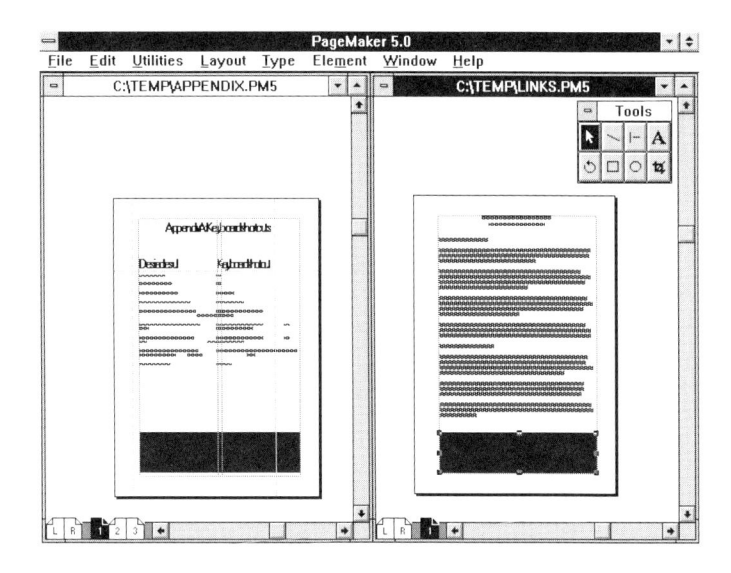

Creating a Table of Contents 15

Table of Contents

PageMaker can generate a table of contents for a single publication or a series of publications contained in a book list. PageMaker searches for specific styles to create the table of contents.

Figure 1. PageMaker generates a table of contents based on how you set up the different paragraph styles. If you define the styles to include in the table of contents, PageMaker searches only for these paragraphs when it generates its contents.

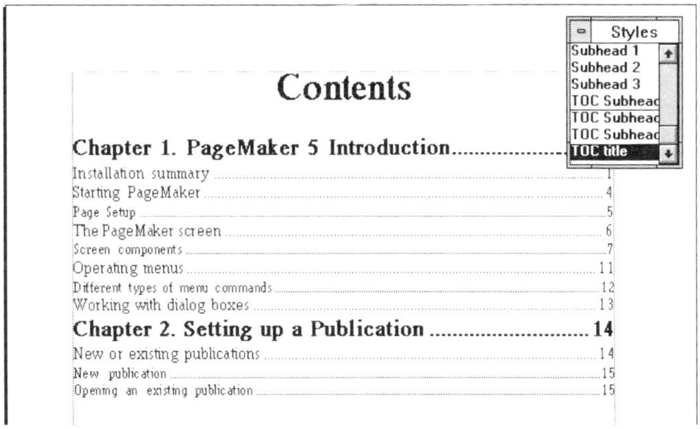

You specify which styles will be included in a table of contents through the *Paragraph specifications* dialog box (Figure 2). In these styles you must select the *Include in table of contents* option before PageMaker can generate the list.

You can also select individual paragraphs (as opposed to applying a style) and apply the *Include in table of contents* option through the same *Paragraph specifications* dialog box (Figure 2).

203

Chapter 15: Creating a Table of Contents

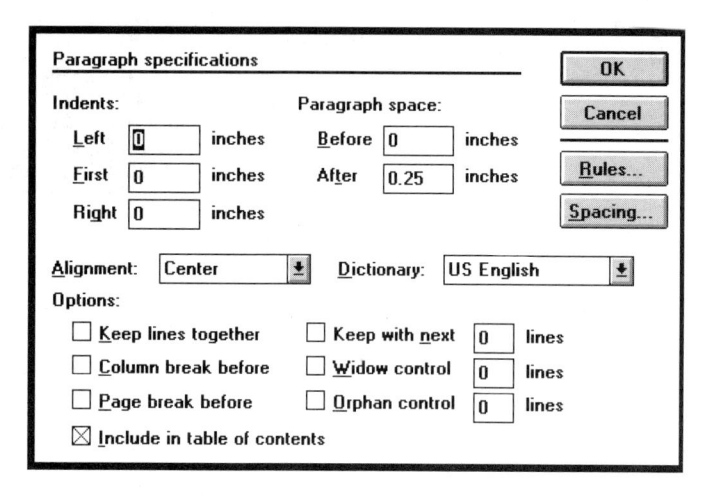

Figure 2. At the bottom of the *Paragraph specifications* dialog box is the option *Include in table of contents*. If you check this option when you create a style, all the paragraphs which you apply this style to will form part of the generated contents.

You can create many different styles within a publication with this option selected (see Chapter 11, **Using Styles** for more information).

Creating Contents

If you are creating a table of contents for more than one publication, it is a good idea to create a new publication and in this publication create your book list before generating your table of contents (see Chapter 14, **Multiple Publication Features**).

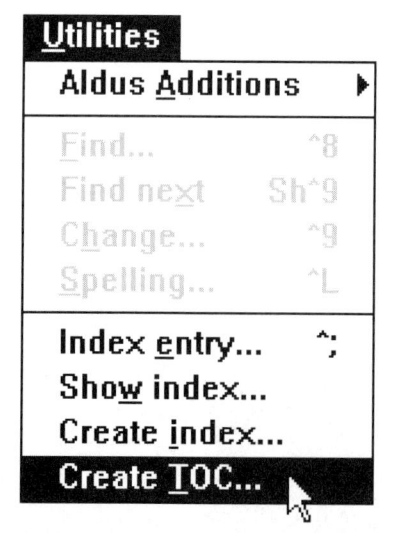

Figure 3. To create the table of contents, you first choose *Create TOC* in the **Utilities** menu.

204

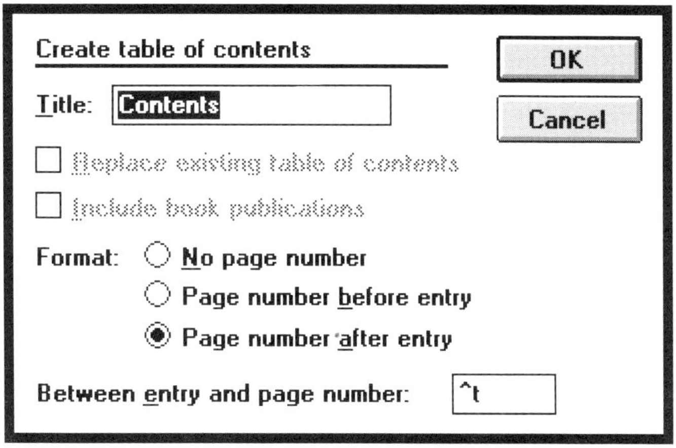

Figure 4. This is the *Create table of contents* dialog box. The word *Contents* appears by default in the *Title* text box. You can delete this and replace it with a title of your own, up to 30 characters in length. This is the word that will appear at the top of the contents.

You can select the *Replace existing table of contents* option only if you have generated a previous table of contents. If you have, this option is automatically checked. You can uncheck it if you want to compare old and new versions.

You can select the *Include book publications* option only if you have included the publication in a book list. If you have, this option is automatically checked. You can uncheck it if you wish to review the contents for that publication only.

You can also choose whether your table of contents includes page numbers with the *No page number* option, and where they appear with *Page number before entry* or *Page number after entry*. The bottom line, *Between entry and page number,* allows you to adjust the spacing between a contents heading and the various page numbers. The default format code is '^t' for a tab with dot leaders. (You can use other codes which you will find listed in Appendix A of the *PageMaker User Manual.*)

Clicking on *OK* in the *Create table of contents* dialog box generates the table of contents. This may take some time, depending on the number of publications you include. You can then place this as you do any text file in PageMaker.

Chapter 15: Creating a Table of Contents

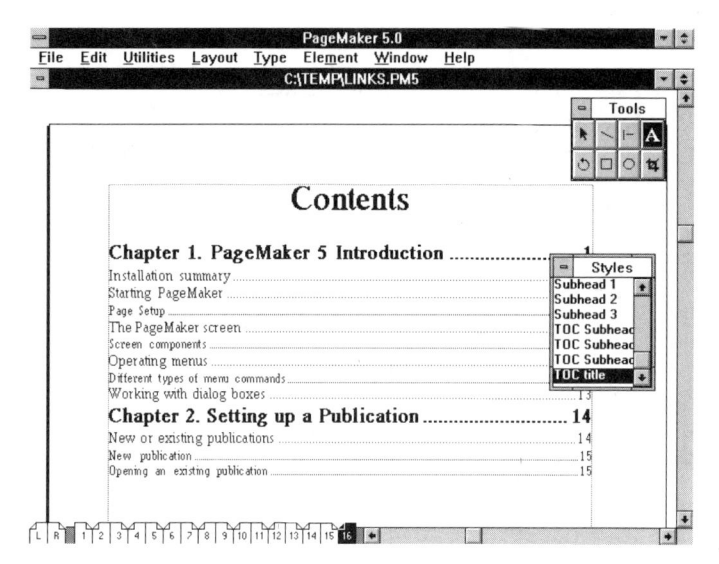

Figure 5. When you generate the contents, PageMaker automatically creates TOC styles based on the styles of the original paragraph but with the word TOC in front of them. TOC style fonts are Times Roman by default.

You can edit these TOC styles in the same way as you edit other paragraph styles.

CREATING AN INDEX 16

INDEXES

PageMaker allows you to generate an index for your publication automatically. Your index can be a simple one based on keywords or a more detailed multi-level index that spans several publications. Index entries contain two elements: a topic and a page reference. In some cases the page reference may be a page range or a cross-reference to another index entry.

CREATING INDEX ENTRIES

Figure 1. When you create an index entry, PageMaker adds an index marker to your text (◘). These are only visible in the Story editor, although you can create index entries both in *Layout* view and Story editor.

To create an individual index entry either:

(a) Insert the text near where you wish to reference a word or topic; or alternatively

(b) select the text you wish to index.

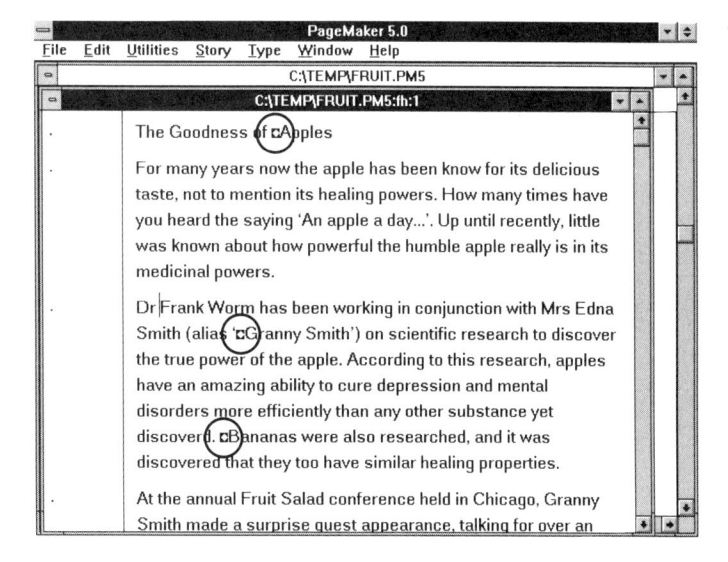

207

Chapter 16: Creating an Index

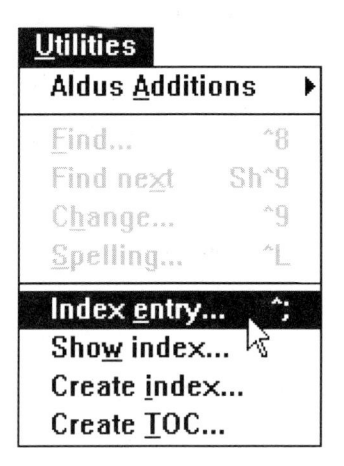

Figure 2. Then use the *Index entry* command in the **Utilities** menu to create the reference.

Figure 3. If you have selected text, then this text will appear as shown here in the level 1 *Topic* text box (in this case *Apples*). If you merely placed the insertion point, then the *Topic* levels will have no text in them. Use this latter method when you wish to insert a different word or phrase in the index than that in your text. You are then free to type in your own index word into the level 1 *Topic* text box. There are three different *Topic* levels available.

You can enter up to three levels of topics. Click on the *Topic* button to see what other topics you have already defined.

Chapter 16: Creating an Index

Figure 4. We now have entered both primary and secondary index entries. We have also entered additional information in the *Sort* rectangles indicating to PageMaker how we want it to sort the *Topic* index entries. If you leave the *Sort* text box blank, you may not get the alphabetic sequence you want when dealing with items such as numbers.

```
Add index entry                                    ┌────────┐
                                                   │   OK   │
Type:    ● Page reference   ○ Cross-reference      └────────┘
Topic:                       Sort:                 ┌────────┐
┌─────────────────────┐  ┌┐ ┌─────────────────────┐│ Cancel │
│ St George           │  │↵│ │ Saint George       │└────────┘
└─────────────────────┘     └─────────────────────┘┌────────┐
┌─────────────────────┐     ┌─────────────────────┐│  Add   │
│ 7-Up                │     │ Seven Up|           │└────────┘
└─────────────────────┘     └─────────────────────┘┌────────┐
┌─────────────────────┐     ┌─────────────────────┐│ Topic..│
└─────────────────────┘     └─────────────────────┘└────────┘

Page range:  ● Current page
             ○ To next style change
             ○ To next use of style:  ┌─────────┐
                                      │Body text│↕
                                      └─────────┘
             ○ For next   [ 1 ]  paragraphs
             ○ Suppress page range
Page # override:   ☐ Bold   ☐ Italic   ☐ Underline
```

The *Page range* options allow you to decide how many pages you want to reference for each index entry.

The *Page # override* option allows you to change the type style of page numbers and cross-referencing for additional emphasis.

Figure 5. The above index entry options produce entries in the index like this example.

```
S
St George
   7-Up   19
```

Figure 6. This is same index entry as in Figure 4 but we have selected different *Page range* and *Page # override* options. See Figure 7 for the result.

```
Add index entry                                    ┌────────┐
                                                   │   OK   │
Type:    ● Page reference   ○ Cross-reference      └────────┘
Topic:                       Sort:                 ┌────────┐
┌─────────────────────┐  ┌┐ ┌─────────────────────┐│ Cancel │
│ St George           │  │↵│ │ Saint George       │└────────┘
└─────────────────────┘     └─────────────────────┘┌────────┐
┌─────────────────────┐     ┌─────────────────────┐│  Add   │
│ 7-Up                │     │ Seven Up            │└────────┘
└─────────────────────┘     └─────────────────────┘┌────────┐
┌─────────────────────┐     ┌─────────────────────┐│ Topic..│
└─────────────────────┘     └─────────────────────┘└────────┘

Page range:  ○ Current page
             ○ To next style change
             ○ To next use of style:  ┌─────────┐
                                      │Body text│↕
                                      └─────────┘
             ● For next   [ 10 ]  paragraphs
             ○ Suppress page range
Page # override:   ☐ Bold   ☒ Italic   ☐ Underline
```

209

Figure 7. The index entry options of Figure 6 produce an entry like this.

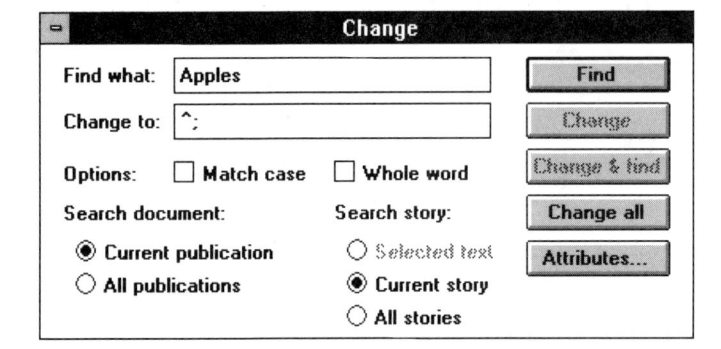

MULTIPLE INDEX ENTRIES

Figure 8. If you want to create multiple index entries of a particular word or phrase that occurs throughout your publication, select *Change* from the **Utilities** menu. (You can select this only when you are in Story editor.) In the *Change* dialog box, enter the text you need to index in the *Find what* edit box and insert '^;' (caret+semicolon) in the *Change to* text box. This is the symbol for an index entry marker.

Then click on the *Change all* button and PageMaker will mark every occurrence of the text with an index entry marker.

Figure 9. PageMaker has marked every occurrence of the word "apples" with an index entry marker.

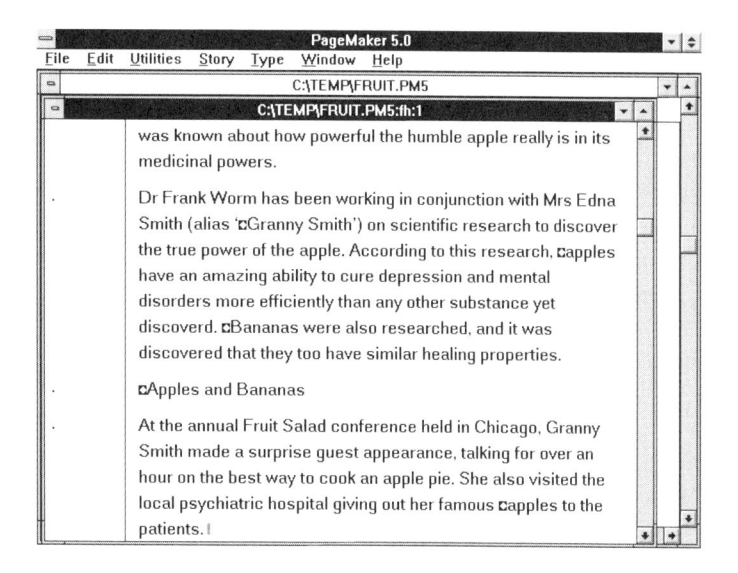

TOPIC AND CROSS-REFERENCING

Figure 10. Use the *Topic* button from the *Add index entry* dialog box to select a topic that you have already created elsewhere in your document. First insert the text cursor near the word and select the *Index entry* command. Activate the *Select topic* dialog box by clicking on the *Topic* button in the *Add index entry* dialog box. Use the *Topic section* to find the letter that begins the word for which you are searching.

This dialog box lets you select an index entry you have already included. This simplifies your work and reduces the possibility of misspelling subsequent entries of an existing index topic.

Chapter 16: Creating an Index

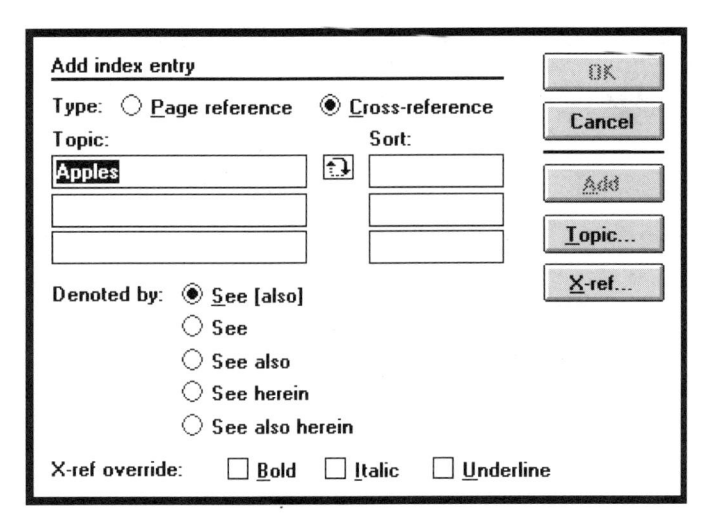

Figure 11. To cross-reference another index entry, first enter the word you wish to cross-reference in the *Add index entry* dialog box. Choose the *Cross-reference* option at the top of the dialog box, and then the *X-ref* button.

In this example, we entered *Apples* and we want to cross-reference it to another entry, called *Bananas* (e.g. Apples. *See* Bananas).

Figure 12. The *X-ref* activates the *Select cross-reference topic* dialog box. In this box, find the *Bananas* entry by selecting the *B* alongside *Topic section,* or click on *Next section* until *Bananas* appears. Select *Bananas* and click on *OK*. That brings you back to the *Add index entry* dialog box. Click on *OK* once more to finish the operation.

212

Chapter 16: Creating an Index

SHOW INDEX COMMAND

Figure 13. To review all index entries before generating the index, choose *Show index* from the **Utilities** menu.

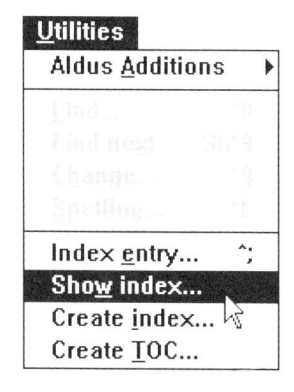

Figure 14. The *Show index* dialog box allows you to add cross-references and edit or remove index entries. For example, if you wish to cross-reference *Bananas* by adding the following: "Bananas. *See also* Apples" you would first find the *Bananas* entry as shown in this figure. Then click on the *Add x-ref* button.

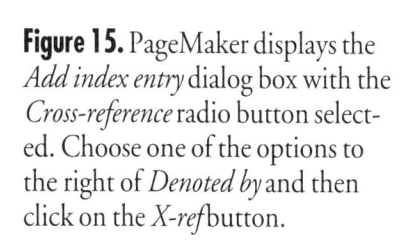

Figure 15. PageMaker displays the *Add index entry* dialog box with the *Cross-reference* radio button selected. Choose one of the options to the right of *Denoted by* and then click on the *X-ref* button.

213

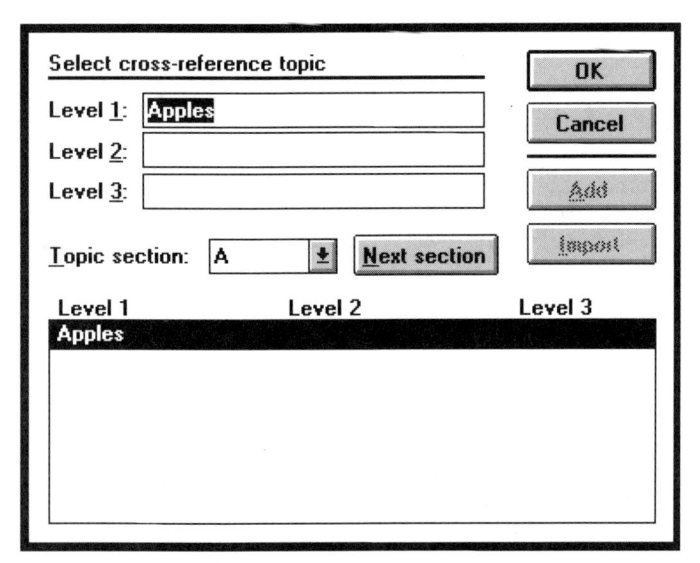

Figure 16. Search for the topic for which you need to cross-reference (in our example "Apples") using the *Topic section* drop-down list. Select the topic you want to cross reference ("Apples") and click on *OK* in the two dialog boxes to return to the *Show index* dialog box.

Figure 17. This dialog box now displays *Bananas*, cross-referenced to *Apples*. Click on *OK* once you have finished reviewing your index entries.

CREATING THE INDEX

Figure 18. Use the *Create index* command to generate the index, once you have entered, cross-referenced and edited all index entries as necessary. This activates the *Create index* dialog box.

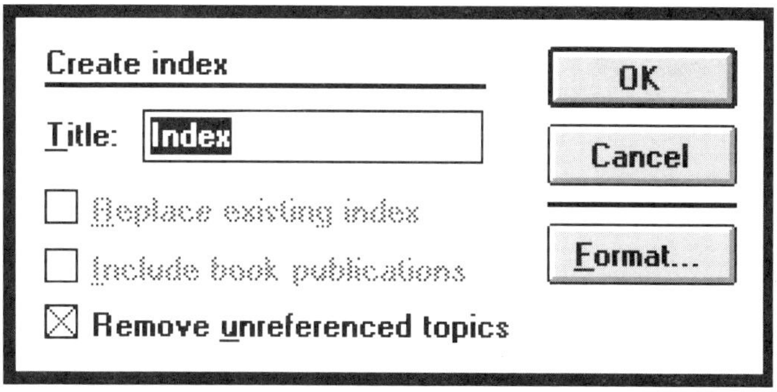

Chapter 16: Creating an Index

Figure 19. The default title shown here is *Index*. You can delete this and include your own—up to 30 characters. *Replace existing index* is unchecked only if this is the first index you have created. You may uncheck this if you wish to keep the existing index.

You can select the *Include book publications* option if this current publication contains a book list and you want the full book list index. Uncheck it if you want only the single publication index.

The *Remove unreferenced topics* option does not include any index items that do not have a page number or cross-reference.

Clicking on *OK* generates the index. Clicking the *Format* button activates the *Index format* dialog box.

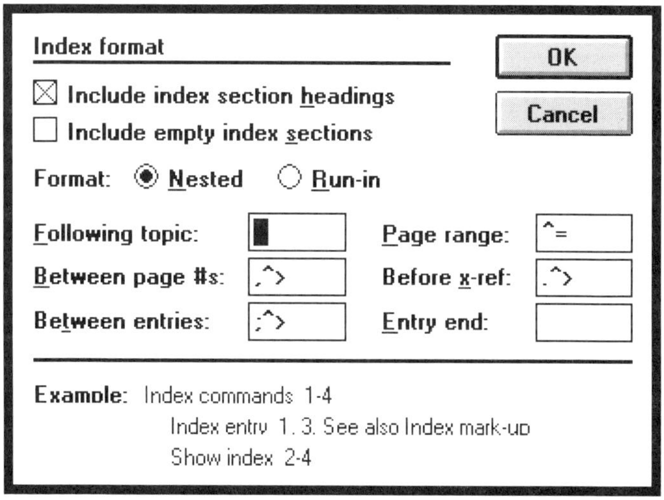

Figure 20. Use the *Index format* dialog box to determine:

- What sections and headings are included in the index.
- Whether the index format is a nested (indented entries) or run-in (entries in a single paragraph). Examples of the *Nested* or *Run-in* format are shown at the bottom of the dialog box as you choose each option.
- What characters separate index entries. More details of these are contained in Appendix A of the *PageMaker User Manual*.

215

Chapter 16: Creating an Index

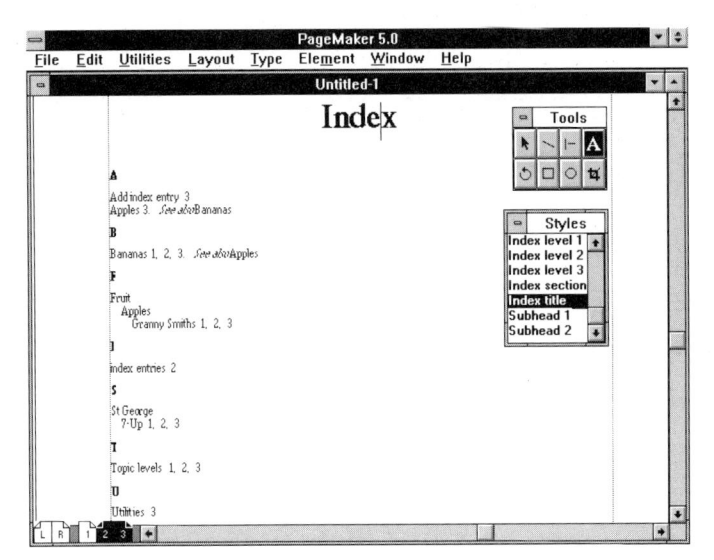

Figure 21. Once generated, you place the index text file on the page as you would any other text file.

You can modify the styles (which are generated by PageMaker) and the text as you would normally.

Utilities 17

Table Editor

Table Editor is a separate program to PageMaker. It enables you to create tables and place them into PageMaker.

STARTING TABLE EDITOR

Figure 1. To start Table Editor, locate the Table Editor icon in the Windows Program Manager, and double-click on it with your mouse.

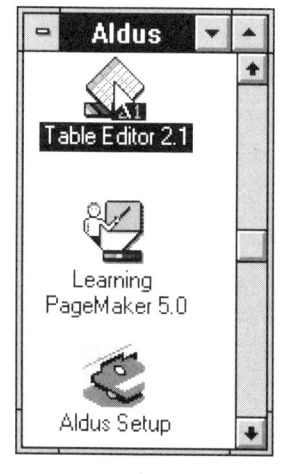

Figure 2. This is the start-up screen you see after launching the Table Editor.

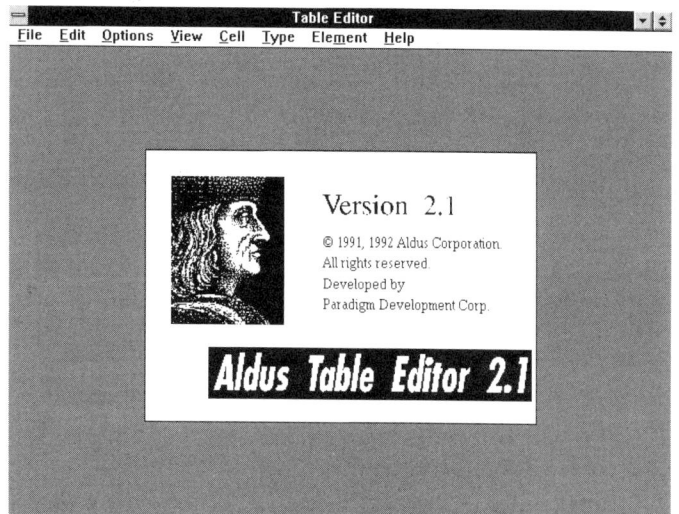

Chapter 17: Utilities

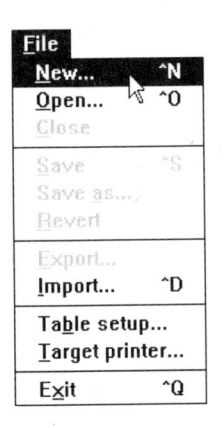

Figure 3. To create a new table, select *New* from the **File** menu. To open a previously saved Table Editor document, select *Open*.

Figure 4. This is the *Table setup* dialog box that appears after you select *New*. It is here that you initially define the number of columns and rows, and the size of your table. You can modify this later in a number of ways, including through the *Table setup* command in the **File** menu. Choose the options you need and click on *OK*.

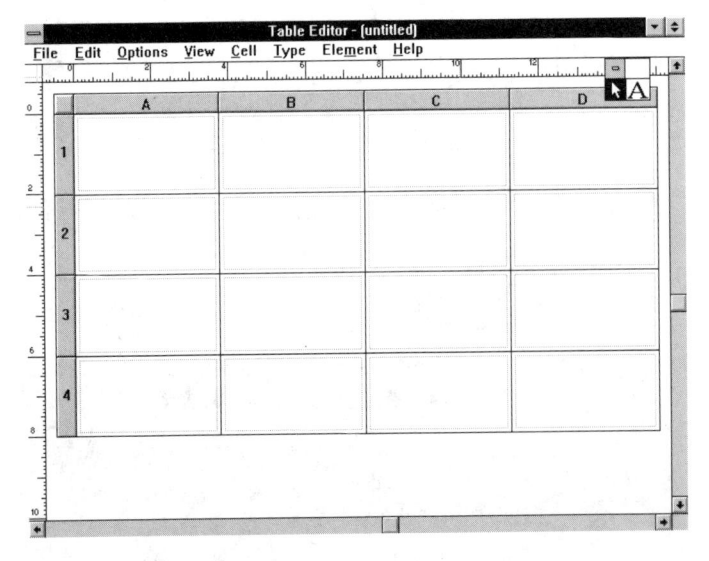

Figure 5. After selecting *OK* in the *Table setup* dialog box, this is how your table looks with the default settings.

Chapter 17: Utilities

TABLE MANIPULATION

Table Editor provides a wide range of features for entering text, formatting text, and changing cell, row, and column features.

ENTERING TEXT

Figure 6. To enter text, simply select the text tool (**A**), click the mouse inside the chosen cell, and start typing.

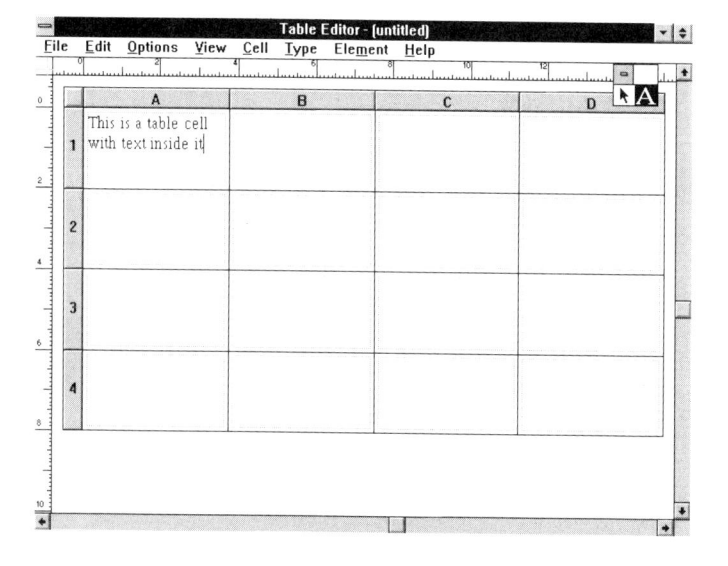

Figure 7. You can move from cell to cell when you are entering information into multiple cells in a number of ways:

1. Use the Tab key to move to the right.

2. Use the Shift+Tab keys to move to the left.

3. Use the Enter key to move downwards.

4. Use the mouse to move to any cell and click to insert text.

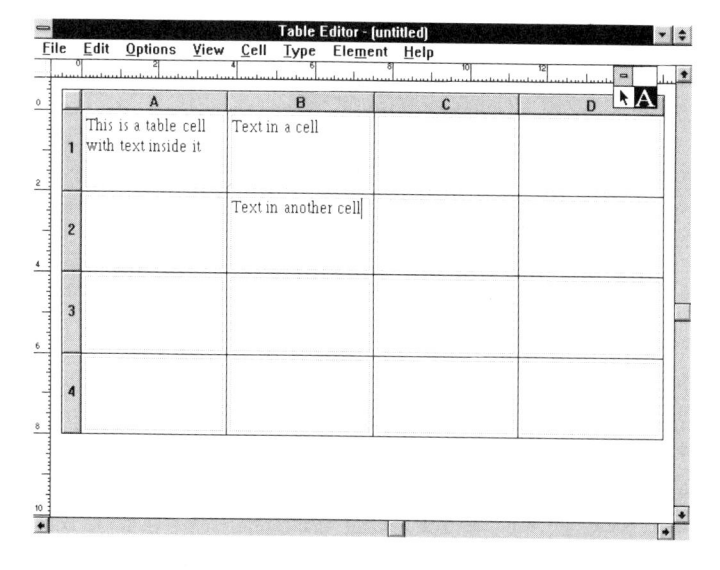

219

Chapter 17: Utilities

SELECTING CELLS WITH THE POINTER TOOL

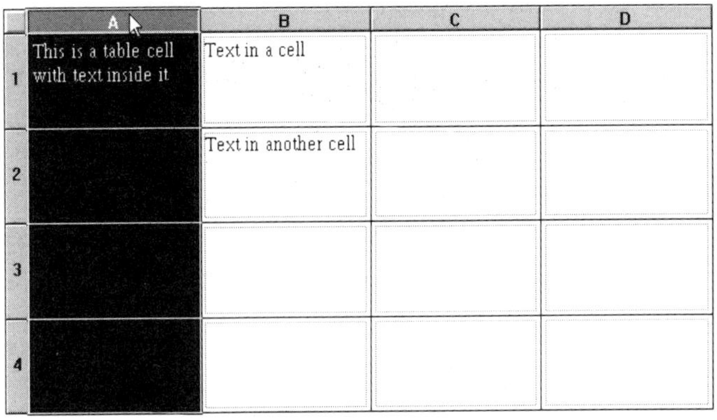

Figure 8. Select a whole column by clicking on its corresponding grid label letter, in this case A.

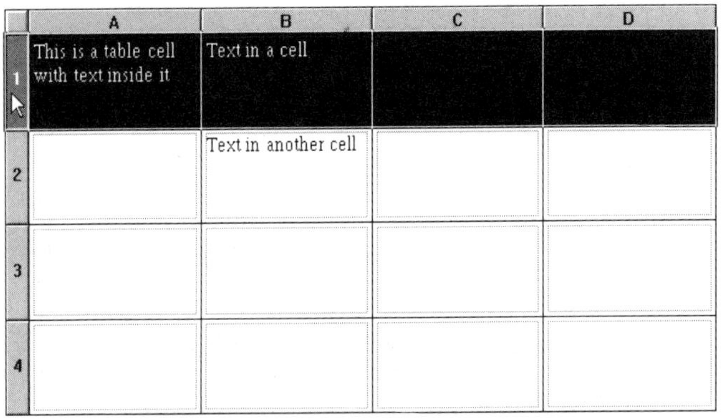

Figure 9. Select a whole row by clicking on its corresponding grid label number, in this case 1.

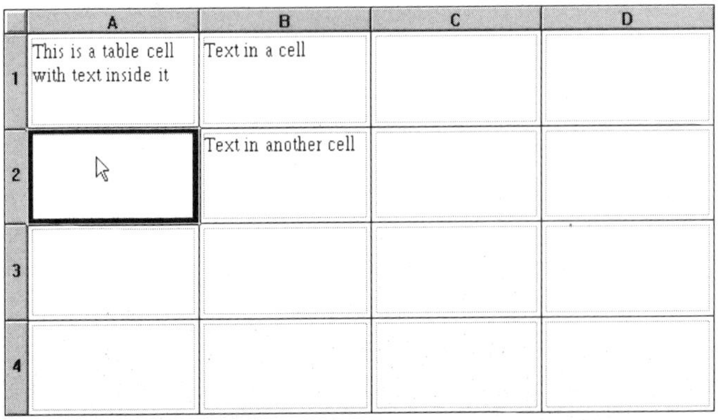

Figure 10. Select individual cells by clicking on the specific cell once with the mouse. This will not highlight the whole cell, only the border of the cell as you can see in this figure.

You can select the whole table by clicking on the button in the top-left corner of the table.

Chapter 17: Utilities

Figure 11. Select multiple cells by holding down the Shift key as you select the cells with the mouse or hold down the mouse button and drag the mouse over the cells you wish to select. In this case, Table Editor highlights the border of the first selected cell, and totally highlights the rest of the selected cells.

SELECTING CELLS WITH THE TEXT TOOL

Figure 12. With the text tool, you may select individual cells for formatting the text. As Table Editor limits each cell to one style of text, simply inserting the cursor is enough to select all the text in the cell.

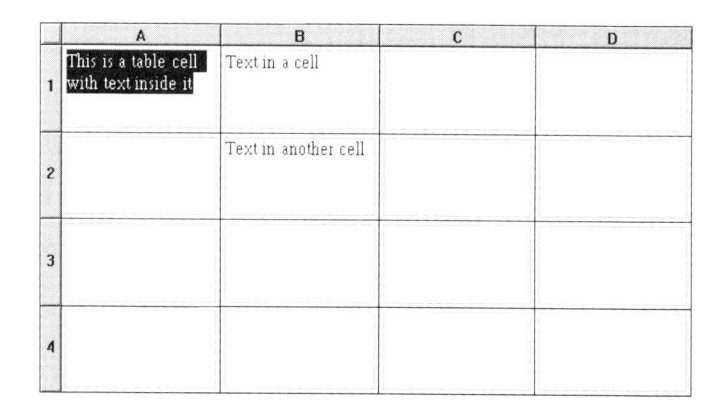

FORMATTING TEXT

Figure 13. To format text, you first select it. Once the text is selected, you can apply any of the text formatting options from the **Type** menu in the same way as you would within PageMaker. Here we are changing the point size of the selected text.

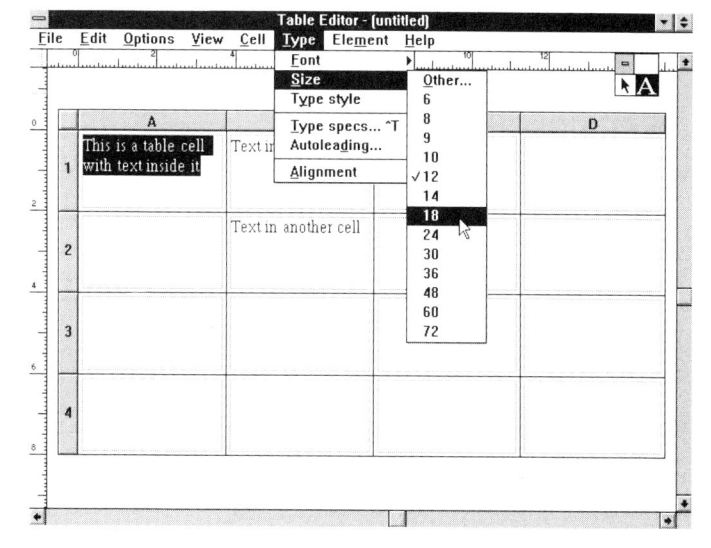

221

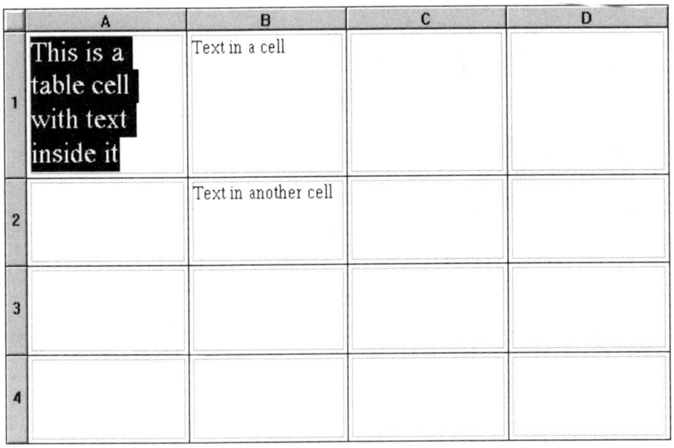

Chapter 17: Utilities

Figure 14. This shows the result of the change in point size.

You can also select text with the pointer tool to change its attributes.

RESIZING ROWS AND COLUMNS

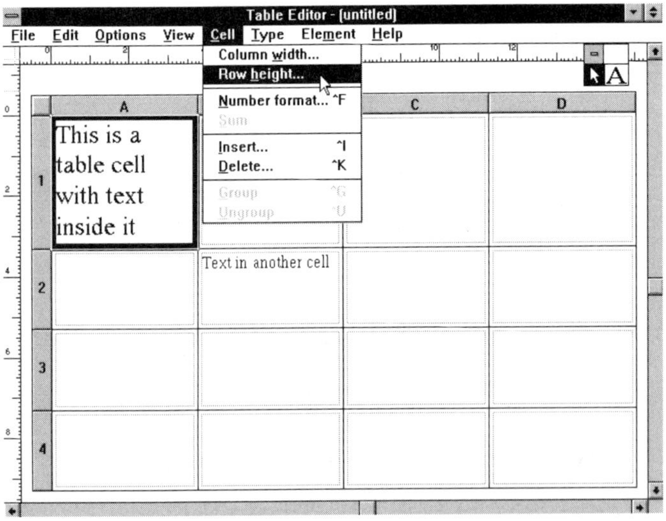

Figure 15. To change the height of a row, select a cell from that row and then select *Row height* from the **Cell** menu.

In this case we have selected the cell in the top left corner. You can use the pointer or text tool to select the cell.

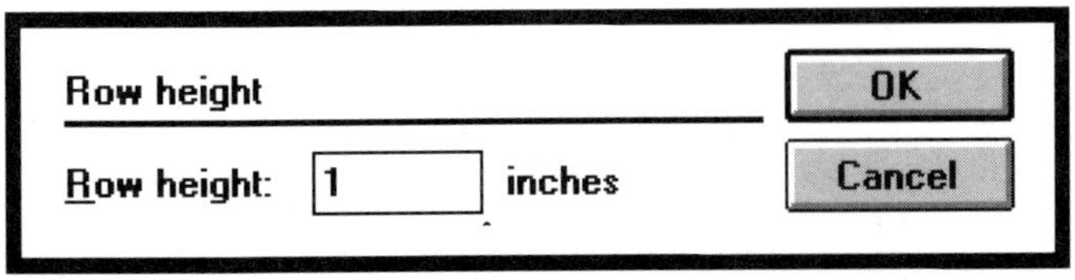

Figure 16. In the *Row height* dialog box, we changed the setting from 0.79 to 1 inch.

Figure 17. This is how the table now looks. You can change the width of columns using the same method as for rows, but choose *Column width* from the **Cell** menu.

Figure 18. You can resize rows or columns manually by placing the cursor between a column or row, as shown here, until a double-headed arrow appears. Hold the mouse down and move to a new position to resize the column (or row).

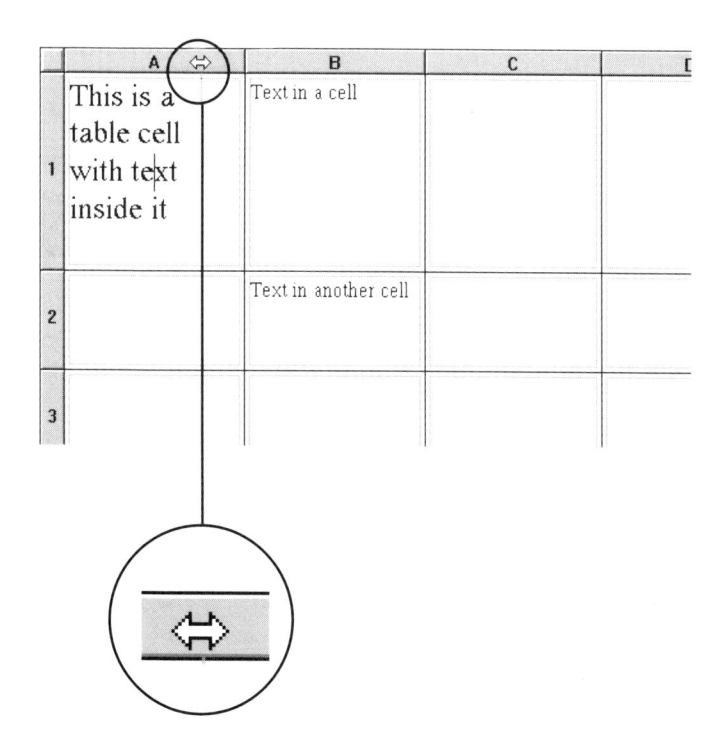

Chapter 17: Utilities

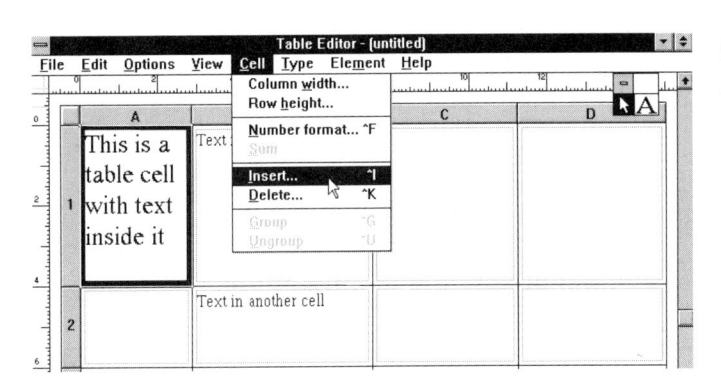

INSERTING ROWS AND COLUMNS

Figure 19. To insert a column or row, highlight a cell and then select *Insert* from the **Cell** menu.

Figure 20. This activates the *Insert* dialog box. This is where you choose to insert either a column or a row. A new row appears above the selected cell, and a new column appears to the left of the selected cell.

Figure 21. The new row appears as row 1 above the old one which is now row 2.

You can also add rows and columns using the *Table setup* command from the **File** menu.

224

DELETING ROWS AND COLUMNS

Figure 22. To delete rows and columns, use the *Delete* command from the **Cell** menu in the same way as you use the *Insert* command.

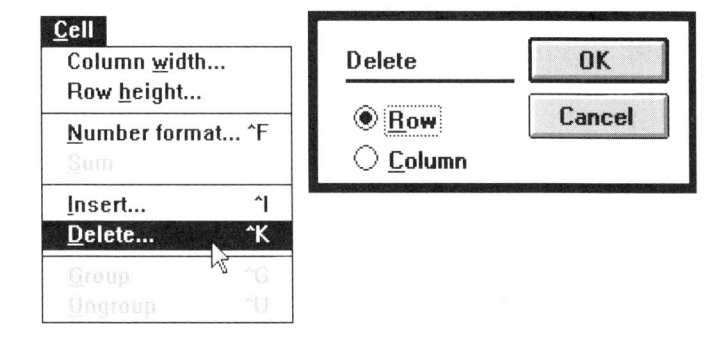

GROUPING CELLS

Figure 23. You can group cells together to create header rows of a table. Highlight, with the pointer tool, the cells you wish to group and select *Group* from the **Cell** menu. In this figure we selected the four cells across the top of the table.

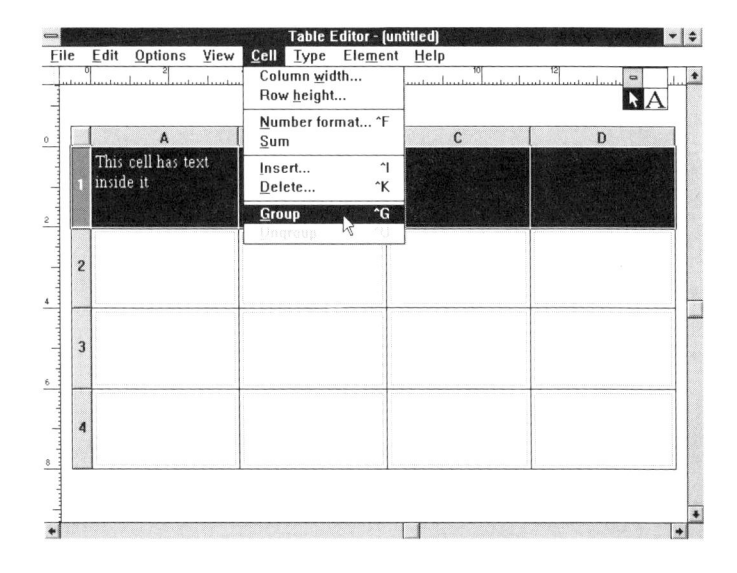

Figure 24. The new, larger cell is ready for you to format or enter more text.

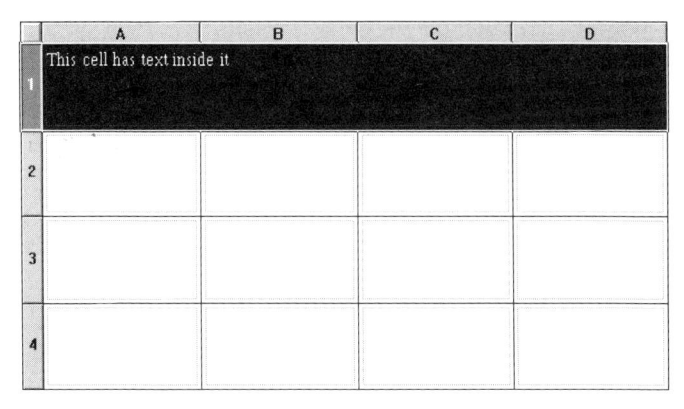

Chapter 17: Utilities

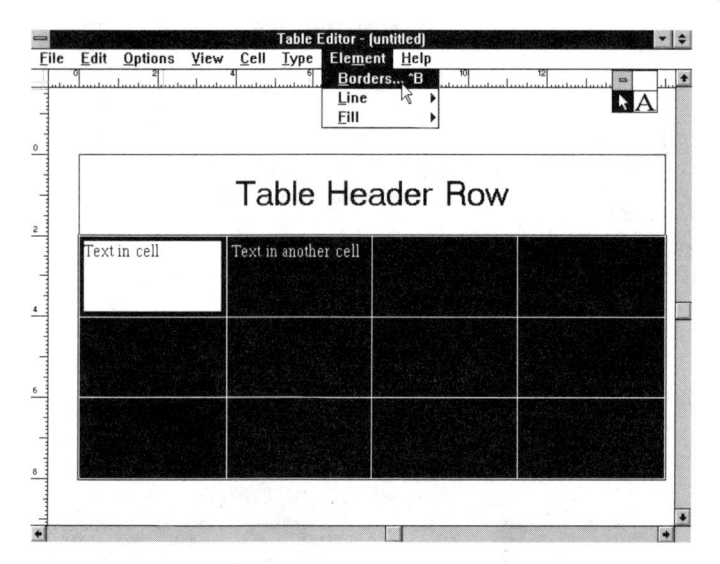

CHANGING LINE ATTRIBUTES

Figure 25. To apply a different line thickness to a table, select the cell or cells required. In this example, we have selected the whole table body, excluding the header row. Now, select *Borders* from the **Element** menu.

In this example of modifying line attributes, we first turned the *Grid lines* and *Grid labels* off in the **Options** menu.

Figure 26. In the Borders dialog box, select only the lines you wish to change. Because we don't want any interior vertical lines, we have selected *Verticals* and then the *None* choice in the *Line* option at the bottom of the *Borders* dialog box.

This selection changes the thickness of all vertical interior lines of selected cells to none, thus making them invisible.

226

Chapter 17: Utilities

Figure 27. This is how the table now looks.

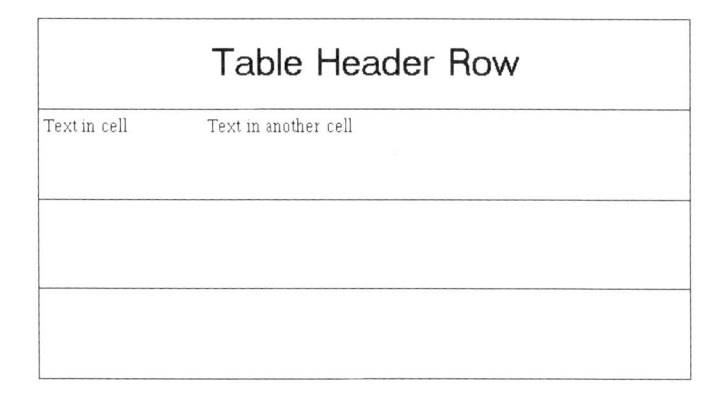

APPLYING SHADES

Figure 28. To shade a cell or cells, first select the required section of the table. Activate the *Fill* submenu from the **Element** menu and select the desired percentage (in our case 10%).

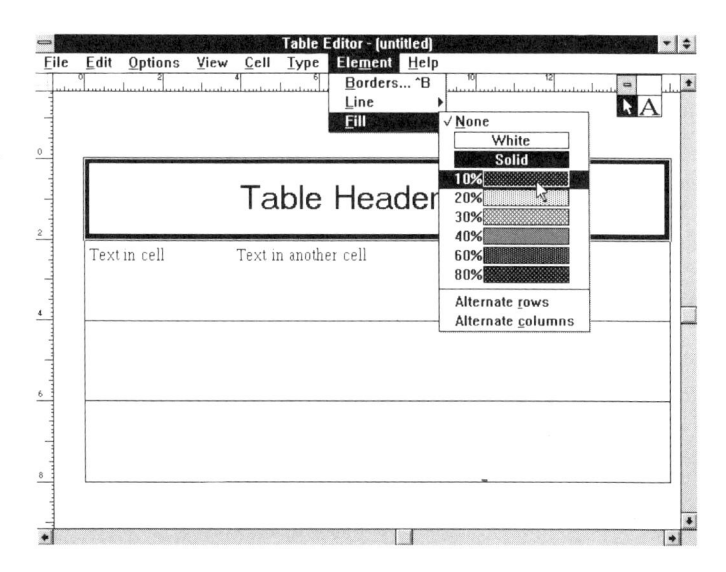

Figure 29. We have given the top row a 10% shade.

227

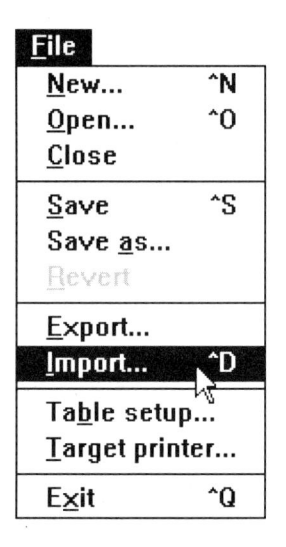

IMPORTING FILES INTO TABLE EDITOR

Figure 30. You can import text files from other programs into the Table Editor with the *Import* command from the **File** menu.

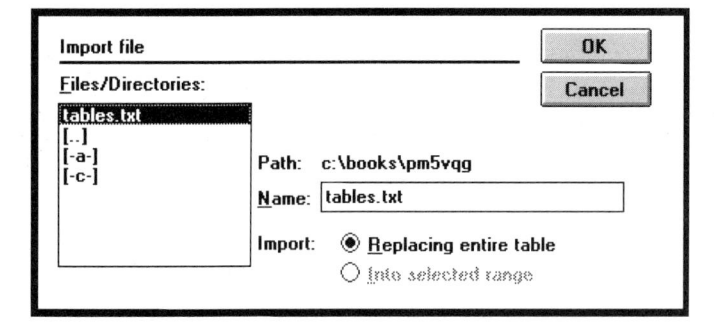

Figure 31. When the *Import file* dialog box appears, find the text file that you would like to import into your table. You can select the *Replacing entire table* option for the text to replace any text that is currently in the table. If you have a portion of the table selected, you can choose the *Into selected range* option to place the text in a specific part of the table.

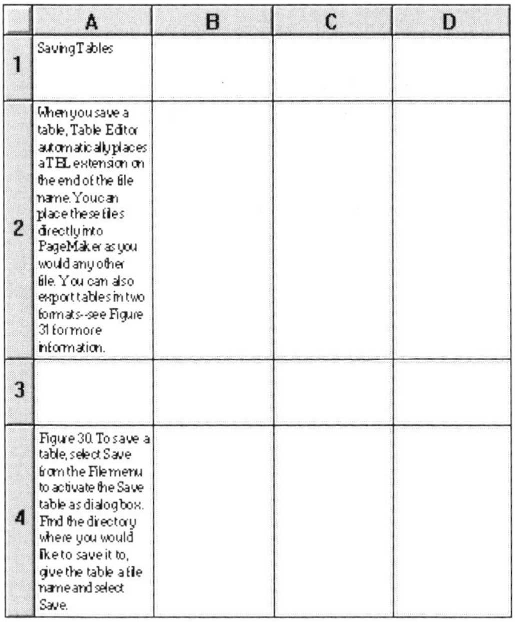

Chapter 17: Utilities

Figure 32. After you select *OK* in the *Import file* dialog box, Table Editor places the text in the table—each cell contains a paragraph of text or block of text that you have separated with a tab.

	A	B	C	D
1	SavingTables			
2	When you save a table, Table Editor automatically places a TBL extension on the end of the file name. You can place these files directly into PageMaker as you would any other file. You can also export tables in two formats–see Figure 31 for more information.			
3				
4	Figure 30. To save a table, select Save from the File menu to activate the Save table as dialog box. Find the directory where you would like to save it to, give the table a file name and select Save.			

SAVING TABLES

When you save a table, Table Editor automatically places a *tbl* extension on the end of the file name. You can place these files directly into PageMaker as you would any other file. You can also export tables in two formats.

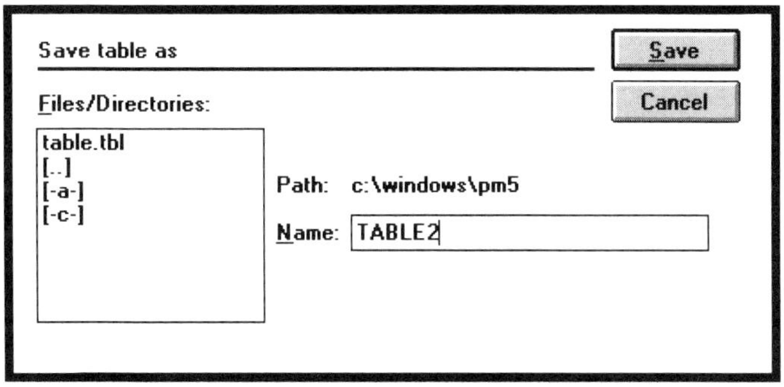

Figure 33. To save a table, select *Save* from the **File** menu to activate the *Save table as* dialog box. Find the directory where you would like to save it, give the table a file name, and select *Save*.

```
Save table as                          [ Save   ]
Files/Directories:                     [ Cancel ]
table.tbl
[..]        Path:  c:\windows\pm5
[-a-]
[-c-]       Name: TABLE2
```

229

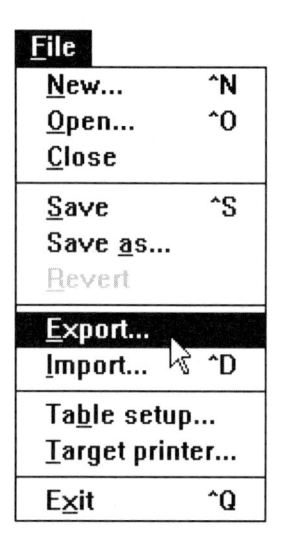

Exporting Files from Table Editor

Figure 34. To allow applications other than PageMaker to read your table file, you need to first export the table file from Table Editor.

Select *Export* from the **File** menu to activate the *Export to file* dialog box.

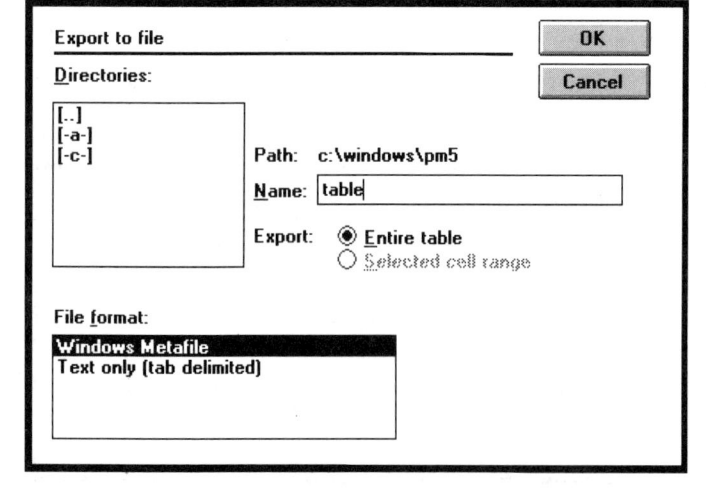

Figure 35. At the bottom of the dialog box you must select a *File format*. If you select the *Text only* option, Table Editor exports only the table text within the cells as a text file. The *Windows Metafile* format allows you to import the table into PageMaker or other applications as a graphics file.

You can also export parts of the table, after selecting the desired section of the table with the mouse, by choosing the *Selected cell range* option.

Name your file after you have selected the required options and click on *OK*. This file will then be saved to disk.

Chapter 17: Utilities

PLACING FILES IN PAGEMAKER

Figure 36. You can place tables into PageMaker in *Text only* or *Windows Metafile* formats. You can also place *tbl* files—Table Editor's native file format. You import tables in the same way as placing any text or graphics.

Open the PageMaker file in which you wish to place the table, then use the *Place* command to place the table file.

Figure 37. In the *Place document* dialog box, you can select any of the three table formats in which you can save a table —**wmf**, **tbl** or **txt**.

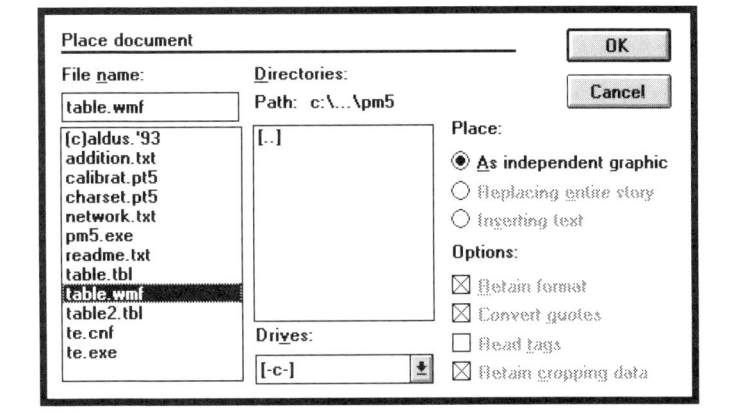

231

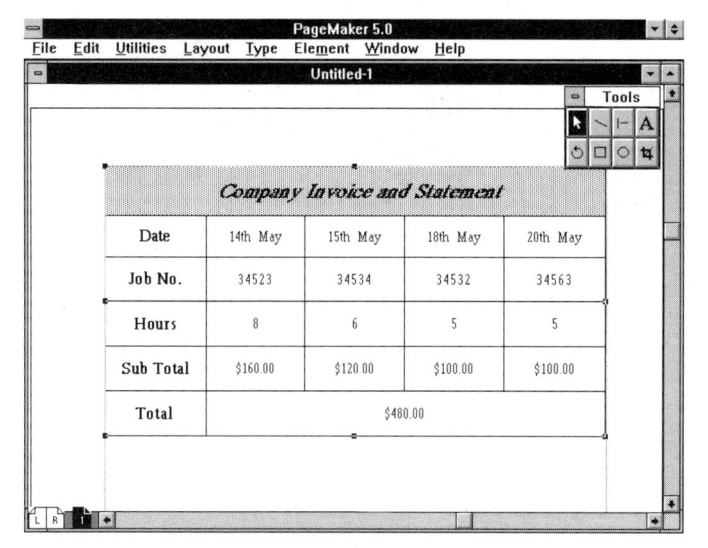

Figure 38. This is how a typical table file looks in PageMaker when you save it in the *Windows Metafile* format.

Because it is a graphic, you can resize, move and crop it in exactly the same way as you would any graphic.

You can also copy Table Editor files to the clipboard and then paste them directly into a PageMaker publication.

EDITING AN IMPORTED TABLE

It is best to import a table into PageMaker in its native file format—**tbl**. With this format you can edit the table easily by holding down the Ctrl key and triple-clicking on the table to reactivate the original table editor file. After you have edited the table, close the file and save the changes. To update these changes in the PageMaker file, activate the *Links* dialog box from the **File** menu, select the table file name in the list, and click on the *Update* button. See Chapter 3 for more information on linking files.

Chapter 17: Utilities

DICTIONARY EDITOR

The Dictionary Editor is another separate utility that you can use to add, edit, find and hyphenate words in PageMaker's dictionary. PageMaker uses the dictionary for spell checking and hyphenating (see Chapter 4, **Text** for more information on spell checking and hyphenation). You can also create your own dictionary.

STARTING DICTIONARY EDITOR

Figure 39. To start Dictionary Editor, locate the Dictionary Editor in the Windows Program Manager, and double-click on it with your mouse.

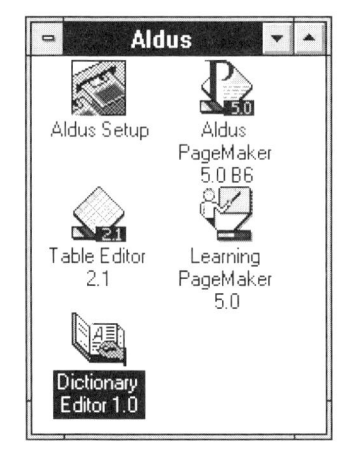

Figure 40. This is the dialog box that appears after activating the Dictionary Editor.

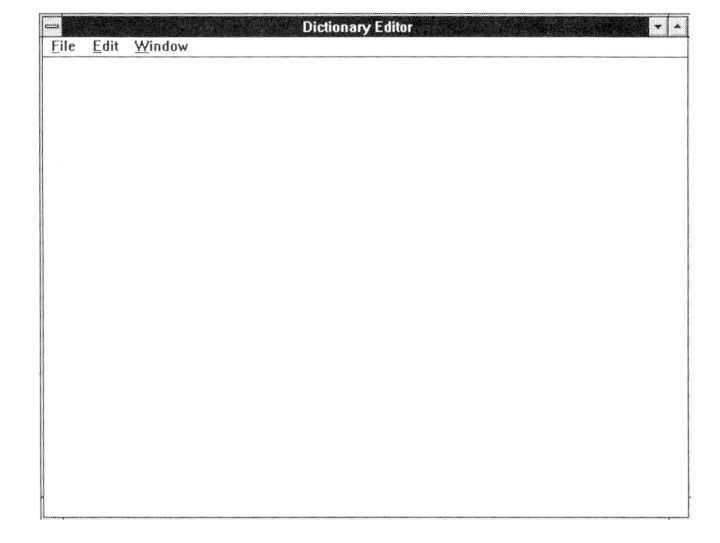

233

OPENING AND CREATING DICTIONARIES

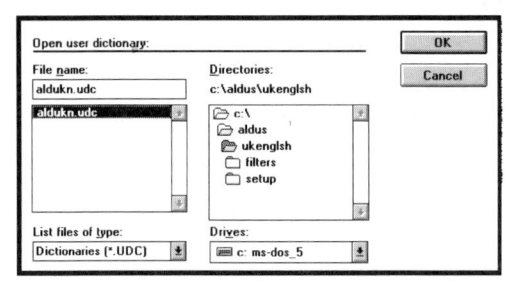

Figure 41. To open an existing dictionary, select *Open* from the **File** menu and choose the dictionary you want to edit. To create a new dictionary, select *New* from the **File** menu.

IMPORTING TEXT FILES

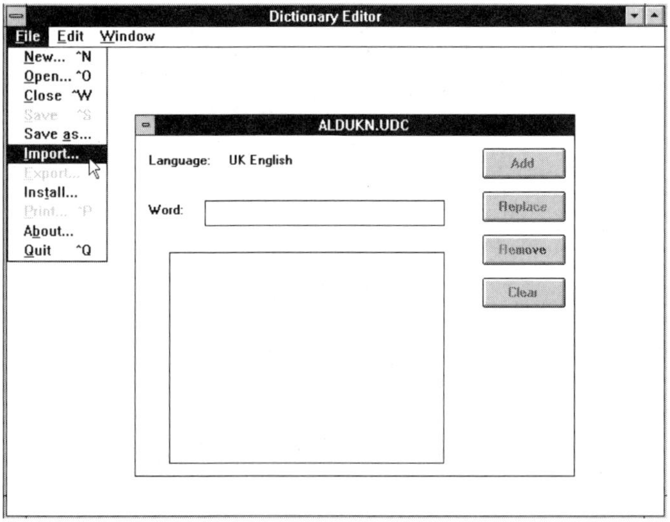

Figure 42. After you have selected a dictionary, this dialog box appears. If you have not added any words to the user dictionary through the *Hyphenation* or the *Spelling* commands, this dialog box will be empty. You can however add words, or import text-only files containing a list of words separated by carriage returns, tabs, or spaces. To do this select *Import* from the **File** menu.

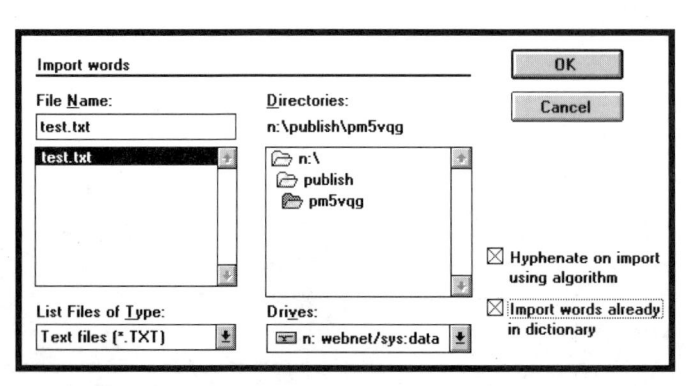

Figure 43. When the *Import file* dialog box appears, find and double-click on the text file you want to import.

Chapter 17: Utilities

Figure 44. When you return to the *Dictionary Editor* dialog box, you will see a list of words in the word list.

SELECTING AND EDITING WORDS

Figure 45. To select a word from the list, double-click on it. It then appears in the *Word* edit box. You can then make any spelling or hyphenation changes in this edit box (see Chapter 4, **Text** for more information on hyphenating words). To save your changes click on the *Replace* button. Clicking on the *Clear* button removes the word and the changes from the *Word* edit box.

REMOVING WORDS

To remove a word, double-click on it and click on the *Remove* button.

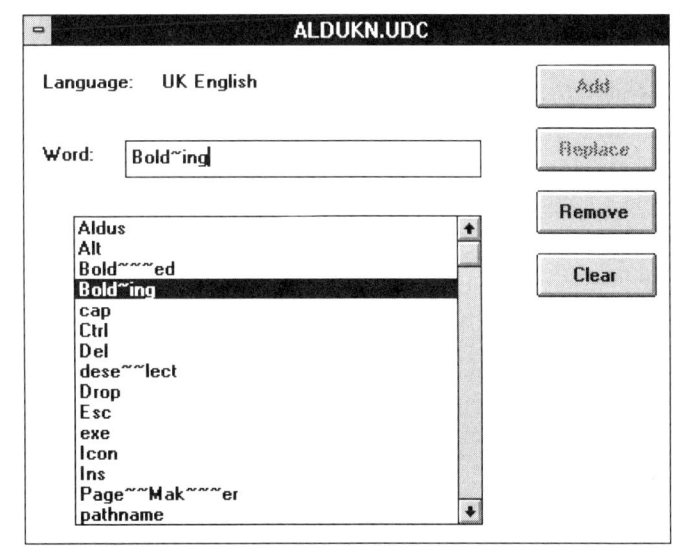

235

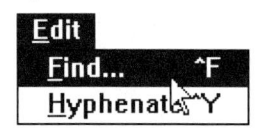

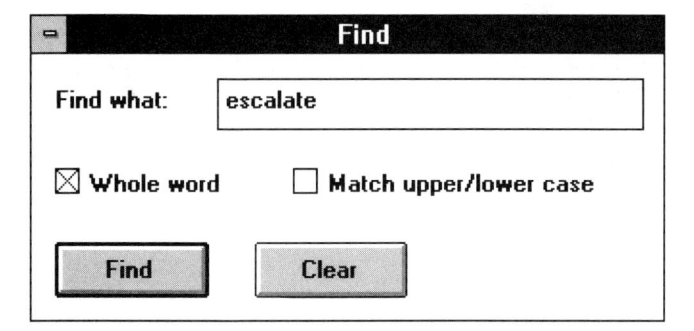

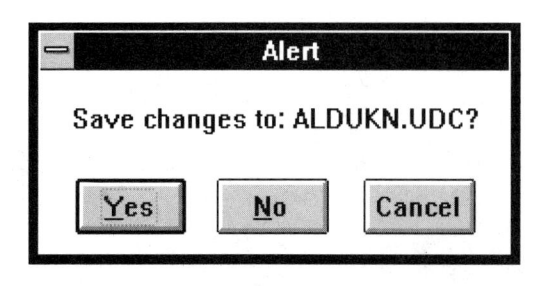

FINDING WORDS

Figure 46. To find a word without having to scroll, select *Find* from the **Edit** menu. Type the word into the *Find what* edit box and click on the *Find* button.

ADDING SINGLE WORDS

Figure 47. Type the word you want to add into the *Word* edit box with the exact spelling and capitalization and click on the *Add* button. PageMaker adds this word to the list.

EXITING DICTIONARY EDITOR

Figure 48. You can leave the Dictionary Editor using the *Quit* command in the **File** menu. If you have not saved the changes you have made, you are prompted to save changes to the current dictionary.

Index

A

accessing multiple file windows, 17
Add Cont'd line addition, 134
adding files to a library, 26
adjusting text blocks, 76
Aldus Additions, 133
    Acquire image, 133
    Add Cont'd line, 134
    Balance columns, 134
    Build booklet, 135
    Bullets and numbering, 140
    Create color library, 142
    Create keyline, 144
    Display pub info, 145
    Display textblock info, 146
    Display story info, 146
    Drop cap, 146
    Edit tracks, 147
    Expert kerning, 149
    Find overset text, 150
    List styles used, 150
    Open stories, 151
    Open template, 151
    PS Group it, 152
    PS Ungroup it, 153
    Printer styles, 153
    Running headers/footers, 156
    Run script, 158
    Sort pages, 159
    Traverse textblocks, 161
    VP converter, 162
Alignment command, 58
application defaults, 167
applying color, 180
arranging windows, 18
    Cascade command, 18
    Tile command, 18
As new story option, 20
Autoflow command, 23
Autoleading option, 53
automatic page numbering, 86
automatic text flow, 21

B

Balance columns addition, 134
Book command, 197
Book list
    adding to, 198
    Book dialog box, 198
    moving, 198
    Print all publications in book option, 191
    removing, 198
Build booklet addition, 135, 136
    creep, 138
    Layout option, 137
    preparing your publication, 136
Bullets and numbering addition, 140
    removing bullets and numbering, 142

C

Cascade command, 18
Change command, 71
changing views, 14
    Actual Size view, 14
    Fit in Window view, 14
    View command, 14
Clear command, 99
color, 142, 179
    applying colors, 180
    CMYK, 184
    color libraries, 185
    copying colors, 180
    editing colors, 183, 186
    fill, 181
    HLS, 184
    knockout, 182
    line, 181
    model type, 183

Index

Overprint option, 182
Pantone, 183
process colors, 179
removing, 180
RGB, 184
spot colors, 179
tint, 186
type option, 183
Color palette, 180, 181, 186
colors
   copying, 187
   creating, 183
   editing, 187
   removing, 187
column guides, 29
Column guides command, 29
constrained line, 91
Control palette, 12, 60, 102, 176
   Align-to-grid button, 67
   alignment, 66
   Apply button, 62, 104
   applying styles, 177
   baseline, 64
   Character view, 61
   creating styles, 178
   cropping graphics, 127
   cursor position, 66
   font, 62
   grid size, 66
   Horizontal reflection button, 110
   indent, 66
   kerning, 64
   keyboard shortcuts, 69
   leading, 63
   moving and resizing graphics, 107
   nudge buttons, 68
   Palette view buttons, 62
   paragraph style, 65
   Paragraph view, 64, 176
   Percent scaling, 109
   Proportional scaling, 106
   Proxy, 83, 104, 107, 109
      reference point, 108
   reflecting graphics, 110
   removing transformations, 83, 111
   rotating graphics, 109
   Set-width option, 63
   Sizing and Percentage Scaling option, 105
   skewing, 110
   Space-before and Space-after options, 66
   Story editor, 73
   Text palette, 61
   transforming graphics, 107
   type style, case and position, 62
   using the Control palette, 67
   Vertical reflection button, 110
Control palette, 80, 102, 126
   text, 60
   tracking, 63
Convert quotes option, 20
Copy command, 43, 99
Copy master guides command, 90
copy text, 41
Create color library addition, 142
Create index command, 214
Create keyline addition, 144
Create TOC command, 204
creating and opening a library, 25
cropping graphics, 127
cropping tool, 118
Cut command, 42, 99
Cut, Copy, and Paste commands, 99

D

defaults, 165
Define colors command, 183
Define printer styles option, 155
Define styles command, 170
delete text, 41
deleting headers/footers, 158
Dictionary Editor, 233
   editing words, 235
   finding words, 236
   removing words, 235
   single words, 236
Display master items command, 88
Display pub info addition, 145
Display story info addition, 146
Display textblock info addition, 146
drawing graphics, 92

Index

drawing tools, 91
Drop cap addition, 146

E

Edit layout command, 70
Edit menu, 42
Edit original command, 38
Edit story command, 70
edit text, 41
Edit tracks addition, 147
   creating a proof, 149
Element menu, 95
ellipse tool, 91
Encapsulated Postscript, 152
Expert kerning addition, 149
Export command, 59
exporting text, 59
   export tags, 59
   file format, 59

F

Fill and line command, 97, 182
Fill command, 96
Find command, 71
Find overset text addition, 150
Font command, 45
footers, 156

G

Graphics
   constraining, 101
   Control palette, 102
     height, 105
     width, 105
     X and Y coordinates, 105
   Cut, Copy, and Paste commands, 99
   defaults, 100
     fill and line, 101
   Fill and line command, 97
   Fill command, 96, 100
   hollow fill, 98
   layering, 98
   Line command, 95, 100
   line style, 96
   Multiple paste command, 99, 100
   percent scaling, 109
   reflecting, 110
   removing transformations, 111
   rotating, 109
   rotation tool, 101
   rounded corners, 92
   Send to back command, 98
   skewing, 110
   solid fill, 98
   transforming graphics, 107

H

headers, 156
Hyphenation command, 56, 234
   hyphenation zone, 57
   Limit consecutive hyphens to option, 57
   Manual only option, 57
   Manual plus algorithm option, 57
   Manual plus dictionary option, 57

I

Image control command, 125
Imported graphics, 113
   As independent graphic option, 123
   Contrast, 125
   Control palette, 126
   cropping, 118, 127
   cropping tool, 118
   cursor shapes, 115
   custom wrap, 121
   formats, 113
   image control, 125
   independent graphics, 124
   inline graphics, 123
   irregular wrap-around, 121, 122
   lightness, 126
   linking, 117
   loading, 115
   Multiple paste command, 126
   OLE, 117
   printing parameters, 126
   proportional resizing, 116

Index

regular wraparound, 120
Replacing entire graphic option, 117
Replacing existing graphics option, 117
Retain cropping data option, 117
text wrap, 120
Wrapping text, 119
Include in table of contents option, 204
Indents/tabs command, 53
   Leader option, 55
Indents/tabs dialog box, 53
independent graphics, 115, 124
Index entry command, 211
indexing, 197, 207
   Create index command, 214
   creating, 214
   cross-referencing, 212, 213
   edit entries, 213
   Include book publications option, 215
   multiple index entries, 210
   primary entry, 209
   Replace existing index option, 215
   secondary entry, 209
   Show index command, 213
   Sort, 209
   Topic, 208, 211
   topic levels, 208
   topic section, 211
inline graphics, 115, 124
   As inline graphic option, 123
Insert object command, 37
installation, 1
internal graphics
   constraining graphics, 101
   drawing graphics, 91
   editing graphics, 99
   graphic defaults, 100
   moving graphics, 94
   multiple graphics, 93
   resizing graphics, 94
   selecting graphics, 93
irregular wrap-around, 122

K

knockout, 182

L

Layout view, 69, 70
leading, 53
Leading command, 46
left and right master pages, 85
Library palette, 12, 25
   adding and editing item information, 27
   closing, 29
   Display both command, 29
   Display images command, 29
   Display names command, 29
   Edit item after adding command, 29
   item information, 26
   Options menu, 29
   placing a library palette object, 27
   removing items, 28
   searching for items, 28
   Show all items command, 29
Line command, 95
line tool, 91
Link info command, 35
Link options, 33, 36
Link options command, 35
linking files, 33, 34
   Edit original command
      OLE, 38
   Insert object command
      OLE, 37
   OLE, 33
   OLE-embedding, 37
   Paste command, 36
   Paste link command, 36
   Paste special command, 36, 37
   updating files, 34
links, 232
Links command, 34
List styles used addition, 150

M

manual text flow, 21
margin guides, 29
master page guides, 87
master pages, 85

Index

column guides, 87
left and right master pages, 85
removing master page items, 88
minimize, maximize and restore buttons, 9
minimizing and maximizing publication windows, 19
moving text blocks, 74
Multiple paste command, 44, 99, 100, 126

N

New command, 6, 15
nudge buttons, 68

O

Open command, 6, 15
Open stories addition, 151
Open template addition, 151
opening multiple publications, 16
Orphan control option, 50
Overprint option, 182

P

Page numbering, 87
Page setup, 7
PageMaker 5.0 Scripting Language, 158
PageMaker defaults
    application defaults, 165
    publication defaults, 167
PageMaker screen, 8
    master page icons, 9
    menu bar, 9
    page area, 11
    page number icons, 9
    rulers, 10
    scroll bars, 10
    title bar, 9
    toolbox, 13
Pantone color, 183, 185
Paragraph command, 49
    Alignment option, 49
    Autoleading option, 53
    Dictionary option, 50
    Leading option, 53

Orphan control option, 50
    Spacing attributes option, 52
    Widow control option, 50
paragraph rules, 51
    Align to grid option, 52
    Options button, 52
Paste command, 36, 43, 99
Paste link command, 36
Paste special command, 37
Place command, 19, 73, 115
placing files, 19
placing graphic files, 24
placing text files, 20
Print command, 189
Print document dialog box, 190
print file information, 154
Printer styles addition, 153
printing
    color, 195
    color separations, 195
    orientation, 191
    Page setup command, 189
    PostScript errors, 194
    Print dialog box, 189
    printer settings, 192
    printing graphics, 193
    screen ruling, 196
    thumbnails, 192
    tiling, 192
process colors, 179
Proxy, 104
PS Group it addition, 152
PS Ungroup it addition, 153

R

rectangle tool, 91
reflecting graphics, 110
reflecting text, 83
Remove transformation command, 83, 111
Replacing entire story option, 20
Replacing existing graphics option, 117
resizing text blocks, 75
Retain cropping data option, 20
Retain format option, 20

241

Index

rotating graphics, 109
rotating text, 80
rotation tool, 81, 91, 101
    rotation lever, 102
    starburst cursor, 102
Rounded corners command, 92
Run script addition, 158
    PageMaker 5.0 Scripting Language, 158
Running headers/footers addition, 156

S

Save As command, 31
    creating a copy, 32
Save command, 31
saving publications, 31
    compressing files, 32
Select all command, 42, 93, 99
Send to back command, 98
Set width command, 46
Show index command, 213
Size command, 45
skewing graphics, 110
skewing text, 82
Sort pages addition, 159
spelling, 234
Spelling command, 72
spot colors, 179
starting PageMaker, 6
Story editor, 69
    accessing Story editor, 69
    Change command, 71
    Close story command, 70
    Control palette, 73
    Display style names, 69
    Find command, 71
    Layout view, 69
    Spelling command, 72
story info, addition, 146
Style palette, 169
Styles, 169
    Applying, 169, 177
    Control palette, 176
    copying, 175
    creating, 170, 178

    editing, 172
    Hyphenation option, 172
    importing, 176
    Indents/tabs option, 171
    Paragraph specifications, 171
    Paragraph view, 176
    removing, 173
    Type specifications, 171

T

Table Editor
    borders, 226
    deleting rows/columns, 225
    exporting from, 230
    formatting text, 221
    grouping cells, 225
    inserting rows/columns, 224
    line attributes, 226
    moving between cells, 219
    resizing rows/columns, 222
    selecting cells, 220
    shading cells, 227
    starting, 217
    Table setup dialog box, 218
    text entry, 219
Table of contents, 197
    book list, 204
    Create TOC command, 204
    creating, 204
    Include book publications option, 205
    Include in table of contents option, 204
    Replace existing table of contents option, 205
    TOC styles, 206
Table setup command, 218
tables, 217
    changing line attributes, 226
    column width, 223
    Delete command, 225
    deleting rows and columns, 225
    editing an imported table, 232
    entering text, 219
    exporting files, 230
    file format, 230
    formatting text, 221

Index

Grid labels command, 226
Grid lines command, 226
Group command, 225
grouping cells, 225
importing files, 228
Insert command, 224
inserting rows and columns, 224
moving around a table, 219
pasting tables, 232
Replacing entire table option, 228
resizing columns, 222
resizing rows, 222
row height, 222
saving, 229
selecting cells, 220
shading cells, 227
templates, 129, 151
   As independent graphic option, 132
   Copy option, 130
   creating templates, 129
   extension, 130
   graphic placeholders, 131
   Inserting text, 131
   opening, 130
   Original option, 130
   Replacing entire graphic option, 132
   Replacing entire story option, 131
   Replacing selected text option, 131
   replacing text, 130
   text placeholders, 131
   using templates, 130
text blocks, 74
   manipulating, 74
   rotating text
      Control palette, 80
Text blocks
   adjusting, 76
   losing text, 77
   reflecting text, 83
   rotating text, 80
   Rotation tool, 81
   skewing text, 82
   threading text, 79
   unthreading text, 78
Text wrap command, 119

textblock info, addition, 146
threading text, 79
Tile command, 18
toolbox, 13, 91
   constrained line tool, 13
   cropping tool, 13
   ellipse tool, 13
   line tool, 13
   pointer tool, 13
   rectangle tool, 13
   rotation tool, 13
   text tool, 13
Track command, 46, 147
transforming text, 80
Traverse textblocks addition, 161
Type menu, 44
Type specifications dialog box, 47
Type specs command, 47
Type style command, 47

U

unthreading text, 78
using the Control palette, 67

V

VP converter addition, 162

W

Widow control option, 50

243

More from Peachpit Press...

101 Windows Tips and Tricks
Jesse Berst and Scott Dunn
This power-packed, user-friendly survival guide gives you power-user tips to make Windows faster, easier, and more fun. Icons and illustrations lead your eye to the key points, and friendly explanations get you up to speed in a hurry. *(216 pages)*

CorelDRAW 3: Visual QuickStart Guide
Webster & Associates
This is a highly visual tour of CorelDRAW, with graphics and screen shots that demonstrate how to use the Draw, Chart, Show, and Photo-Paint modules of the package. This book is so easy to read that you'll be able to enjoy using Corel's versatile features right away! *(400 pages)*

Desktop Publishing Secrets
Robert Eckhardt, Bob Weibel, and Ted Nace
This is a compilation of hundreds of the best desktop publishing tips from five years of *Publish* magazine. The tips cover all the major desktop publishing software and hardware products, including Ventura Publisher, PageMaker, WordPerfect, CorelDRAW, Windows, PostScript, fonts, laser printers, clip art, and more. *(550 pages)*

Everyone's Guide to Successful Publications
Elizabeth Adler
This comprehensive reference book pulls together all the information essential to developing and producing printed marketing materials. Packed with ideas, practical advice, and hundreds of photographs and illustrations, it discusses planning the printed piece, writing strong copy, basic design, desktop publishing, preparation for printing, and distribution. *(412 pages)*

Jargon
Robin Williams
This friendly, informative book is a comprehensive guide to current computer terminology and culture. It explains what the terms mean, and then gives useful background information related to the subject. *Example*: the entry for "reboot" defines the term, and then tells both Mac and PC users how to reboot their machines. Often humorous, always helpful, and essential for every computer user's library. *(688 pages)*

The Little DOS 6 Book
Kay Yarborough Nelson
A quick and accessible guide to DOS 6. This book is packed with plenty of tips as well as an easy-to-use "cookbook" section on DOS commands. It also covers DOS basics, working with files and directories, disk management, and more. *(232 pages)*

The Little Windows Book, 3.1 Edition
Kay Yarborough Nelson
This second edition of Peachpit's popular book will get you acquainted with Windows quickly. Topics include switching between programs, using the Program and File Managers, working with fonts, and troubleshooting printing problems. Each chapter includes a handy summary chart of keyboard shortcuts and quick tips. *(144 pages)*

The Little WordPerfect for Windows Book
Kay Yarborough Nelson
This book gives you the basic skills you need to create simple documents and get familiar with WordPerfect's new Windows interface. It also covers more advanced topics, such as formatting pages, working with blocks of text, and using different fonts. Special features include WordPerfect's new mail merge, tables, equations, indexes, and footnotes. *(200 pages)*

Mastering CorelDRAW 3
Chris Dickman
Packed with field-tested tutorials, this book leads you through the inner workings of this top-rated graphics program. In addition to teaching Corel's sophisticated drawing and paint tools, the book also covers slide creation, scanners, sign making, using service bureaus, and working with other software. Included are two disks containing Windows utilities, CorelDRAW templates, and 26 Castcraft fonts. *(600 pages)*

PageMaker 5 for Windows: Visual QuickStart Guide
Webster and Associates
Provides a fast, highly visual introduction to desktop publishing in PageMaker 5 for Windows. Packed with hundreds of illustrations, the book shows how to set up a publication, work with text, import graphics, use Aldus Additions, and more. *(256 pages)*

The PC is not a typewriter
Robin Williams
PC users can now learn Robin Williams's secrets for creating beautiful type. Here are the principles behind the techniques for professional typesetting, including punctuation, leading, special characters, kerning, fonts, justification, and more. *(96 pages)*

The QuarkXPress Book, Windows Edition
David Blatner and Bob Weibel
This best-selling guide, coveted by knowledgeable Quark users, is now available in the Windows edition. Better than the user manual, this book teaches you how to work with Quark's sophisticated type tools, import graphics, modify pictures, work with color, prepare files for a service bureau, and more. The inside cover features three panels of useful keyboard shortcuts. *(576 pages)*

The Underground Guide to Laser Printers
Editorial Staff of The Flash
This book shows how to save hundreds of dollars in laser printer supplies, repairs, maintenance, and upgrades; how to get the best quality and productivity out of your printer; how to troubleshoot printing problems; and how to push the limits of your printer with special techniques for creating negatives, overheads, separations, and iron-on transfers. *(176 pages)*

Ventura Tips and Tricks, 3rd Edition
Ted Nace and Daniel Will-Harris
This book was described by Ventura President John Meyer as "the most complete reference for anyone serious enough about using Ventura." Packed with inside information, speed-up tips, special tricks for reviving a crashed chapter, ways to overcome memory limitations, and more Features a directory of over 700 products and resources that enhance Ventura's performance. *(790 pages)*

The Windows 3.1 Bible
Fred Davis
Compiled by one of America's leading Windows experts, this book is a wall-to-wall compendium of tips, tricks, warnings, shortcuts, reviews, and resources that will inform, entertain, and empower Windows users of every ability level. It details the software's general principles, such as managing programs and files, multi-tasking, and working with fonts. Thoroughly indexed, the book also contains information on how to install and configure Windows 3.1 for optimal performance. *(1,154 pages)*

The Windows 3.1 Font Book
David Angell and Brent Heslop
This book is the first hands-on font guide for Windows users. It explains managing, choosing, and using fonts to enhance all kinds of documents, with instructions for working with TrueType and PostScript font manager programs. Included is a comprehensive listing of font vendors and over 100 font samples. *(184 pages)*

WordPerfect: Desktop Publishing in Style, 2nd Edition
Daniel Will-Harris
Peachpit's popular guide to producing documents with WordPerfect 5.1 or 5.0 opens with a simple tutorial and proceeds through 20 sample documents, each complete with all keystroke instructions. Humorous and insightful, this book is an asset to any WordPerfect user's library. *(650 pages)*

Word for Windows Essentials
Geoffrey Mandel
This book covers all of Word's features, including editing, formatting, printing, adding graphics, making tables, creating macros, and customizing your program. Scores of shortcuts and tips show how to maximize this powerful software. *(216 pages)*

WordPerfect for Windows with Style
Daniel Will-Harris
Daniel Will-Harris delights readers again with this generously illustrated handbook that gives step-by-step instructions for creating good-looking business documents using WordPerfect for Windows. The book shows a variety of documents and provides the exact commands, codes, and keystrokes used to create each one. Includes valuable insights into styles, graphics, fonts, tables, macros, clip art, printers, and utilities. Like its predecessor *(WordPerfect: Desktop Publishing in Style)*, you'll find this book to be detailed, easy-to-understand, and just plain fun. *(528 pages)*

Order Information:

How soon will I get my books?
UPS Ground orders arrive within 10 days on the West Coast and within three weeks on the East Coast. UPS Blue orders arrive within two working days anywhere in the U.S., provided we receive a fax or a phone call by 11 a.m. Pacific Time.

What about backorders?
Any book that is not available yet will be shipped separately when it is printed. *Requesting such books will not hold up your regular order.*

What if I don't like it?
Since we're asking you to buy our books sight unseen, we back them with an *unconditional money-back guarantee*. Whether you're a first time or a repeat customer, we want you to be completely satisfied in all your dealings with Peachpit Press.

What about shipping to Canada and overseas?
Shipping to Canada and overseas is via air mail. Orders must be prepaid in U.S. dollars.

Order Form

to order, call:
(800) 283-9444 or (510) 548-4393 or (510) 548-5991 (fax)

#	Title	Price	Total
	101 Windows Tips & Tricks	12.95	
	CorelDRAW 3: Visual QuickStart Guide	16.00	
	Desktop Publishing Secrets	27.95	
	Everyone's Guide to Successful Publications	28.00	
	Jargon	22.00	
	The Little DOS 6 Book	13.00	
	The Little Windows Book, 3.1 Edition	12.95	
	The Little WordPerfect for Windows Book	12.95	
	Mastering Corel Draw 3 (with 2 disks)	38.00	
	PageMaker 5 for Windows: Visual QuickStart Guide	14.00	
	The PC is not a typewriter	9.95	
	The QuarkXPress Book, Windows Edition	28.00	
	The Underground Guide to Laser Printers	14.00	
	Ventura Tips and Tricks, 3rd Edition	27.95	
	Windows 3.1 Bible	28.00	
	Windows 3.1 Font Book	12.95	
	Word for Windows Essentials	14.00	
	WordPerfect: Desktop Publishing in Style, 2nd Edition	23.95	
	WordPerfect for Windows with Style	24.95	

SHIPPING:	First Item	Each Additional	Subtotal		
UPS Ground	$4	$1	8.25% Tax (CA only)		
UPS Blue	$7	$2			
Canada	$6	$4	Shipping		
Overseas	$14	$14	**TOTAL**		

Name
Company
Address
City   State   Zip
Phone   Fax
❏ Check enclosed   ❏ Visa   ❏ MasterCard
Company purchase order #
Credit card #   Expiration Date

Peachpit Press, Inc. • 2414 Sixth Street • Berkeley, CA • 94710
Your satisfaction is guaranteed or your money will be cheerfully refunded!